TAMARA

TAMARA

Memoirs of St Petersburg, Paris,
Oxford and Byzantium

TAMARA TALBOT RICE
Edited by Elizabeth Talbot Rice

JOHN MURRAY
Albemarle Street, London

First published in 1996
by John Murray (Publishers) Ltd.,
50 Albemarle Street, London W1X 4BD

A catalogue record for this book is available
from the British Library

ISBN 0-7195-5721 6

Typeset in Monotype Sabon
by Servis Filmsetting Ltd, Manchester
Printed and bound in Great Britain by
The University Press, Cambridge.

To Harry, Jay, Sophia, Zoe

The whitewashed cottage of poverty, or the vermilion gate
of affluence, have each seemed to last but a day in turn.

Po Chu-i, T'ang dynasty poet

Contents

Illustrations

The editor and publishers would like to thank Auberon Waugh for kind permission to reproduce the line drawing by his father Evelyn in Plate 6.

Preface

Encouraged by family and friends, my mother began writing her memoirs in the mid-1970s, continuing, despite increasing pain, until some six months before her death in 1993. Her failing health can be inferred from the increasing illegibility of the manual corrections to her typescript. Had serious operations not intervened, the manuscript might have been longer, for several handwritten lists still exist of people and events she presumably had intended to include. Obvious omissions include gardening friends such as Lawrence Johnston, creator of the garden at Hidcote which she so loved; Gloucestershire friends – those seen most frequently, before as well as after the war, Robert and Vi Henriques, lived just two fields away; others visited often. Pre-war, the River Coln abounded in crayfish and I remember lively crayfishing parties during the summers. Round, flat nets baited with hunks of meat were lowered on to the river bed, then, once the crayfish had clambered on, they had to be kept carefully level as, with the aid of a forked stick, they were lifted on to the bank.

Visiting, after the war, was curtailed for some years because of the petrol shortage, but I recall an evening spent at Daneway with the architect Oliver Hill and his young wife Tania. Tamara had brought visiting guests with her, so had felt constrained to contribute an apple strudel to the dinner. After lengthy pre-dinner drinks and talk we made our way indoors where the Hills' huge white poodle, a look of ecstasy on its face, was just finishing off the strudel.

Would she also have included a chapter on the dogs which were valued members of the family, both at Pigeon House and after her widowhood? Once in Edinburgh, one of a succession of Bedlingtons went missing for two or three days. Tamara was distraught. The streets nearby resounded to her calls; the police were notified. More plates were needed for a dinner party which could not be cancelled, although the hosts were not in the mood; the full-length china cupboard was opened and there, cowering in the dark, was the missing Bedlington.

For reasons given in her opening paragraphs, Tamara said little about her family background. However, memoirs are of little point unless one knows something about the writer and her family: an introductory note was therefore necessary.

The reminiscences end with the death of my father in 1972. For my mother, her *raison d'être* probably ended then too, for her life was entirely bound up with that of her husband. Yet the next two decades were certainly not years of procrastination or self-pity; although a projected biography of Tsar Paul failed to find a publisher, Tamara contributed articles and reviews to several learned publications, lectured on many trips organized by Swan Hellenic and Serenissima to Russia and Eastern Europe, and was invited to Pakistan to give the Chughtai Memorial Lecture.

Perhaps inhibited by the Official Secrets Act she did not write about the war years. Yet she held an important and responsible job in the Ministry of Information. Sadly it was not possible to find anyone still alive who had worked in the same department as her. I have therefore attempted to show the importance and scope of the work in which she was involved, although I have not explored the friendships she formed at that period of her life, several of which were lifelong and included the godparents of her son, born in 1944.

It was thus necessary to provide a beginning, a middle and an end to these memoirs. However, there was a further reason for offering additional commentary. Tamara's friends included people of many ages and backgrounds. Some of her younger readers may know little about the Russian Revolution and other historical events to which she refers. Again, although she was at Oxford with contemporaries about whom much has been written, these were all male undergraduates. Little has been published on the life of women students, who had only just been accepted as full members of the university. Among my mother's papers were copies of regulations and of examination papers which were so interesting that it seemed a pity not to draw on them.

Readers will notice occasional errors of dates or facts. As Tamara says, she kept no diaries. In most cases, rather than disturb the dramatic flow of her narrative, I have preferred to amplify or correct her memories, where needed, by the use of footnotes. I hope these, together with the introductory notes to the chapters, will help to illuminate her memoirs: memoirs which are a vivid testimony to my mother's wide interests, her zest for life, for art and for people.

ELIZABETH TALBOT RICE
London, 1995

Acknowledgements

There are many people who must be thanked for their help with this volume. However any errors will be entirely my fault, because, contrary to the training given me by Bill Reid, former Director of the National Army Museum, Chelsea, although I checked and rechecked, I clearly omitted to check yet a further time. In particular I would like to thank my brother-in-law, Hugh Bredin, for the help and encouragement he has given me, especially with attempts to cut – and thanks to him almost succeeding – 145,000 words down to 90,000. I must also single out for special thanks Rodney Keeble and James Gormley, the former for typing a first draft from my mother's tangled and at times illegible manuscript; Jim for kindly agreeing to supply recollections of my mother as guide lecturer, as well as providing me with copies of letters she wrote to him, and for help in other matters.

Andrew Harris generously photocopied correspondence between my mother and grandmother and his cousin, Dr Morris Davidson, who in 1917/18 was working amongst refugees, for the US Legation in Stockholm. My cousins Genia Lang and Evelyn Waley provided useful family background and George Schmerling most kindly read and advised on the chapters dealing with Russia. Dr David Smith, Librarian and Archivist of St Anne's College, Oxford, turned up invaluable documentation regarding my mother's time as a home student, and the Trustees of St Anne's kindly allowed me to reproduce from the correspondence.

Others who have helped on various points include Selina Ballance; Joan Bennet; Chris Dale of the BBC Scottish Symphony Orchestra; Digital Drawings, Cirencester; Enriqueta Frankfort; David Herring with Russian translations; John V. Howard of Edinburgh University Library; Sidney C. Hutchison, Hon. Archivist of the Royal Academy of Arts; Colin O'Brien with photography; Miss D. C. Quare, Librarian and Archivist of St Hugh's

College, Oxford; Helen Smailes of the National Gallery of Scotland; D. C. Reid of Whytock & Reid, Edinburgh.

Dr Stanislav Dumin of the Historico-Genealogical Society in Moscow conducted a thorough search of the State Archives in St Petersburg, finding the relevant marriage and birth certificates to substantiate my mother's parentage. The Ministère de la Culture et de la Francophonie and the Centre d'Histoire de la Résistance et de la Déportation both searched, sadly in vain, for documentation regarding my mother's brother Volodia. Mr Arif Rahman Chughtai of the Chughtai Museum Trust gave me unqualified permission to use material from the scrapbook presented to my mother after her visit to Pakistan.

Many others have given advice and encouragement and I hope they will accept this general expression of gratitude as a personal thank-you.

The following have generously allowed me to quote from printed works: Sir John Gielgud CH from his autobiography, *An Actor and His Time* published by Sidgwick & Jackson; Jane Emery from her biography, *Rose Macaulay: A Writer's Life*; Edinburgh University Press for Gervase Mathew's translation from Gregory's treatise of the Soul and the Resurrection, printed in *Studies in Memory of David Talbot Rice*; Chambers Harrap, publisher of *Bohemian Literary and Social Life in Paris* by S. Huddleston; Columbia University Press, publishers of Carlton J. H. Hayes, *France: A Nation of Patriots*; J. M. Dent, publishers of A. Symons, *Cities*; Faber & Faber Ltd, publishers of *Murder in the Cathedral* by T. S. Eliot; Robert Hale Ltd, publishers of H. E. Counsell, *37, The Broad*; David Higham Associates for the American rights and Reed Books for English language rights of Anthony Powell, *To Keep the Ball Rolling*, published by Heinemann; International Thomson Publishing Services Ltd for R. Pascal, *Design and Truth in Autobiography*, published by Routledge; Macmillan General Books, publishers of *An Edwardian Youth* by L. E. Jones; Oxford University Press, publishers of *Collected Poems of Ivor Gurney* edited by P. J. Kavanagh, 1982, and also for permission to quote from L. H. Dudley Buxton and S. Gibson, *Oxford University Ceremonies*; George Sassoon for the line from *Memories*; the Society of Authors as the literary representative of the Estate of

John Masefield; the Literary Trustees of Walter de la Mare, and the Society of Authors as their representatives for the quotations from *Vain Questions* by Walter de la Mare; the publishers Weatherhill for an excerpt from Po Chu-i in L. Kuck, *The World of the Japanese Garden*; Weidenfeld & Nicolson, publishers of Harold Hobson, *Indirect Journey*; quotations from *Russian Hussar*, originally published by J. A. Allen & Co., are now the copyright of Mary A. Littauer, White Mane Publishing Inc., Shippensberg, Pennsylvania.

Crown copyright material in PRO/INF 1/83 is reproduced with the permission of the Controller of Her Majesty's Stationery Office.

Material for the biographical footnotes and the dates of individuals listed in the Index have been taken from the *Dictionary of National Biography*, various editions of *Who's Who*, *Chambers Biographical Dictionary* and similar reference books. Grateful acknowledgement is made to the editors.

It has unfortunately not been possible to trace the remaining copyright holders.

ON THE FAMILY

TAMARA says little about herself in her memoirs. This may be because, as she writes, memories were too bitter. But, in a letter of 1981 written to an American friend, she mentioned that she was having difficulty with the Russian chapters since she was afraid of incriminating friends there. 'I cannot', she wrote, 'bring myself to describe any incidents which, if the political situation became difficult, could even by the wildest stretch of the imagination, land them in difficulties.' How can we, who have lived our lives in security and freedom, appreciate the fear of retaliation which a young child would remember throughout life? We may regret, but cannot criticize, her caution.

However, despite her apprehensions, it seems essential to give her memoirs a biographical setting, even if only to identify the relatives who flit in and out of these pages. In the course of reading it should also be noted that until February 1918 the Russians used the Julian calendar, which was thirteen days behind the Gregorian calendar used in the West. The dates in the early chapters of the memoirs follow the Gregorian calendar unless otherwise stated.

The record of Elena Tamara's birth on 19 June 1904 (Julian calendar), registered by the rabbi, is preserved in the Russian State Historical Archive of St Petersburg. Her parents, Israel Boris Abelevich Abelson and Louisa Elisabeth (Lifa) Vilenkin, had married in St Petersburg on 16 February 1897. The couple had one other child, a son Vladimir (Volodia), born on 4 December 1897.

Although the Abelson births and marriage were recorded by the rabbi, there is no indication that Tamara was brought up in the Jewish faith. She certainly attended Orthodox services and celebrated Christian festivals. However, in later life she was a non-believer.

The Abelsons originated in Lithuania where Israel Boris was born in July 1864, probably one of five brothers; no sisters have yet been identified. At the time of Boris's marriage his father Abel was a merchant 'of the first class', trading in Kiev in the Ukraine and also in St Petersburg.

With the rank of 'personal honorary citizen' he must have received either a gold or a silver medal from the Ministry of Finance for exemplary conduct in trade or manufacturing. In 1911, Boris himself is listed as a member of the St Petersburg Stock Exchange and, in 1914, as a member of the Russian-English Bank Revisory Inspection Committee.

Russian society was rooted in a hierarchical class system dependent on wealth rather than birth. To oversimplify, there were two estates, the non-taxable and the taxable. The former was subdivided into the hereditary nobility; the personal nobility or life peers and honoured citizens; the merchants. The taxable estate included small shopkeepers, artisans and peasantry. The clergy were outside both groupings.

The merchants – managers of wholesale and retail businesses and factory owners – were subdivided into three grades according to wealth. They paid an annual tax for a certificate guaranteeing the right to trade and to manufacture. Non-renewal of this certificate rendered the right void. A first-class merchant could engage in foreign or domestic commerce, own ships and factories, and perform banking functions. Exempt from military service and (except for the third-class merchant) from corporal punishment as well as from the poll tax, merchants were however obliged to undertake unpaid service as judges, police constables and local government officials. The merchant class was never very numerous. At the end of the nineteenth century, it accounted for at most 6 per cent of the population of Moscow, the centre of the merchant culture.

After ten years' blameless service a first-class merchant could apply for promotion to 'honorary citizen' (*pochetnyi grazhdanin*), which absolved the holder from purchase of the yearly certificate. The honour, also awarded to holders of the Orders of St Stanislaus and of St Vladimir, could be personal, for life, or hereditary. Boris, his wife and children were confirmed as Hereditary Honorary Citizens on 15 December 1914 (certificate nos. 5781–4), an honour already accorded to Abel and also bestowed on Boris's father-in-law, Abraham Markovich Vilenkin.

Sadly, Tamara does not describe how either her father or her brother escaped from Russia after the Revolution. Both reached Paris in 1921. Tamara writes that Volodia later took French citizenship. A search for his naturalization papers proved negative, but I was told that Volodia was probably stripped of French citizenship by the Vichy régime in 1941; files relating to Jewish citizens were destroyed by the collaborators. On the outbreak of the Second World War he was called up. After the fall of France, he joined the Maquis, perhaps forging passports in a ring based on Nice headed by Mrs David Seligman. After the war, he returned to Paris, living there until his death in 1958.

Tamara's mother spent the Second World War in Gloucestershire, walking twice a week 'through all weathers' the two or three miles to and from the local railway station to take a train to Cirencester, where she helped in the YWCA canteen and 'washed up, made sandwiches & served etc.', so a letter of gratitude reads. In 1947 she took British nationality (PRO/HO334/173/AZ23978) and lived in a one-room flat in Chelsea, her Paris flat having been ransacked by the Germans during the occupation. She died in Cheltenham in 1954 and is buried in Coln Rogers, in Gloucestershire.

More information is available on Tamara's maternal ancestors, the Vilenkins, than on the Abelsons. Her mother Lifa was the third of eight children of a prominent Jewish family of timber merchants and land-owners. The two country estates Tamara so loved, Ostrogovitza and Volgovo, probably belonged to her Vilenkin grandfather.

The subsequent histories of the Vilenkins make sad reading, several escaping the Revolution only to fall victim to the Nazis. Tamara's mater-nal grandfather, Abraham, came to England by sea from Reval (now Tallinn) in 1921, after the death of his wife from ill health. He eventually settled in France.

Of the children Gregory (Grisha), the eldest, studied law at the uni-versities of Dorpat (now Tartu), Estonia, and St Petersburg before enter-ing public service, first in the Ministry of Public Instruction then the Ministry of Finance. He served in Tokyo, 1906–10, then the United States, as Financial Agent. In 1912 he was posted to the Imperial Russian Embassy in London. Correspondence in the Foreign Office papers in the Public Record Office relates to the nature of his appointment (PRO/FO372/383/40144/p278). Informed of his attachment to the embassy in an honorific capacity, the ambassador is asked how Vilenkin should be described in the Diplomatic List. The reply states that he is attached 'à titre honoraire, et pas en qualité spéciale' and should be listed as attaché after the Military, Naval and Commercial Agents. Grisha's granddaughter, Evelyn, tells me that he was offered ennoblement if he would convert to the Orthodox religion, but refused. Despite this, he was awarded the Orders of St Stanislaus and of St Anne by the Tsar, and held several decorations from other countries. Being abroad during the Revolution, he was in a position to help relatives gain entry into England. Grisha and his family settled in London.

The Vilenkin Family

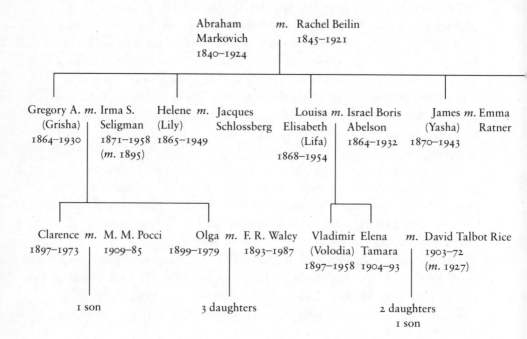

Abraham Markovich 1840–1924 *m.* Rachel Beilin 1845–1921

- Gregory A. (Grisha) 1864–1930 *m.* Irma S. Seligman 1871–1958 (*m.* 1895)
- Helene (Lily) 1865–1949 *m.* Jacques Schlossberg
- Louisa Elisabeth (Lifa) 1868–1954 *m.* Israel Boris Abelson 1864–1932
- James (Yasha) 1870–1943 *m.* Emma Ratner

- Clarence 1897–1973 *m.* M. M. Pocci 1909–85
- Olga 1899–1979 *m.* F. R. Waley 1893–1987
- Vladimir (Volodia) 1897–1958
- Elena Tamara 1904–93 *m.* David Talbot Rice 1903–72 (*m.* 1927)

1 son   3 daughters   2 daughters 1 son

Next in age came Helene (Lily). She escaped to Constantinople in 1919 and then to Germany, finally settling in Nice in 1923. James (Yasha) also escaped, making his home in Paris.

Amalia (Malia), the next Vilenkin daughter, married Matthew (Mitia) Ponisovsky. She died in 1918. Matthew fled Russia with their children at the same time as Tamara and her mother. In hiding in Nice during the Second World War, he escaped detection by the Nazis, and died in Paris in old age. Of their four children, the twins James (Jim) and Alexander (Alec) were Tamara's special chums. Jim was artistic, and played the piano well. He was a great reader, more of an introvert than his twin. He graduated in mechanical engineering at Imperial College, London, in 1923 and then found employment with the American Smelting and Refining Co., as European Technical Representative, based in Brussels. He died of meningitis. Alec graduated in 1923 from St John's College, Cambridge, where his main interest was rowing. He then went into banking, becoming in due course financial adviser to the Monaco Government. Although this was a neutral country in the war, he was an

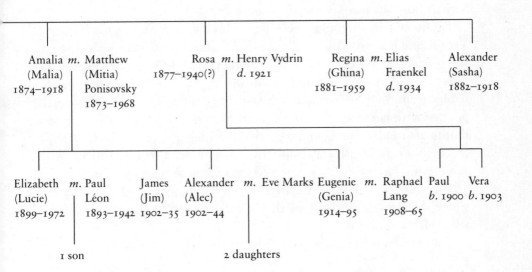

active member of the Resistance, helping escaping Allied airmen; unmasked by a careless escapee, he was arrested, deported to Auschwitz in 1944 and murdered.

Their elder sister Lucie eloped to Paris in 1921 to marry Paul Léon, a classicist specializing in the works of Rousseau and Benjamin Constant and a close friend of James Joyce. In her booklet, *James Joyce and Paul Léon: the Story of a Friendship*, New York, 1948, Lucie describes the panic which ensued when Léon left the corrected proofs of Joyce's *Finnegans Wake* in a Paris taxi. Anxiety continued for two days until a fat cab driver rang the doorbell and handed in the missing parcel. During the war the Léon family remained in France. Lucie, suspected of helping British escapees, was repeatedly questioned by the Gestapo. In August 1941, Léon was amongst fifty Jews taken hostage by the Germans. He was murdered by them while being moved from Auschwitz to Birkenau. Meanwhile Lucie smuggled letters, money and food into the concentration camps until, warned that she was on the wanted list, she escaped to Monaco in December 1942. After the Allied invasion of southern France in 1944 she was employed as an interpreter by the American army. Peace declared, she resumed her occupation as Paris fashion editor of the New York *Herald Tribune*.

Genia, the younger Ponisovsky sister, was brought up in Nice. She earned her living as a secretary and a tour guide for TWA, marrying a Swiss whom she met on one of the tours.

The next two Vilenkins were girls. Rosa married a doctor, Henry Vydrin, and had two children, Paul and Vera. Since, to begin with, doctors were protected by Lenin, the Vydrins remained in Russia. Henry died 'after ten weeks of suffering from his heart' in 1921. There are several letters from Vera to Tamara, the last dated 1922; her mother corresponded with her siblings until the early thirties when they were warned that further letters might endanger her. Nothing more has been heard of the family: unobtrusive attempts by Tamara, who returned to Russia several times in the 1960s and 70s, to trace them were unsuccessful.

The youngest Vilenkin daughter, Regina (Ghina), escaped to Germany where she married. In 1938, by then a widow, she fled again, to join her sister Helene in Nice.

Tamara's favourite uncle, Alexander (Sasha), is described in Chapter 3.

I

A Russian Childhood

There must be a sense . . . of belonging to something old,
and honourable, and beneficent; a sense of being possessed
as well as of possessing.

L. E. Jones, *An Edwardian Youth*

ACCORDING to Roy Pascal, 'the centre of interest in an autobiography is the self, not the outside world.'* If that were so,
surely only those whose thoughts or actions have affected the lives
of many others would be justified in writing about themselves. Yet
it seems to me possible to maintain that the life of each individual,
regardless of its influence on others, has a unique quality which
may occasionally serve to divert or interest others. Perhaps my life
is no more deserving of notice than are those of countless contemporaries who have, like me, witnessed the death throes of the Age
of Reason and the birth pangs of the Age of the Atom, the
Computer and the Chip, yet, because the 'self' which Pascal had in
mind cannot completely dissociate itself from the outside world,
so, conversely, is that outer world forced to impinge to a greater or
lesser degree upon the 'self'.

Chance, as Conrad called it, fate as others regard it, decreed that
my life was to evolve in a succession of settings each of which
formed a world complete in itself. Some of those worlds ceased to
exist in my youth, others have undergone changes of varying inten-
sities in the course of my life and several are evolving as I write.
Each had faults as well as merits, yet in my eyes none deserves to be
relegated to oblivion, and it is of them rather than of myself that I
intend to write, all the more so since I consider the 'self' a private
place which should be treated as such. In describing the societies in
which I lived, I shall of course be obliged also to write about myself,

---

*Roy Pascal, *Design and Truth in Autobiography*, London, 1960, p. 9.

7

yet it will seldom be of that inner 'self', nor even of the numerous distinguished people whom it has been my good fortune to meet; rather will I try to describe the communities to which I at times belonged, striving to depict them as faithfully as a halting memory and hesitant pen permit.

Conforming to the custom of the period my beloved English governess, May Gilchrist, decided, when I was still very young, that I should keep a diary. Although she met with stubborn resistance on my part she too had a determined streak in her character. Noticing my fondness for fine, shiny white paper and polished leather bindings, she attempted to overcome my dislike of writing by sending annually to Harrods for a large, sumptuous diary, beautifully bound in shiny morocco leather and fitted with a lock and key. When she confronted me with the volume's blank pages tears poured from my eyes and, notwithstanding the jollifications which had delighted me on New Year's Eve, I could think of nothing to record. The events which had really mattered during the preceding day seemed too private to confide to paper, whilst minor happenings seemed too trivial and boring to justify the effort of recording them. The contest over the diary was re-enacted during the opening weeks of each year, then postponed for a twelvemonth till, after three or four years of endeavour, it lapsed, never to be resumed. Within another couple of years even a childish account of schoolroom life in a privileged Russian family such as mine would have been considered so dangerous as to have been forbidden, and so, supposing I had kept a diary, I would be no better fitted for my present task, since my diaries would almost certainly have been destroyed by my parents soon after the outbreak of the 1917 Revolution.

I was born in 1904 and lived in St Petersburg, in Mokhovaya Street, at a time when little girls, and also quite big ones, curtsied to their elders and betters. Boys bowed when shaking hands with young girls but greeted married ladies by raising the lady's right hand, generally encased in a white kid glove, to their lips.

The world in which we moved as children, although secure and loving, was also complex and exacting. No real or imaginary baize doors existed to separate the generations. In addition to our own quarters we had the freedom of the entire house. Everyone except toddlers met at luncheon, the children occupying the ends of the dining-room table, the boys grouped round their tutors, the girls round their governesses. Their parents sat opposite each other at the centre of the table, guests ranged at their sides. No child spoke unless spoken to by an adult. At the end of its meal, each child went first to its mother, then to its father, to thank them for the luncheon. Children were expected to eat the food served them and, once they had started a slice of bread, were forbidden to leave even a scrap, because bread, we were told, was produced at the sweat of a peasant's brow.

We addressed all visitors by their names and patronymics* but were expected to regard our parents' intimate friends as honorary uncles and aunts, calling them such even if we disliked them. We spoke French in our parents' reception rooms where we addressed them as *vous* (you). In private rooms, that is to say in our parents' bedrooms, boudoir and study, we could speak in whatever language we liked and there it was possible to address them using the intimate *tu* (thou). In our schoolrooms, where French, English and German were spoken, our teachers insisted on a certain degree of formality, but constraint was lifted in our playrooms. However, we relied on forbidden sallies into the servants' quarters for light-hearted gaiety, complete freedom, unrestrained laughter and unsuppressed giggles. Yet, although they never reported our misdeeds, the servants were no slower or less ready to chide rudeness than were parents, teachers, tutors and governesses.

The servants who meant most to me were Ilya, our major-domo, an even keener stamp collector than I; Ivan, our superlative chef; our fat, tearful and earnest head laundress, Polish Tonya, and my own maid, gay Nastya. Minna, mother's Lettish lady's maid, was bad-tempered and as quick with her tongue as she was neat with her hands. Whilst with us she learnt to speak quite fluent French, English and German, and was clearly bent on bettering herself.

All our servants, excepting clever and ambitious Minna and foolish, tearful Tonya, came from our country estates. Their forebears had known our forebears, they had known us from our birth, we knew their parents and children and, at any rate to us, we

---

*Russians use a masculine or feminine patronymic in addition to the first name when addressing others. Tamara would be greeted as Tamara Borisovna – Tamara, daughter of Boris; her brother as Vladimir Borisovich.

seemed to belong to each other. From them we children learnt most of what we knew about rural Russia. They kept us in touch with the villagers. Whenever one of their relatives arrived in Petersburg from the country, generally to break a piece of bad news or to borrow money, we knew of it first and rushed to our parents to demand their help. When the trouble had been dealt with we showered the newcomer with questions about the village, our particular cronies, our ponies and dogs, and other pets.

My beloved nurse, Anna, was the only member of the household who never found fault with me. Her constant love and devotion, her unshakeable conviction that I could do no wrong, enveloped me in a cocoon of security grievously dented by her departure when I was six years old. She left amidst floods of our tears to look after a baby cousin. The pain of that parting lost none of its acuteness until war and revolution inflicted griefs which blunted the earlier sorrow without, however, obliterating it.

Anna had had a hard life but when she came to us her life was her only possession. She was fond of it, liked to recall it and to philosophize over it. Her parents had been serfs at birth but young enough to prosper from their liberation in 1861. Yet it was her father who had been the first to treat Anna with violence amounting to brutality; then her husband had done so. To begin with Anna was cowed by her husband's harshness, then her indomitable spirit revived and being childless, strong and young, she suddenly walked away from her native village, determined to explore the vast and unknown world lying beyond its boundaries. Devout from childhood, she remained so until death. She made use of her independence to visit a number of monasteries, praying before their icons, savouring the hospitality offered by each, revelling in the vivid descriptions of the outlandish places which her fellow pilgrims had visited. Eventually she came to my mother in St Petersburg to ask for work. She became my nurse and I loved to question her about her childhood and her wanderings through Russia. She had a keen sense of the ridiculous and her replies, vivid and racy like those of many articulate women of her class and background, often took the form of a *chastushka* – a witty rhymed couplet coined and delivered in a high-pitched, singsong tone of voice.

In her day village life made great physical demands on the peasants – as it was to do on Soviet manual workers. However, it also had its lighter side. There were swings, as popular with young girls as with children; there was much singing and dancing among the young people; there were fairs at which the girls bought finery and the men drink, gossiping, often quarrelling as they did so. The peasants were uninhibited. Many were gay and witty. Most were quick to give way to their feelings, whether of sympathy or hate, but however violent the anger it was generally short-lived. Religious festivals, of which there were many, brought the entire village together, whilst births, weddings or deaths resulted in equally large gatherings. Each reunion was accompanied by feasting which, even at funerals, gave rise to some merriment. The older women encouraged the observance of ancient customs and superstitions. Fortune-telling was widely practised, yet neither divination nor superstition imperilled the Christian piety of the people, for it was their faith that enabled them to endure their misfortunes, even to accept them as expressions of God's will.

Like Pushkin's nurse, mine accepted life's trials without question or complaint, but it seemed to me that Anna deserved nothing but felicity. I felt that God had been unfair to her. When I realized that Mother devoted her mornings to charitable work I assumed that she too questioned the nature of the existing order of things. When challenged, she hedged, but my doubts increased when the older boys returned from school provocatively chanting, 'Si Dieu le veut et ne le peut Il n'est pas tout puissant; s'Il le peut et ne le veut Il n'est pas bienfaisant; s'Il le veut et le peut pourquoi ne le fait-Il pas?' Greatly perturbed, I sought an explanation from the good, kind, simple and not very clever priest who taught us divinity. His inability to solve the riddle, coinciding as it did with Anna's departure, destroyed my faith in the deity without, however, diminishing my delight in the beauties of the Orthodox Church's ritual.

In my mother's youth many well-to-do parents disliked sending their daughters to school. Mother and her sisters received a good deal of their education from an English governess called Margaret Rate. In addition to English, Miss Rate taught her charges world history, geography, literature with special emphasis on the works of Shakespeare and Richardson, painting, needlework, deportment and good manners. She was a veritable martinet and everyone was a little afraid of her. When I knew her Miss Rate seemed a very old lady. Standing little more than four feet-odd high, thin and straight as a bodkin, her black hair heavily streaked with grey and pulled straight back from her severe, unsmiling face to be rolled into a hard, dangerous-looking bun, her appearance was chilling. Nevertheless her former pupils were devoted to her and cared for her until her death in 1918. Nothing was known of her origin but it was assumed that she was close on ninety when she died.

Miss Rate deserved her pupils' gratitude for she had turned them into cultivated women. My mother was nevertheless determined that I should receive a sounder education. I think I was about four years old when I started to puzzle over the intricacies of the English language in a book called, erroneously from my point of view, *Reading Without Tears*,* but I cannot recollect when I learnt to read Russian and French; I must have done so painlessly and when still quite young. From early childhood until the outbreak of the First World War I was provided with three resident governesses, one French, one German and one English. Each took it in turn to look after me from breakfast-time to bedtime, although it was the English governess who had daily care of me, getting me up, putting me to bed and taking me for walks. My French governess, Mlle Jeanne Séjourner, was gay, flighty and flirtatious, and I think that Mother never fully trusted her, and was perhaps a trifle jealous of her youth and liveliness. The daughter of a Parisian market gardener, Mademoiselle Jeanne returned to France in the spring of 1914 for her annual holiday and we never heard from her again.

My German governesses changed frequently. Each found me a difficult child, which was precisely what I intended, since Anna's accounts of the harshness with which many German bailiffs treated Russian peasants had already led me to distrust Germans. The last of my German governesses believed in spiritualism which we encouraged by tying cotton to the legs of the table which she used for her seances. By pulling the cotton we unobtrusively jerked the table when, with her fingertips resting lightly on it, she would screw up her eyes and purse her lips in expectation of a manifestation. In 1914, when returning to Germany for her summer holiday, she asked for the loan of an eiderdown. Mother told her to take

---

*F. L. Bevan, *Reading Without Tears, or A Pleasant Mode of Learning to Read*, London, 1857. Despite its publication date, Tamara's elder daughter remembers reading from the same textbook some thirty years later.

whatever she liked from the children's rooms. She chose one covered in an unattractive, Oscar Wildean shade of lilac satin. Seven years later we were living in Paris in a state bordering on penury. One day, to our astonishment, the postman delivered a large parcel. It contained the eiderdown, still in perfect condition. No letter or sender's address was attached. Touched, slightly abashed and considerably amused, we wondered whether the spirits had enabled her to trace us. Unanimously we bestowed the luxurious, perfectly hideous article on Father. He grew to love it. When feeling ill or acutely miserable he would roll himself in it and lie on his bed, refusing to speak or eat, transported back to the houses and country which he adored and so poignantly missed. At such times we felt deeply grateful to my former long-suffering governess and it was as much a tribute to her as to provide Father with a link with his homeland that we buried him in that soft, ugly, satin quilt.

Even when England was at the height of her prosperity she owed an immense debt to the young Englishwomen who went abroad to become governesses to foreign children. Miss Rate had seen to it that my mother and her sisters became ardent Anglophiles. My mother may have visited England first in 1907 when the stable, relaxed atmosphere of Edwardian London contrasted sharply with that which prevailed in war-weary, revolution-torn St Petersburg. She fell in love with everything English and decided to entrust the moral and physical upbringing of her children to an Englishwoman with the duty also of teaching them her language. As a result it was the English language, English customs and standards of behaviour that predominated in our wing. My first English nursery governess was a pretty young woman with lovely deep blue eyes called Miss Booth, who flirted so outrageously with my younger uncles that her stay was of short duration. She was succeeded by a stern disciplinarian called Miss Bell.

Miss Bell disapproved of the delicious food provided by Ivan and, perhaps in reaction, insisted on my swallowing the thick, greyish, crinkled skins which clotted my milk, for throughout my childhood it was necessary in Russia for milk and all drinking water to be boiled. The skins made me vomit. Realizing that my revulsion was genuine, my darling Nastya came to my help. She secreted milk skins for a whole week, then one Wednesday, my mother's at-home day – when I had changed into a freshly laundered white frock, generally made of tulle or broderie anglaise, with a wide blue satin ribbon tied round my hips, as was then the fashion, with another blue satin ribbon knotted into my straight, fine hair which was twisted into bulky curlers every night so as to be brushed into corkscrews round a hoop stick each morning – I entered the drawing-room with Nastya's collection of repellent milk skins suspended from my fingers. These, I wailed, are what the Englishwoman feeds me. The assembled ladies were horrified. The skins were removed. I was hugged and petted, comforted, stuffed with delicious *petits fours* and was absolved for once from the weekly ordeal of having to entertain the assembled company either by playing a piece on the piano or by reciting a poem. Best of all, however, was the instant dismissal of Miss Bell.

Soon after my sixth birthday her place was taken by May Gilchrist.* Although Nastya and I had practised pronouncing her surname for several days before her arrival she almost instantly became Maykins to us, and Maykins she remained until her death.

On my seventh birthday I was enrolled as an externe pupil, as distinct from an interne, at the Tagantzeva girls' school, a few doors from where we lived. Neither my enrolment nor the school's proximity resulted in my attending school daily, for my parents thought it undesirable for me to go to school until I was in my teens. As an externe I would attend only for the last three weeks or so of the academic year in order to sit the annual exams with my interne contemporaries so as, on passing, to be able to move into the next form.† I discarded the pastel-coloured dresses of my customary

---

*Gilchrist, May Beatrice (Maykins). Tamara's English governess from *c.* 1910, and family friend. Much against her will, her employers insisted on her leaving Russia in 1918, but she returned to them after Tamara's escape. After the Second World War, which she spent in Gloucestershire, she was set up in a house in Oxford, where she took student lodgers. Eventually their exuberance became too much. Tamara persuaded the Nuffield Foundation to find room for her in their Banbury Road home where Maykins silenced residents' moans with her cheeriness. She died shortly after her hundredth birthday. Asked to what she attributed her longevity, she replied, 'Sleeping with the window open, taking plenty of exercise and keeping cheerful.'

† In a contribution entitled 'Legal Status of Jews in Russia', which appears in *Russian Jewry (1860–1917)*, ed. J. Frumkin, G. Aronson and A. Goldenweiser, New York, 1966, Goldenweiser states that, because of the quota system which limited the numbers of Jews who could attend secondary and higher education institutions, 'thousands of young people studied at home and took matric examinations as so called "externes".' They would then go on to foreign universities.

existence to wear a Russian schoolgirl's uniform of a long-sleeved, high-necked brown woollen or gabardine frock, depending on the season, with a small white collar of cotton or lace, and a black apron. Virtually the same uniform was still worn in the 1980s by Soviet girls of all ages although a red tie, the badge of the Pioneer Corps, and a white apron, a nice contrast to the black, had been added. Therefore, annually, in April, trembling with apprehension and excitement, I entered my school and met my contemporaries. They always greeted me warmly and it was not until I went to school in London that I appreciated their innate kindliness for, instead of making fun of me, they showed me my desk, and the loo, and told me my timetable. They made me feel that I belonged. I considered their attitude natural, and I believe that they did too.

Throughout the rest of the academic year the five teachers who taught my nominal classmates visited me daily, each giving me close on an hour of private tuition. In addition I studied music and dancing and, on Saturday mornings, drawing and painting. All my teachers were dedicated to their calling but my teacher of Russian, Olga Ivanovna Voznessenskaya, exercised a lasting and profound influence on me. She was tall and plump and used no make-up. She had few clothes, none of which was at all becoming for she never considered either her appearance or her health, but she was a dedicated and inspired teacher. Her love of Russia, its literature, landscape and peasantry was shared, if to a lesser degree, by my elegant art master, yet it was she who was chiefly responsible for the delight I took in Russia's vast and unspectacular expanses. She also encouraged the fondness which Anna had taught me to feel for Russia's turbulent yet patient peasants, whose talents and intelligence Anna had already trained me to respect.

Examinations were regarded with the utmost seriousness alike by teachers, parents and pupils. The school papers were corrected by outside examiners and children who failed were obliged to spend a second year in the same form. My brother Volodia was no scholar. He hated book work. His school, the Tenyshev Gymnasium, prided itself on its liberal methods and opinions.* It was situated as close

---

*School and curriculum are described in B. Boyd, *Vladimir Nabokov: The Russian Years*, London, 1990, pp. 86–7. The building now houses the Practice Theatre of the Institute of Theatre, Music and Cinematograph.

to one side of our house as my school was to the other. Volodia went to school daily but refused to join in any of its sporting activities. In the spring the thought of the approaching examinations so distressed him, for he was well aware that he had idled the winter away, that he always had to be dosed with valerian drops before each test. Miraculously he always just scraped through whilst I, who studied so conscientiously, failed one year to pass the Russian spelling test. The news was greeted with consternation. The servants shook their heads, looked dismayed, muttered 'Learning is light: ignorance is darkness', reminding me how lucky I was to be receiving an education when so many children were deprived of one. Ilya, our stamp-collecting major-domo, wondered whether I would ever be able to use Stanley Gibbons' stamp catalogue unaided. Father refused to speak to me for a fortnight or to allow me to read the difficult leader in the daily newspaper, the *Novoe Vremia* (New Times), an equivalent of the London *Times*, to him. Maykins felt that too much fuss was being made over my failure, yet she too was unable to appreciate how difficult I found it to concentrate on exams, coinciding as they did with the excitement of going to school.

Mother gave me only a mild scolding for she had never liked bookwork, but she resorted to the customary remedy of engaging a poor student to coach me during the holidays. She found an attractive-looking, sweet-tempered youth who travelled to our country estate with us. Mother attended his first few lessons. She must either have been satisfied with his method or bored, for she soon ceased to appear. Meanwhile, my young tutor and I discovered we were both deeply interested in archaeology. Although I knew very little about the subject and I doubt that he knew a great deal more than I, we proceeded to excavate one of several small and unimportant nomadic burials situated in the grounds. No objections were raised and we became so absorbed in our hobby that, as digging progressed, spelling regressed, and was soon set aside in favour of a study of the Scythians and their allied nomads.* Neither of us noted the passage of time but Mother must have been on the alert, for she suddenly appeared at one of my lessons. She

---

*Tamara dedicated her book, *The Scythians*, to 'those who lived at Volgovo', presumably the country estate where the excavation took place.

had come to assess the improvement in my spelling. Sadly there was none. Deeply shamed, my tutor and I devoted the rest of the holidays to spelling and fortunately, although I have remained a bad speller in all languages, I managed to pass the autumn test. My young tutor and I parted with moist eyes, never to meet again.

When I was still very young the battle against illiteracy was gathering momentum in Russia. In the poorer streets the shop signs still displayed illustrations with little or no text, a baker's board advertising its wares by means of a picture of a loaf of bread, a fishmonger's by a fish reposing on a dish. Now these pictorial signs were gradually being replaced by inscriptions written in either large orange-coloured letters, for which gold was substituted in the richer districts, or black ones set against a blue background. Yearly the letters seemed to become smaller and more numerous.

Troikas could still be seen in Petersburg but were rare enough to arouse interest; by about 1912 motor cars ceased to be a novelty, but private carriages outnumbered them, and only horse-drawn cabs were available for hire. Most of these consisted of a spacious carriage harnessed to a single horse, although smarter turn-outs were generally drawn by a pair of horses. In winter the carriage was replaced by a sledge. However, it was the single, very fast horse, usually a spirited stallion, pulling a lighter and smaller vehicle driven by an intrepid daredevil, that was sought after by dashing young gentlemen. Known as *likhachi*, these express cabs were driven with scant regard for safety and as a result, in winter, the skids of their sledges were apt to catch in the tramlines, spilling passenger and driver.

I revelled in the liveliness of the streets where people laughed, shouted, kissed and squabbled. The roads were paved with cobblestones which, reverberating to the traffic, added to the noise. In cases of severe illness the sound of horses' hoofs and hard-surfaced wheels was deadened by straw spread outside the sufferer's house. In winter snow muffled most of the noise of sledges drawn by trotting horses, but the laughter and chatter of the coachmen who stopped to warm themselves at the braziers kept alight at many street corners carried far in the still air. Beggars were numerous and, however dirty, were never ignored or sent away from the braziers. Officers, officials, students and most schoolboys wore uniform. The military, with splendid, gold-tasselled epaulettes, carried long, curved, slender swords; most wore vicious spurs and clanking medals. The students' uniforms were often shabby but the long-coated policemen were neatly turned out.

My parents kept open house in both town and country but several of their annual dinner parties were particularly formal and important occasions. For these, flowers and fruit were ordered well in advance from the South of France. Ivan spent many hours making spun sugar centre-pieces, often shaped like galleons or temples, which he filled with sweets or fruits he himself had glazed. He used to send a miniature version of the great set-piece up to my day nursery for me.

Several days before these dinner parties there was much activity in the pantry and laundry as well as the kitchen, and Ivan became increasingly short-tempered with his underlings. On the day itself he would attempt to steady his nerves by resorting to the vodka bottle so that by breakfast-time he was gloriously drunk. Then it was only a matter of minutes before he seized a large carving knife and proceeded to chase the immensely fat Tonya round the house, cursing all Poles as he did so. With something of the clumsiness and agility of an elephant Tonya careered from room to room, squealing like a piglet. We children watched entranced, cheering Ivan as he pursued her, encouraging Tonya as she sped past, whilst Mother wailed in anguish and Father yelled orders to both servants, which both ignored. Then Ilya would appear, stately, even majestic, very calm. His shout of command was like a clap of thunder. Instantly pursuer and pursued halted; footmen emerged to take Ivan's arms, lead him to his room and put him to bed. Meanwhile Tonya was placated with cups of tea laced with blackcurrant jam, and chocolate cakes. A couple of hours later, now completely sober, Ivan would enter his kitchens and that evening our parents' guests would be regaled with a splendid repast.

Two or three times during the winter Mother gave a luncheon party for me from which all adults were excluded. Some forty of my friends were invited. We sat on small chairs around small tables. Our plates and cutlery were also small versions of the dining-room ones. Our meal was served by our servants' older children. Ivan took as much trouble in producing small spun sugar centre-pieces for my tables as he did over the larger ones required for my parents' banquets. Following the custom in force at the Congress of Vienna, many of the decorations were architectural.* Unlike our elders, without hesitation we devoured them at the end of the meal. It was not until many years later, when working on my biography of the Empress Elizabeth of Russia, that I discovered with surprise that the Empress gave similar children's parties from which she excluded adults.† My luncheon parties were followed by games, with hide and seek being by far the most popular. They ended with dances, chiefly the waltz, minuet and gavotte, as well as the Georgian *lesghinka* and the Polish mazurka. By this time adults had joined the party. Two of my younger uncles excelled at the mazurka and the *krakoviak* and brought fresh vigour into the dancing.

Shortly before the war we acquired our first gramophone. One afternoon two footmen carried an enormous packing case into my schoolroom with orders not to open it until Father had joined us. We could not imagine what such an immense chest could possibly contain and were wild with excitement when it disclosed a huge horn mounted on a smallish square base. We adored playing it, yet it was Father who derived the keenest pleasure from it, delighting especially in the records of Adelina Patti.

From an early age I was fond of reading and spent most of my time doing so. The English books which I read when I reached schoolroom age included *Uncle Tom's Cabin*, *Little Lord Fauntleroy*, *Tom Brown's Schooldays*, *The Tapestry Room*, *The Secret Garden*, *Children of the New Forest*, much of Dickens and Scott, neither of which I enjoyed, and Shakespeare. In French, I read the books of the Bibliothèques Rose and Bleu, Daudet's *Lettres de mon moulin*, and later Jules Verne. I adored Selma Lagerlöf's *Adventures of Nils* and *The Queens of Kungahella* and also Jerome K. Jerome's *Three Men in a Boat*, but I preferred above all others the books which were kept in Father's study. In *War and Peace* old Prince Bolkonsky spends much of his time lying on the sofa in his study. The study sofa was an indispensable piece of furniture to a Russian gentleman. It was his place of refuge from

---

*Architectural pâtisseries had been popularized by the French chef, Marie-Antoine Carême (1784–1833), whose employers included Talleyrand, the Prince Regent and Tsar Alexander I. His designs for these confections were published in *Le Pâtissier pittoresque – précédé d'un traité sur les cinq ordres d'architecture* (1815).
† Tamara Talbot Rice, *Elizabeth Empress of Russia*, London, 1970, p. 138.

boredom – that Russian malady – from ill health or depression. Father's library was furnished with Dutch marquetry furniture and several sombre, either German or Portuguese, pieces, and contained the essential sofa. The pictures were chiefly the works of Russian artists but also included a couple of genre paintings by the Dutch seventeenth-century artist David Teniers which amused us and embarrassed our governesses because each included a man relieving nature.

I had very little free time but it never occurred to me to wish for more, any unexpected break in my strictly ordered routine sufficing to delight me. Sometimes such treats took the form of a drive with Mother to buy delicious cakes at the French confectioner Ballet and Einem sweets from Berlin or going to Eliseev's great emporium where caviare was sold from large wooden barrels and dazzling groceries, beautifully displayed, were imported from both the Eastern and Western worlds. Another treat was to walk with Maykins to Druce's, the English shop at the top of the Nevsky Prospekt where, as at Harrods, almost everything could be bought. A large poster of Bubbles hung just inside its entrance and after seeing it I too took to blowing bubbles. Many years later I was to meet in Scotland the elderly admiral who had suffered in his youth for having, as a child, sat to Millais for that painting but who, I believe, in old age, enjoyed hearing that it had indirectly provided a child in far-distant Russia with a good deal of pleasure.*

There were certain popular events which my parents felt that I should not miss. On one such occasion, with rain threatening, I drove out of town with Father to watch the flight of what I fancy to have been the first Russian-made aeroplane to take to the air. If that is correct it must have been in 1913, when the first four-engined Russian bomber flew over the capital. Igor Sikorsky designed it and I think it was called the *Vityaz* (Knight). It weighed four tons and could stay in the air for almost two hours with eight aboard. A large crowd had assembled to watch the aircraft. At some point – I cannot remember whether it was on take-off or landing – the plane flew so low that, in a moment of panic, Father opened his umbrella and raised it protectively above my head, blotting out my view of the aircraft. All those carrying umbrellas followed his example so

*Admiral Sir William Melbourne James GCB (1881–1970), the artist's grandson.

that, for years to come, I mentally associated aeroplanes with umbrellas.

At weekends we sometimes drove to the Islands in the delta of the Neva.* Although they were part of St Petersburg the expanses of water, groves of birches and shrubs, and the open spaces seemed so little urbanized that I was allowed to take off my hat and gloves and run about instead of walking sedately at the side of a grown-up. Longer day excursions by train took us to Peterhof (now Petrodvoretz), even to Oranienbaum (now Lomonosova) from where the naval base of Kronstadt could be seen on a clear day. These outings were a welcome change from the customary walk with Maykins through the formal, statue-lined alleys of Peter the Great's Summer Garden to the Neva embankment, past the British Embassy and the Winter Palace to the Senate Square where, under the gaze of Falconet's majestic equestrian statue of Peter the Great, plump women and cheeky youths sold large balloons, beribboned wet nurses, their finery flying in the breeze, pushed their charges in large prams, and smartly uniformed court officials and civil servants hurried to their offices. It was a long and tiring walk, and I preferred the all too rare occasions when, seated in a Bath chair mounted on skids, we were pushed across the frozen Neva by brawny skaters, returning home by walking across the nearest bridge. The Neva was at its most exciting in the spring when its thick coating of ice broke into miniature icebergs or fantastic shapes of such massive proportions that, on colliding as they rushed towards the open sea, they emitted a threatening, ear-splitting roar. Then, as soon as the great river was clear of ice, it filled with countless barges, steamboats of various sizes and large ships, to become as lively and busy a thoroughfare as the crowded Nevsky Prospekt.

Holidays were printed in red on our calendars, ordinary days in black. There were almost as many red-numbered days in a good week as ordinary black ones, for all the church festivals as well as the anniversaries of every member of the imperial family, in addition to certain saints' days and some state occasions, ranked as holidays. Those were veritable red-letter days, each seeming a gift

---

*The 1914 Baedeker states that the Islands sometimes flooded in spring but by summer were verdant parks. They contained many *dachas* or country villas.

from God. Each therefore called for some special celebration and even the least inventive diversion, representing as it did a break from routine, gave us intense pleasure. Although our own birthdays and name-days were not printed in red in our calendars they ranked as if they had been, and we looked forward to them with special delight. A birthday child's dining-room chair was exquisitely festooned with flowers; there were quantities of presents but, most precious of all, was the impression I had on those days of owning time. It was only then that I had the right to dispose of time exactly as I wished; I became its master, its dispenser, and by delaying one activity could make myself believe that I had stopped time at a moment of bliss, and would think of myself as omnipotent. Nevertheless, Christmas and Easter, the Church's two main festivals, surpassed even birthdays in splendour and solemnity, the gravity of All Souls' Day* insidiously heralding the joys of Christmas, whilst the unrestrained gaiety of Butter Week (Carnival) presaged Easter's profound significance. Christmas and Easter were universal as opposed to personal festivals and, as such, could be anticipated and talked about.

Preparations for Christmas occupied several weeks, for Mother was determined to provide presents not only for the entire household, but also for the parents and children of most of the servants. The number of these gifts ran into three figures. Few were starkly utilitarian, for on that festive occasion Mother was at pains to satisfy the younger maids' craving for finery, the children's longing for toys, the footmen's desire for trinkets, a page-boy's wish for some foreign novelty. Each present had to be attractively wrapped and carefully labelled. Annually until 1917 a large Christmas tree was sent up from the country. In December the sight of cart tracks in the snow of our courtyard was a signal to rush to the kitchen where a couple of laughing peasants were being feasted. Later, the tree they had brought was carried to the prettiest drawing-room and set on a cross-piece of wood covered by a sheet, puckered to resemble snow drifts. The tree reached almost to the ceiling. On the 23rd most of the time was spent decorating it. Our parents' fear of

---

*Tamara is probably referring here to 'Ancestors' Saturday', the Saturday preceding 26 October. Instituted in 1380 to commemorate casualties of a victory against the Tartars, it came with time to include not only soldiers but all the dead.

fire was part of the fun, for each candle gave rise to an amicable argument as to whether it had been safely placed. Sponges were tied to very long poles resting in buckets of water ready for the footmen to use in extinguishing any dangerously burning candle. Presents were put round the base of the tree. When everything had been done, the doors to the room were locked and we were told to direct our thoughts to the religious aspects of the festival. That was difficult because the staff party started at midnight on the 24th, when the tree was lit for the first time. After presents had been distributed we younger children were sent to bed and the servants sat down to a splendid supper.

By the afternoon of the 25th the tree had been refreshed, our presents laid at its base and the room made splendidly festive for our family celebrations. We exchanged presents, good wishes, kisses, played games, danced and stayed up for dinner. On the 26th the tree was lit for the third and last time, on this occasion for a children's party. No presents were grouped round the tree but at the end of the afternoon each guest received a fairing from its branches. On the 27th we generally left for Moscow to spend a fortnight or so with my favourite cousins. Here too there was a tree, more presents, much gaiety and more delights. Twelfth Night marked their end.

Twelfth Night was the best night of all, for it was devoted to fortune-telling. The maids were even keener to probe the future than we were, for in their case the whole of their happiness was at stake. Whom would they marry? How would life work out? Many of the maids would at intervals slip out into the street carrying a looking-glass; stationing themselves near a street light, their backs to the pavement, they would raise the mirror when a man walked past, hoping to catch a glimpse of his features in the glass in order to gain an impression of those which would belong to the man they would marry. Saucier maids would stop the first man they met and, with the darkness concealing their blushes, ask his Christian name, for it would be the same as that of their future husband. Uncle Sasha, Mother's youngest brother, used to draw up lists of preposterous names, such as Melchizedek or Agaphon and, wearing a hideous mask, prowl the streets in order to reduce girls to a state of horrified giggles by his answers. Although prevented from getting too involved in the fortune-telling, we were allowed to join the maids when they resorted to the wax method of divination. It entailed having a row of buckets filled with icy cold water, lumps of white wax and lots of shovels. A lump of wax on a shovel was held over a fire until it melted when it had to be tipped very rapidly into the near-freezing water. As it solidified the wax formed into shapes which were regarded as omens. Oddly enough, year after year, my wax solidified into a galleon or boat – a symbol of travel.

Butter Week was celebrated by almost everybody. It was a week of gluttony, of abandonment to sheer delight, a time when we children could be almost as foolish as we felt inclined, and when even the poor shared in the feasting and fun, for the week's dissipations served as a prelude to the Lenten fasts and abnegations which succeeded it. In St Petersburg Butter Week was heralded by the arrival of the *veika*, an enticing little rustic sledge drawn by a single, sturdy, fast-pacing pony with bells and coloured streamers suspended from its harness. For that one week in the year the *veikas* could carry passengers in the capital's streets and it was difficult to walk past an empty *veika* without hiring it. Their peasant drivers were keen to pit their ponies against those of the *likhachi*, the rakish cabs, and the spontaneous races developed into exciting contests, turning many a street into a tricky racecourse. Forgetful of safety, ignoring the menace of the tramlines, the drivers, wildly cracking their whips, raced headlong to their goal accompanied by the cheers or yells of despair of their passengers. Inevitably the *likhachi* won.

We had money to fritter away in Butter Week because our real uncles and many of the nominal ones pressed silver or gold coins into our hands. We were allowed to accept that money and spend it as we wished at the fair, which was called the *Verba*, the synonym for a willow twig and for Palm Sunday when, in Russia, catkins were used as a symbol for palm fronds. In my childhood the booths which inspired Alexander Benois and Diaghilev to create the ballet *Petrushka* had been banished from the Palace Circus to a site close to the Horse Guards, near the Field of Mars, still in the town's centre. Food stalls abounded, and although the wealthy feasted at home on pancakes filled with caviare and other delicacies, the poor gorged at the fair on hot pancakes dripping with butter and on bulbous doughnuts; others walked about skilfully and rhythmically throwing sunflower seeds into their mouths. Caged birds could be bought for release on 24 March in celebration of spring;

finery could be purchased, cheap jewellery, lace collars, satin ribbons, vividly patterned cotton and woollen headscarves, wooden toys intricately carved and gaily painted by village craftsmen and, most exciting of all, small glass tubes filled with pink or mauve-coloured liquid – I believe some sort of spirit – in which little black glass imps were imprisoned; called for some inexplicable reason either Carthusian Devils or American Inhabitants these imps could be made to career up and down their cages merely by warming the tubes in one's hands. The noise was gloriously deafening, the gaiety sublime.

Sometimes during Lent I was taken to a jeweller, generally Fabergé, to buy miniature Easter eggs to be worn as bracelet or necklace charms, as presents for my governesses and teachers. Until the war I preferred the gold eggs decorated with enamel inlays or those made of semi-precious stones to those decorated with the letters XV and VV standing for Christ is Risen and Verily He is Risen, but during the war I chose eggs displaying the flags of Russia and her allies. As Easter approached, it fell to us children to colour seemingly endless numbers of hard-boiled eggs, since each member of the household was to receive twelve.

In contrast to the gaiety of Christmas, Easter was a solemn, spiritual occasion. Its spirit was especially marked in Moscow. Services were held in all the Kremlin's churches and chapels, as they were in each of Moscow's 1,600 churches and in all those throughout the land. Before leaving for the midnight service the lights burning in front of each family's domestic icons were extinguished and fresh candles were taken for lighting at the moment of Christ's resurrection. As midnight struck, the great bells of the Kremlin's St John's belfry gave the signal for all the monasteries and churches to ring out the glad news. The darkness in which the churches had been plunged since the dawn of Good Friday was lifted as the priest lit a taper from the single flame kept burning on the altar, passing its light and message of hope from candle to candle and icon lamp to icon lamp until the church was ablaze with light. The voices of the choir rose in glorious song as the priest blessed the Easter fare which members of the congregation had brought to church for that purpose. The traditional Easter greeting of *Christós Voskrésse* – *Voistinu Voskrésse*, Christ is Risen – Verily He is Risen, accompanied by the traditional three kisses, echoed on all sides as the worshippers hurried home, shielding their burning tapers, trying to preserve their flames in order to use them for relighting the icon lamps which they had extinguished a few hours earlier.

In the morning a marvellous, almost tangible feeling of pure happiness permeated the house. It acquired an earthier element when poor Maykins ventured into the streets because her Titian-coloured hair and glowing cheeks proved irresistible to many bearded, none-too-clean peasants or saucy youths who took advantage of the day to bestow the traditional three kisses whilst she, blushing a deeper crimson, was obliged as she broke away to mutter the expected reply of 'Verily, He is Risen.'

I enjoyed looking at paintings and it was probably because I was fascinated by two of Makovski's winter landscapes that Mother arranged for me to visit him in his St Petersburg studio.* It was late autumn, the weather damp and grey, depressing to foreigners but sharpening a Petersburgian's sensibilities. Winter could be sensed waiting to strike. Meanwhile the mustard-coloured air was disturbing, the sky was changing into a sound box ready to relay the hoofbeats of the town's equestrian statues.

My visit, the first of several, was sheer delight. As the door opened I encountered that tingling, rather oily smell of an artist's studio. Although it made me sneeze I thought it delicious, breathtakingly exciting. I saw before me, on a platform, a chair set against glowing drapery, stacks of canvases, and the entire paraphernalia of a studio. I liked what I saw and I liked my host who, although he seemed old, treated me as a contemporary. He was to make a habit of talking to me of rural Russia, of the beauty of its landscape, the luminous quality of its colours, the poetry of its customs. Did he and others who shared his love of Russia sense that the country they knew and loved, and regarded as essential to their own identity, was to disappear – to survive only as memories shared by a small group of people? He also talked at length of the theatre, of its evocative powers, of its duty to create its own reality in order correctly to portray authentic, everyday life. Makovski was perhaps

---

*The genre painter Vladimir Egorovich Makovski (1846–1920) studied in Moscow, then taught there until 1894 when he was appointed to the St Petersburg Academy of Arts. A year after, he became rector of the Academy's School of Arts. He spent the remainder of his life in St Petersburg. Although some works are hung in the Russian Museum in St Petersburg, the greater part of his output is in the Tretiakov Gallery, Moscow.

responsible for the habit I formed of making close friendships with people far older than myself, friendships which enriched the greater part of my life, but inevitably left deep gaps in my later years.

In St Petersburg I was often taken to concerts, especially to those given by young celebrities such as the teenaged Yasha Heifetz or the child prodigy Willy Ferrero who conducted the Petersburg Symphony Orchestra wearing a Lord Fauntleroy suit.* I went to the cinema to see *The Last Days of Pompeii* and, later, a Russian version of *War and Peace*. A visit to Cinizelli's Circus when I was very young to see a train pulled by a small steam-engine manned entirely by piglets failed to amuse me. All attempts to persuade me to enjoy the circus were abandoned after I had seen an acrobat fall to his death through a safety net too rotten to serve its purpose.

In contrast I adored the theatre. In Moscow we were taken to *Twelfth Night* admirably produced against a backcloth of curtains, and to Maeterlinck's *Blue Bird*. But the opera, especially Russian operas such as *Sadko*, *Boris Godunov*, *A Life for the Tsar* (now called *Ivan Susanin*), enchanted me. Even more I enjoyed the ballets which, like the opera, I watched spellbound from my parents' box in the Mariinsky (later renamed the Kirov). As a rule I was taken to matinées but occasionally, for a particular production such as that of *Don Quixote* in which Cecchetti appeared as Sancho, I was allowed to attend an evening performance. Although Maykins disapproved of late nights she enjoyed them almost as much as me, but insisted on putting me to bed in the afternoon, hoping that I would sleep.

I knew what to expect from the dancers because I attended two dancing classes a week, both taken by Mr Berestovsky of the Mariinsky ballet. One was devoted to ballroom dancing, curtseying, waltzing, dancing the polka, minuet, *pas d'Espagne* and, later, the quickstep and tango, as well as national dances such as the Russian *gopak*, the Polish *krakoviak* and mazurka, and the Caucasian *lesghinka*, but the second lesson concentrated on ballet. Mr Berestovsky was tall, elegant, strict and very formal. He wore a morning coat and white kid gloves. I loved dancing the waltz and polka and, later, the tango, but in the evenings, when my young uncles were in the house, I clamoured for the mazurka and

---

*In 1914 the eight-year-old boy toured Europe, starting in Russia.

krakoviak, for they danced these with great panache. Yet it was the Russian *gopak* which really stirred me. Anna had taught it to me when I was still very young and, not unlike Tolstoy's Natasha Rostova, I strove when dancing it to express what I assumed to be the spirit of Russia.

Military parades and regiments on the march provided splendid spectacles. I loved their brass bands, their uniforms, their medals. Probably the finest sight I was to see was the great procession down the Nevsky from the Winter Palace to mark the three-hundredth anniversary of the Romanov dynasty in March 1913. The Astoria Hotel overlooking St Isaac's Cathedral had been built to receive the foreign guests expected in St Petersburg for the celebrations. My parents had been favourably impressed when they attended the hotel's opening. In the 1940s Hitler planned a victory banquet there, preparing invitations which gave a month and a year but left the date blank. In the 1980s the hotel was rebuilt and now ranks with the Grand Hotel Europe as the best in the city.

The anniversary procession was magnificent, yet I felt that a general's funeral was even more impressive a sight, the music more solemn and stirring. Many generals seemed to qualify for a splendid funeral. The black hearse was drawn by six superb black horses wearing black horse furniture, black masks and magnificent black ostrich feathers. The dead man's charger, led by his groom, walked immediately behind, bridled and saddled, its master's boots slung across the empty saddle. The dead man's batman followed, carrying his master's orders and decorations neatly arranged in rows on a red velvet cushion. Also spectacular was the long funeral procession that unfolded in a ribbon behind him.

2

The Riches of Diversity

I remember, I remember
The fir trees dark and high;
I used to think their slender tops
Were close against the sky.

Thomas Hood, *Past and Present*

I ADORED rural Russia, and the short periods which we spent
annually in each of our estates, Ostrogovitza near Narva, and
Volgovo on the middle reaches of the Volga, passed all too quickly.
Volgovo was our favourite house, perhaps because it was less fine
architecturally and therefore cosier than Ostrogovitza. Both were
built in the Rastrelli style which became fashionable in the mid-
eighteenth century, each displaying along their main façades the
columns and pediments, niches and vistas of rooms characterizing
their interiors, which the Italian-born architect had introduced
to St Petersburg. Both were of wood, but the columns had been
so skilfully painted to resemble Siberian marble that, aided by
malachite-topped tables and marble urns mounted in ormolu, the
subterfuge became evident only to the touch. The house at Volgovo
was a trifle smaller than that at Ostrogovitza and was built in a
more rustic style. Replacing Ostrogovitza's terrace were columns
aligned along the outer edge of the veranda. These did not
attempt to conceal their forest origin.

Some impoverished relatives and close friends of our parents
lived permanently in both houses. Distances were great in Russia:
the nearest country town could be as much as seventy miles away,
the roads were poor, the stations remote. Parties were such fun that
house guests were apt to stay for a couple of weeks, luncheon or
dinner guests for a night or so.

Whereas at Ostrogovitza bachelors who visited us lived in one
wing of the house and the servants in another, at Volgovo the young

men were housed in a square-shaped chalet, whilst the maids, under the supervision of an inefficient duenna, lived in another, situated at some distance from that assigned to visiting young men.

At Ostrogovitza, a wide terrace at the back of the house overlooked parkland and an ornamental lake. We assembled there for tea; whilst they waited for it, our elders, when not playing tennis or croquet, sat for hours on end talking, playing cards, embroidering. Both afternoon and evening tea were focal points of the day, in town and country. The samovar presided over both, but lost some of its magic when there were so many guests that it had to stand on a sideboard with a footman instead of Mother pouring the tea. The samovar was lit in the kitchen by a youth employed especially for the purpose. When it reached boiling point it was carried to the table by a footman. Mother had seen several people badly scalded because of a dropped samovar, generally as a result of a child colliding with it. She therefore insisted on the samovar-carrying footman being preceded by a page-boy, the lad announcing their approach in an enchanting singsong. We looked forward to his chant, although my mother's idiosyncrasy amused us.

In the spring, both at Ostrogovitza and at Volgovo, the air was heavy with the heady scent of lilacs, lilies of the valley, acacias and elderberry trees. At both estates there was boating on the lake or river, paddling and fishing in clear, cold, swift-flowing streams rich in fish and crayfish. Later in the year, in the north, there were wild raspberries in the woods, later still cranberries and bilberries, and finally came the time for mushrooming picnics. Since vast numbers of mushrooms were needed both for immediate use and for drying and pickling, these expeditions into the forests were serious as well as gay occasions. Everyone took part. The footmen were the first to leave the house, setting out in a cart loaded with provisions, napery and cutlery. Mother was a great walker. Accompanied by her walking companions she was the next to depart. Then we children, with our governesses, tutors and nannies, scrambled on to a brake and hurried to the meeting place. The staider and older members of the party followed at their leisure in carriages.

Our route led past cornfields before turning to skirt one of the woods. The dust which coated the roads inches deep rose at the slightest disturbance in a dense cloud, drier yet as clinging as snowflakes, to mask our faces, making our eyes smart and parching our lips, but on arrival there was always a clear stream or pool in which to wash. The picnic was delicious, but mushroom-picking so serious a business that we did not dawdle over it. On 13 August, the day of Florus and Laurus, patron saints of horses and grooms, no horses were worked. Instead they were bathed in the river, adorned with ribbons and allowed to graze.

Jam-making often coincided with hay-making, in itself a busy time. Sometimes both tasks were interrupted by fierce, generally short storms. These were heralded by a sudden stillness. Then the sultry midsummer heat made way for heavy billows of violent, ominous gusts of wind. Instantly the house was in a turmoil. Doors banged, windows shook. Servants of both sexes and various ages rushed from room to room, the women and girls shrieking and twittering as they hastened to close windows and doors. Whilst they were doing so the wind seemed to reach hurricane force, the flashes of lightning were dazzling, whilst each ear-splitting crash of thunder evoked fresh and even louder wails from the maids. Then, quite suddenly, the wind dropped, there was a moment of stillness, then the rain would come down in torrents to be greedily absorbed by the parched earth. Whilst some bewailed the damage the storm was likely to cause to the hay and fruit, the dry soil sucked up the moisture, gathering freshness from the life-giving downpour, manifesting its satisfaction by exuding gentle steam and a most delicious scent. The rain seldom caused any very severe damage and work was quickly resumed both in the fields and gardens.

Although the boys, and almost as often we girls, had for days gorged on fruit in the kitchen gardens there was never a shortage. The jam was made outdoors in vast copper pans poised above temporary brick braziers. Village girls helped the maids stir the fruit; they worked under the supervision of the head cook, the housekeeper and the kitchen maids. All wore their prettiest blouses, fullest skirts and gayest ribbons; all cajoled the passers-by, insisting on them tasting the hot jam and pronouncing upon it; they showed off before the men, flirted, sang catchy songs, coined *chastushki*, excelled at repartee. Wasps buzzed, evoking shrieks and laughter. Immense quantities of jam, syrups and preserved fruits had to be made to last the winter in a household where large amounts were consumed both upstairs and downstairs. Sugar was bought in bulk as a cure against chills. It came in tall, cylindrical cones wrapped in saxe blue paper, to be broken into lumps by the sugar-boy during the coldest months. Many preferred to sweeten their tea with black-currant or raspberry jam instead of drinking it through a lump of sugar held in the mouth, *v prikusku.*

The pilgrims who called at the house fascinated me more than the jam-making, and very much more than did the majority of our parents' guests. Although the kitchens were forbidden to us, we were thoroughly at home in them. First my beloved Anna, then Nastya would tell me when an especially entertaining pilgrim was entrancing the servants. Within minutes we were in the dining-hall set aside for pilgrims, plying the visitors with questions, delighting in their racy, picturesque language and pious sentiments spiced with picaresque wit.

In town a room was also set aside for the hungry and there too we listened spellbound to the pilgrims, enthralled by their powers of evocation, their masterly use of the Russian language. The room in which Mother provided free meals for students had a sadder, grimmer atmosphere. Though also forbidden to us through fear of infectious diseases – cholera, diphtheria and typhus being common epidemics – we knew it well. We often felt compelled to try and cheer up those using it. I don't suppose we succeeded in doing so, but we were always welcomed by our visitors and it was from them that we learnt to esteem scholarship and respect teachers. Many of the students came from very poor homes; many lived on the verge of starvation, yet for them knowledge served as a beacon; it guided and encouraged them, and invested even the most venial of them with a touch of dignity.

I loved our forests of oak, birch, pine and aspen, our parks rich in lilacs and acacias, with alleys of the French type intersecting them at unexpected angles. I loved the columned terrace of Ostrogovitza, the wooden verandas at Volgovo, but I especially rev-elled in the freedom I was given in the country, a freedom which I soon learnt to extend by climbing some tall tree to lie hidden among its branches, ignoring calls to return to the house. My dresses suffered, I was considered a tomboy and, to my delight, was nicknamed Tommy.

Since I was considered delicate I spent part of April and early May with Maykins in our villa at Pavlovsk, which was as much of a royal village as neighbouring Tsarskoe Selo. Sometimes we went by train, sometimes by car, but once there we bicycled for miles, often going on picnics. In 1915, we were there at harvest time when the corn was taller than I, and studded with cornflowers and poppies. I loved creeping into it and listening to it murmuring to itself as I gazed up into the intensely blue sky. Although war raged, peace prevailed; the world was familiar, secure, enduring; so must Russia have looked in the past; so, I presumed, would it look in the future.

The long Petersburgian winter, which set in towards mid-October and extended well into April, was heralded by the arrival of the workmen responsible for the insertion of inner sets of windows, double glazing helping to retain indoor heat. The window-sills between the double frames were filled with fresh moss or cotton wool before the woodwork was sealed, leaving only one small pane – a *fortochka* – in each window with which to air the room. One inner set of frames was also left unsealed in the warmest corridor for Volodia's tortoise. The snowflakes which fell on the outer windows were somehow magnified by the inner ones, the star-shaped outlines of the first winter snowfall becoming distorted and as fascinating as any shape produced by a kaleidoscope. The floor polishers provided another diversion. They came weekly to give the parquet floors, many of which were elaborately inlaid, a glorious sheen. Encasing their boots in layers of felt they glided along the floors with the elegance and speed of skaters, whistling and singing as they performed intricate turns to skirt the heavier pieces of furniture.

My exacting winter timetable came into force soon after our return to town. When the ice was thick and firm, instead of going for a walk I went skating on the frozen Fontanka,* but I tired easily and as my pace slackened so did my resistance to the cold diminish. I would then sidle up to the large braziers burning at each end of the rink and stand there gazing happily at the reflections of the darting, bright red flames on the polished, bluish ice. When the weather was very bad I was allowed to stay indoors and toboggan on a wooden hill some fifteen feet high set up in a seldom-used corridor.

---

*One of the four waterways, two natural, two man-made, which drain the formerly marshy ground on which the southern part of St Petersburg was built.

In winter I seemed to spend most of my free time dressing to go out and undressing on my return. Houses were so well heated that I wore pastel-coloured shantung or white broderie anglaise dresses and cotton underclothes throughout the year. As a result I had to wear a prodigious amount of warm outdoor clothes during the coldest months. Mother, and doubtless most of her friends, considered external pockets unladylike and I was not allowed them in my over-coats, not even on the outside of the black sealskin fur coat which I wore for longer periods than any of the others. Although a pocket was inserted in its lining it was inaccessible since I wore a quilted lining under the fur. I had therefore to rely on the pocket in the lining of my muff. I craved for external pockets and, being denied them, longed to be a boy, and thereby qualify for a plethora of pockets.

During the winter months, that longing twice daily verged on bitterness as I struggled to lace the knee-high, black leather boots lined with fleece which I wore out of doors over knitted woollen leggings. The boots were provided by Harrods, as were those worn by the boys, but whilst the laces on their boots were held in place by hooks, mine had to be threaded through eyelets and, to make matters worse, I was not allowed to lace them, as boys could, in the easier horizontal way, but was obliged to cross-lace them. A single mistake, if made at the start, was apt to pass undetected until just short of the top, and in that case the slow and irksome operation had to be started afresh. Since I was not allowed any help in dress-ing, dread of making a mistake when lacing my boots generally ensured my doing so, often reducing me to tears. During my child-hood I expended so many tears over such trifles that I must have exhausted the supply, for I have seldom been able to cry over the great sorrows of my life.

Mother adored going abroad. We went every year, generally at the start of the summer holidays, often for a couple of months. Our journeys usually took us first to Berlin and then on to a spa such as Carlsbad or Marienbad where Mother would spend three weeks drinking the waters and taking mud baths. We children were often deposited in some quieter, less fashionable resort. Sometimes we went to Engelberg in Switzerland where the prizes at the rifle ranges consisted of delicious, amusingly shaped gingerbreads lavishly covered in coloured icing – a great incentive for good shooting.

Sometimes I was sent to a Swiss mountain village where the wild strawberries, edelweiss and the sound of distant cattle bells to some extent compensated for the terror which the free-ranging, angry cows aroused in me. Father seldom accompanied us. He preferred to go to Biarritz later in the year.

On leaving Petersburg we always had a railway carriage to ourselves and, given the amount of our luggage, we needed it. Our light luggage included carpet bags, holdalls, umbrella and walking-stick cases, Mother's large leather dressing-case with numerous silver-topped glass containers and ivory brushes and combs, and our own smallish suitcases. We seemed always to travel with thirty-three pieces of heavy luggage, mostly very large trunks, but also several big square hatboxes. Until I saw Visconti's film *Death in Venice*, I had forgotten that, like the Polish girls in the film, I too wore a straw boater, or that Mother, who joined us for our hotel luncheons, more especially at the Excelsior on the Lido, sported vast hats trimmed with wax replicas of the produce of a large kitchen garden. In London, in the 1930s, Freya Stark wore only slightly smaller versions of my mother's elaborate, highly bedecked hats. By that time, Mother's variation on the style had been reduced to a modest straw boater trimmed with only a few imitation flowers and several cherries.

Whenever we were on the point of leaving home for a fairly long time, everyone living in the house assembled in the inner hall to sit in silence for two minutes, while each of us mentally invoked God's blessing on travellers and stay-at-homes alike. On returning to any of our country houses, though not to town, we were greeted with a tray of bread and salt. Much though I enjoyed travelling, seeing new sights, gathering fresh impressions, tasting unaccustomed dishes, those few minutes of silent leave-taking tore at my heart, perhaps in divination of the final, permanent, enforced parting. Swallowing tears, I would make my farewells. However, it was the custom for friends to assemble at the station to bid the travellers God speed, increasing the mound of luggage by gifts of huge bouquets of exotic flowers, great baskets of fruit and luscious boxes of expensive sweets. I quickly cheered up.

The train from Petersburg to Berlin stopped frequently. Volodia knew the culinary specialities of each station restaurant and, during daylight stops, he could not be prevented from bounding off the train before it had halted to rush to the restaurant and sample his favourite dish. He seldom came back before the station-master had rung his departure bell for the second time, and my distraught mother had taken up a position with one foot resting on the bottom step of the carriage, while the other swayed above the platform. She hung there, imploring Volodia to return; he invariably succeeded in doing so just as the bell was being rung for the third and last time. When the train reached the German frontier post of Verzbolovo (now Virbolis in Lithuania), all passengers were obliged to abandon the comfortable, broad-gauged Russian train for the narrow-gauged Western equivalent. The commotion was intense as travellers from all three classes collected their numerous belongings and staggered to the customs sheds where all luggage and passports were laboriously and slowly examined. Our trunks and suitcases, drooping flowers, messy sweets, toys, books and overnight bags were eventually transported to the rather cramped two-berth compartments of the Compagnie Internationale des Wagons-Lits et des Grands Express Européens.

We never stayed in Berlin for as long as we did in Paris or even in London, where my coats, boots and shoes were made, and where orders were placed for stocks of marmalade and other English delicacies enjoyed by Maykins. It was in Paris that Mother bought her clothes and underwear, even though some of her dresses were made in Petersburg by Madame de Brissac, the Russian court dressmaker. Life in Paris was delightful even for the very young. The town's beauty and elegance, the lively streets, the amusing side-shows, donkey and goat carriages in the Champs-Élysées, the *bateaux-mouches* on the Seine and the delicious cakes, bouchées and ice-creams obtainable in all bakeries, cafés and tea-rooms, provided a seemingly endless succession of pleasures.

These delights were epitomized in a magnificent present I received from Monsieur Poiret, the French fashion designer, in the spring of 1914. I had recently been given a very large doll which, notwithstanding its weight, I insisted on taking everywhere, even to one of Mother's fittings at Poiret. The great couturier was present but paid no more attention to my doll than to me, concentrating instead on Mother's clothes. Nevertheless, when her order was delivered it was accompanied by a miniature trunk containing replicas of many of her dresses made to fit my doll. At the time, that generous and splendid gift left me speechless. It was to give me endless pleasure during the depressing war years which followed, and in retrospect it acquired the quality of one of those exquisite tailpieces with which eighteenth-century printers adorned the end of a chapter. Poiret's present set its seal on a way of life doomed, perhaps not undeservedly, by the outbreak of the First World War.

In the summer of 1914 we left for Carlsbad earlier than usual, for a number of us were to meet on the Isle of Wight to watch the great review of the British Fleet. This decision was surprising, for neither Mother, nor the brother and sister who were to join her there, were nautically minded; indeed, they tended to dislike the sea. We were still at Carlsbad when Archduke Ferdinand was murdered at Sarajevo. We were having tea at the Kurhaus and the band was playing a Strauss waltz; the music suddenly stopped, voices died down and, in an ominous silence, the Grand Duke's death was announced. Political murders were not rare in the St Petersburg of my childhood and it did not occur to Mother to change her plans. We left for England on the appointed day.

A large Victorian house complete with staff had been rented in Shanklin, on the Isle of Wight, halfway up Luccombe Road. As promised it did overlook the sea, yet it was some distance from it, the large garden being separated from the beach by a high and very steep cliff. The road to the sea, downhill for a bit, then bending sharply to the left along the top of the cliff, sloped down to the coastal road. Our garden contained a tennis court and a flag-pole.

We came to adore Shanklin, but it did not occur to us to wonder what its inhabitants thought of us. Yet we can hardly have failed to make some impression for there were twelve of us, of whom ten at least were determined thoroughly to explore the town. Volodia was then a plump and adventurous teenager whom Mother delighted in dressing in white sailor suits. Within minutes of our arrival in Luccombe Road he had disappeared in search of the shops. They were some way from the house and his absence passed unnoticed until evening. When no trace of him could be found either in the house or garden, indeed, even in the neighbourhood, Mother assumed that he had fallen off the cliff and drowned. Others thought this unlikely but were equally anxious about him and were on the point of informing the police of his disappearance when a benign constable appeared accompanied by a tearful boy. Volodia had lost his bearings and his requests for directions to Cucumber Road had been in vain.

On the following morning it fell to me to reveal our presence to the local inhabitants for, whilst shopping in the High Street, a bee flew up my knickers and stung my bottom; my roars and the most unlady-like frenzy with which I tore off my knickers attracted a crowd which followed Maykins and me to the chemist's shop. In the meantime, in accordance with Russian custom, the boys' tutor was bathing in the nude. Little time was lost in informing the vicar of the immodesty; and he also lost none in coming to the house to protest.

Other events distinguished our stay in Shanklin, in our eyes largely eclipsing the splendid spectacle provided by the Navy. Volodia, teased beyond endurance at his inability to catch a fish, brought a large brown one to Mother which he said he had caught. Having been duly complimented, he was told to ask cook to serve the strange creature in a white sauce. To our astonishment our haughty, disapproving but glacially polite cook entered the drawing-room to protest at having to cook a kipper in so unusual a way.

There was the pier with its enticing side-shows and automatic vending-machines, and the fortune-teller who foretold our futures with what proved to be remarkable prescience. Above all there were the Pierrots with white cone-shaped hats. They delighted us and we somehow contrived daily to attend at least one show. Motor cars were all the rage, and the boys were mad about them. Back in Russia we had recently acquired our first car, a Delaunay-Belleville, which could negotiate Moscow's hills only in reverse gear. The Pierrots were prob-ably equally interested in cars for they sang a song about a man who was always having to 'Get out and get under his little machine'. At Shanklin Volodia was of an age to giggle when the Pierrots sang 'Who were you with last night?' Then there was the tennis championship when my pretty cousin Lucie reached the semi-finals partnered by one of the Kaiser's sons, to find that the prince was not available for the crucial final match, having suddenly left for Germany without bidding anyone farewell.* A few days later our countries were at war.

---

*Considering the short time spent on the Isle, it made a deep impression on Tamara. The Review of the Fleet was on 18 July. The *Isle of Wight Guardian* of 1 August reported the recall of the prince, who had been staying at the Spa Hotel, Shanklin: 'The necessity for haste was so great that His Highness did not wait for the car to go to the hotel enclosure, but met it in the road opposite the pier.'

Uncle Sasha was staying with us. He became desperately anxious to rejoin the Sumsky Hussars; his sisters were equally keen to return to Russia. Whilst they tried to telephone their eldest brother at the Russian Embassy in London, we rushed to our trunks in search of a Russian flag and were not in the least surprised at finding one of the right size for our flag-pole. It was a perfect summer day. We got very hot trying to haul the flag up the pole. Having done so to our satisfaction we went down to bathe. Returning to the house for luncheon we found our elders in an even greater state of agitation. A neighbour had called during our absence to condole over the death of the Tsar. Once again our elders gathered round the telephone trying to call the embassy in London. Eventually they succeeded. The official to whom they spoke, although shocked to learn of the Tsar's death, was not astonished for there had, after all, been several attempts on the sovereign's life. He promised to check and ring back, but at that moment the vicar appeared to enquire why our flag was being flown at half-mast. Once again we were scolded – unfairly we thought. A few days later we left Shanklin for London determined to get back to Russia as soon as possible. We were astonished to hear as we travelled across England that, although it was still summer, some Russian soldiers were said to have arrived in London, their clothes covered in snow.*

Leaving England proved difficult, for sailings to Scandinavia had been cancelled.† Uncle Sasha spent his days discussing our departure with shipping agents. We were told to be ready to leave at short notice. Meanwhile there was time for frequent visits to Harrods. We also went sightseeing. Volodia insisted on visiting Madame Tussaud's for he had been told that anyone who succeeded in spending a night in the Chamber of Horrors would be rewarded

---

*The story that Russian troops had landed in Scotland and were making their way south to surprise the Germans in western Europe, may have originated in Yorkshire. A party of Lovat Scouts, Territorials from the Highlands, passing through the station, were served tea by local ladies who asked where they came from. They replied, in strong Celtic accents, 'Ross-shire.'

† The normal routes to Russia were no longer possible once the war broke out. Quickest had been the train from Charing Cross to St Petersburg, which took two days. Steamers to St Petersburg from London via the Kiel Canal had sailed weekly, the journey taking four days. Sailings from Hull took half a day longer. See *Baedeker's Russia*, 1914, reprinted London and Newton Abbot, 1971.

with a hundred pounds. He wanted to buy a motor car and was bitterly disappointed when told that the story was false. When we were notified to prepare for immediate departure for Newcastle, Volodia and his tutor could not be found. They had gone to the fairground at White City, seated themselves in the Great Wheel which stopped on reaching the highest point of its trajectory. They were dismayed to find themselves suspended upside-down and immobilized in mid-air. The wheel had stuck. Fortunately for us all, or perhaps not, they were eventually winched down and appeared just in time for us to catch our train to Newcastle.

THE FIRST WORLD WAR

O N 28 JUNE 1914 Archduke Franz Ferdinand, heir to the Austro-Hungarian throne, was assassinated by a Serb nationalist. A month later Austria-Hungary declared war on Serbia. Russia had no option but to support her co-religionists. On 1 August, Austria's ally, Germany, declared war on Russia and the following day on France. France would have been involved anyway, for she and Russia had signed a treaty of economic and commercial co-operation, secretly extending it to cover military assistance should either country be attacked by Germany. Britain did not enter the war until 4 August, when Germany violated Belgium whose neutrality both countries had guaranteed.

Russia's military strength lay in her manpower. At the age of twenty, men were liable for three to four years' national service, followed by thirteen to fifteen years on the reserve, then a further five or six years in the militia, exact timings depending on the arm of service. The regular army of 1,423,000 could, on mobilization, rapidly be expanded to 6,800,000.

The army was, however, woefully ill-equipped. There were only 4,652,000 rifles, insufficient for the expanded force. The manufacturing base was too small to make good the deficiency, let alone replace losses incurred by war and wear and tear. There were 48 field guns per division, half the number deployed by the Germans, and the Russians had 60 batteries of heavy guns compared with the 381 batteries of the Germans. Communications were even more rudimentary. The railroad westward was a mixture of broad and narrow gauge, necessitating frequent transfer of goods and men to other rail stock. The army had only 679 motor vehicles with a call on a further 475 civilian vehicles. Telephone lines were scarce and, since there were virtually no signallers, all messages had to be sent unencoded.

Russia's western frontier, some 1,500 miles long, abutted East Prussia in the north, Silesia to the west and the Austrian-Polish province of Galicia in the south. Her plan was to attack the Austrians on the outbreak of hostilities, but France pressed the Tsar to direct his principal effort at the Germans, to draw enemy battalions eastward. So waves of ill-equipped men were prematurely hurled into battle. Casualties were immense.

After initial success, particularly in the south, disaster struck the Russians in late August 1914. Their 2nd Army of five élite corps outstripped the troops on its flanks and was surrounded by the Germans at Tannenberg. Over 90,000 Russians were taken prisoner, 30,000 killed or missing. David Eggenberger, in his *Dictionary of Battles*, calls this 'one of the great disasters in military history'. Meanwhile the Germans, when within twenty miles of Paris, were forced to transfer two army corps and one cavalry division to their eastern front. A French counter-attack on 6 September, coupled with a British assault, succeeded in repulsing the Germans. Paris had been saved, but its salvation was due in no small part to a huge Russian sacrifice in manpower.

Despite Russian successes against Austria, the French continued to beseech the Tsar to make Germany the prime target, and the Tsar urged this on his generals, ignoring the increasingly pitiful state of his troops, short of ammunition and winter clothing. Deserters and refugees joined train-loads of wounded moving east, clogging railways and hindering the westward-moving reinforcements.

The Russians at first welcomed the war against their traditional enemy, Austria. But in St Petersburg especially, dissatisfaction with the tsarist autocracy permeated all classes. As casualty lists lengthened, the war became increasingly unpopular. In the autumn of 1915 the Russian front was pushed back. A December offensive was a failure. Another counter-offensive in the spring of 1916 came to nothing, owing to a sudden thaw which rendered the marshland of the intended battle area impassable in the absence of metalled roads. Yet in early 1916 Russia routed the Turkish army, capturing Erzerum. Their main offensive, against the Austrians in the south-west that June and July, forced the Austrians to retreat sixty to seventy miles and absorbed large numbers of enemy troops.

Russian military prospects for 1917 were good and morale on the front still high. But on 12 March elements of regiments in Petrograd mutinied. Although it forced the Germans to transfer yet more troops from west to east, another Russian offensive failed. Gradually, as demoralization spread to the front, the Russian front line was forced back. On 15 December the Bolsheviks unilaterally signed an armistice, ratified by the humiliating Treaty of Brest-Litovsk in March 1918. Her casualties are estimated as at least 1.7 million dead, 5 million wounded – appreciably more than Germany suffered on her two fronts, throughout the entire war.

The decade preceding the outbreak of the First World War had witnessed a struggle to liberalize the Tsar's autocratic regime. 1905 was a particularly tumultuous year. In January, in St Petersburg, on what became known as Bloody Sunday, tens of thousands of workers took part in an organized march to petition the Tsar for improved working conditions. They set off in holiday atmosphere, carrying icons, singing hymns and patriotic songs. Instead of receiving the petitioners, the Tsar retreated to his summer palace, leaving orders for the dispersal of the demonstration. The army opened fire without warning; over one thousand were killed, many more wounded.

Sporadic riots and strikes followed in different parts of the country. Some targeted Jews, others landowners. Elsewhere the military rebelled, the crew of the battleship *Potemkin* mutinied. Professional classes demanded a constitution. In October, an Assembly of Workers' Deputies (or Soviet) was established in St Petersburg and the Tsar issued a manifesto granting a handful of liberties and agreeing to the election of a State Duma, or Parliament, but with very restricted powers. Of the twenty or so political groupings returned in 1906 the largest, with 179 out of 478 seats, was the Constitutional Democrats (Kadets or Liberals), mainly lawyers, university professors, scientists. Other important parties included the intelligentsia; the Octobrists who thought that the October concessions went sufficiently far along the path of liberalism; the Social Democrats (Marxists), mostly factory workers; and the Socialist Revolutionaries (non-Marxist revolutionaries), mainly from the countryside. But the Tsar found the reforms advocated by the Assembly so outrageous that he ordered its dissolution. Three more short-lived Dumas were elected between then and 1912. Yet despite continued unrest, from 1907 until 1912 Russia enjoyed economic progress and industrial expansion. By 1914 support for the Tsar had rallied.

Meriel Buchanan, daughter of the British ambassador, in her book *Petrograd, the City of Trouble*, written shortly after the events, draws a vivid picture of the excitement and joy of the populace at the declaration of war, and of their veneration of the Tsar at a solemn intercession for peace held in August 1914 in Moscow. However, the exceptionally cold winter of 1915/16, coupled with serious food shortages and bad news from the front, brought disillusion and despair.

On 12 March 1917, regiments garrisoning Petrograd mutinied. The Tsar, away with the army, ordered the prorogation of the Duma, which had been recalled in 1915. Many of its members ignored the order and proclaimed a Provisional Government and, on 15 March, forced the Tsar to abdicate. The imperial family were imprisoned in the Summer Palace until moved to Tobolsk in Siberia in August. The following year, the Tsar and Tsarina and three of their four daughters were assassinated at Ekaterinburg. The fate of their son and of a fourth princess is unknown: although the survival of Anastasia has frequently been asserted, Anna Anderson's claim to that identity has been disproved by DNA testing. More recently it has been suggested that the surviving sister was Tatiana. However, a Russian commission of enquiry has now stated that it was Maria who escaped murder.

The Provisional Government, composed mainly of Constitutional Democrats but including representatives from other parties, hoped to maintain law and order until such time as a Constituent Assembly could be formed to draw up a new constitution. Unwisely, it deferred an election until the end of the war, the continuation of which was considered an honourable obligation. However, by the autumn, few troops remained loyal – some military students, a women's battalion and a few hundred Cossacks – and in the streets of the capital armed robbery and assault, often the work of petty crooks calling themselves Anarchists, was rife.

The loyalist women were members of Bochkareva's 'Battalion of Death'. Disguised as a man, Maria Leontievna Bochkareva had served on the front through much of the war, reaching the rank of sergeant. Then, dismayed by the dismal morale, she raised a battalion of 300 women, reasoning that men would be shamed into fighting when alongside their wives and daughters. A first detachment was quickly filled and, after a service of dedication at Kazan Cathedral, took its place on the south-west front. The women fought valiantly, taking over 200 prisoners in their first battle and suffering many casualties but, instead of being inspired, the men on both flanks fled. In Petrograd another detachment, the 1st Petrograd Women's Battalion, along with the cadets and Cossacks, remained loyal to the Provisional Government.

On 7 November 1917 (25 October, Julian Calendar, hence the 'October Revolution'), the Bolsheviks seized power in Petrograd, and then gained Moscow after a week of fighting. A mid-November election returned Bolsheviks in a quarter of the seats, but attempts to convene the Assembly were thwarted by Lenin who outlawed the Constitutional

Democratic Party, arresting its members. Finally the Duma opened on 18 January and sat for some twelve hours before being dispersed by the Red Guards: thus ended the attempt at democracy. In April 1918 the secret police surrounded and captured Anarchist strongholds in Moscow. From July 1918 political executions were ordered. Yet it was not until 1922, with the capture of Vladivostock in the east, that the Bolsheviks finally won the Revolution.

At the centre of these events had been the curious figure of Rasputin. A peasant from Tobolsk in Siberia, he was something of an enigma, a split personality. A pleasure-seeker, frequenting drinking places and houses of ill repute, over-indulging his appetites, both sexual and sensual, he was also deeply religious, spent hours in prayer, and was venerated as a *staretz*, or holy man.

One day in 1904, when working in the fields, he saw a vision of the Virgin Mary. As a result, he set off on a pilgrimage. This was not unusual – Tamara's beloved nurse, Anna, had done much the same. Eventually Rasputin reached St Petersburg, where he aroused the interest of society. When sober his was a pleasing personality and he was attractive to women. Also he had powers of healing: his hands could calm a fever, soothe a headache.

The imperial family, curious about so unusual a subject, extended an invitation. The young Tsarevich suffered from the hereditary disease, haemophilia, the least knock bringing on severe bleeding. It is said that on Rasputin's first visit in 1905, the bleeding had started from a knock on the Tsarevich's knee. Rasputin knelt beside the child's bed, prayed, and almost immediately the bleeding stopped. On another occasion, in 1912, the bleeding was so severe that the doctors had given up hope; a telegram was despatched to Rasputin, then in Tobolsk; after a long period of prayer, the *staretz* cabled that the boy should be kept quiet; a second telegram followed, saying that Rasputin's prayers had been heard. Understandably the Tsarina felt beholden to the one person who seemed capable of healing her son. The imperial family could not reconcile reports of Rasputin's increasing debauchery with the religious peasant they knew and revered.

On the outbreak of war, the Tsar took personal command of his army, leaving the Empress in charge of affairs in the capital. In her loneliness she became increasingly dependent on Rasputin. Rumours, almost certainly false, circulated that their relationship was closer than that of religious adviser and disciple. Moreover, since she was German by birth, disasters at the front were attributed to their treachery. Recent research has established that she was totally loyal to Russia. However, fear and loathing of Rasputin were so great that his name was not spoken aloud; he was referred to in whispers as 'the unmentionable one' or 'the nameless one'.

On 30 December 1916 things came to a head, with Prince Felix Yusupov masterminding a plot to assassinate the *staretz*. Inviting Rasputin to supper, the prince plied his guest with madeira and poisoned cakes. These seemingly having no effect, Yusupov took out his revolver and fired. Though hit through the heart, Rasputin struggled to the road where he was eventually overcome by the assassins. Two days later the police found the monk's body frozen under ice in the Neva.

Alas, the situation at the front did not improve with Rasputin's assassination and, there being no other convenient scapegoat, criticisms were increasingly directed at the Tsar himself.

Tamara's youngest uncle, Alexander (Sasha) Vilenkin, was a great favourite with all the family. Like his eldest brother, he had studied law and practised in Moscow, where he was lawyer to the British consulate. Although exemption should have been possible, on the grounds of his father's honourable citizenship, Sasha did his military service in the élite 1st Hussars, Sumsky Regiment. Vladimir Littauer, in his history of the regiment *Royal Hussar*, explains that, being of Jewish descent, Vilenkin could not be promoted, even to non-commissioned rank. However, many officers of the regiment knew him socially. When war broke out it was decided to appoint Sasha permanent messenger to the commanding officer; as such he would live and eat in the officers' mess.

Littauer describes Vilenkin as

in his thirties and a very cultivated man . . . he behaved very bravely and had more decorations than any other soldier in the regiment – seven out of a possible eight . . . His bravery was not based on a lack of imagination . . . the basis of Wilenkin's bravery was great will-power. He would take big chances, although pale and biting his lips . . . Wilenkin's will-power was such that even when he was wounded and sitting on a fallen tree being bandaged he wrote verses about how he had been hit.

The Sumsky Hussars was raised in Moscow in 1651. In 1914 it formed part of the 1st Cavalry Division serving on the East Prussian front in a reconnaissance role. Between August 1914 and February 1915 the regiment advanced twice into Prussia. Losses were heavy. Reduced to one-third of its establishment, in mid-April 1915 the regiment was withdrawn for rest and retraining.

In March 1917, it paraded, along with its officers, to demonstrate loyalty to the new regime. A soldiers' committee was established. 'Fortunately', writes Littauer, 'its first chairman was Wilenkin.' R. H. Bruce Lockhart, in his *Memoirs of a British Agent* (1932), writes that, although regarded by some as a fop, since he was known as the best-dressed man in Moscow, Vilenkin proved himself 'a lion of Judah'. Lockhart continues that Vilenkin, 'by his physical courage, as much as by his intelligence, rose from the ranks to be a junior officer'.

After the Tsar's abdication, numerous secret organizations were set up in Moscow. Sasha headed one of these, aiming to replace the Bolsheviks with a more democratic government. The conspirators were divided into groups, detachments and units, only the commander knowing the identities of all members. But the secrecy was more supposed than real, and as the Bolshevik Secret Service (Cheka) became more efficient, spies infiltrated the groups.

The Order of St George, founded in 1769, was awarded to officers for exceptional bravery. In 1807 two gold and two silver crosses, as opposed to the enamel ones presented to officers, were introduced for non-commissioned officers. For each there were four grades, gained progressively: the fourth being presented for the first deed of outstanding bravery, the third class only to those who already held the fourth class, and the second for a third outstanding action. The first class was an extremely rare award. In 1916 a lesser decoration was introduced, again in four grades, two gold and two silver. Tamara refers to Sasha having been awarded four St George Crosses; Littauer to his having received seven out of a possible eight decorations, more than any other soldier in the regiment. It has not as yet been possible to obtain details of his awards.

3

War and Revolution

A human life, I think, should be well rooted in some spot of
a native land, where it may get the love and tender kinship
for the face of the earth, for the labours men go forth to, for
the sounds and accents that haunt it, for whatever will give
that early home a familiar unmistakable difference amidst
the future widening of knowledge.

George Eliot, *Daniel Deronda*

THE Petersburg to which we returned in the early autumn of
1914 was fervently patriotic. The nation as a whole supported
the Tsar's decision to fulfil his obligations to his allies by defending
the political and religious aspirations of the Balkan Slavs. The
army's rapid advance deep into enemy territory was a source of
pride. Few realized that it was undertaken heedless of self-interest,
chiefly to draw enemy troops from the Western Front and save Paris
from falling into German hands, as it had in 1870. The Tannenberg
disaster was the direct result of that policy. It was a blow not only
to complacency but also to hope, even to confidence, for it revived
memories of the defeat inflicted by Japan ten years earlier.

Tannenberg scarred all Russians old enough to appreciate the
extent of that catastrophe. Those who later emigrated to France
were to suffer anew on realizing that, by the 1920s, the average
Frenchman had forgotten the help his country received from Russia
during those perilous weeks. Feeling betrayed by the Soviet Union's
withdrawal from the war only months before Germany's capitula-
tion, the French refused to acknowledge their debt to the thousands
of Russians killed in that battle. Lady Sybil Grey was one of the few
foreigners who appreciated Russia's contribution to the war effort.
In a letter written in late 1915 to her parents from the Anglo-
Russian Hospital in Petersburg of which she was administrator, she
suggested that Russia 'has not got over the fact that, long before she
was ready, she had to alter all her own plans of campaign and move
forward to help save Paris. By this she sacrificed well over 100,000

men. Last spring, when she in turn wanted help, we said we would advance – but did nothing; just folded our arms and watched the Russians retreat. They don't realize our difficulties, and I quite understand their not understanding.'*

The heavy casualties incurred on the retreat from Tannenberg led Mother to convert part of the house into a ward for wounded privates. As she had no nursing experience she made herself responsible for administering and provisioning the ward, whilst devoting her morning to assembling and despatching comforts to the men in Uncle Sasha's regiment at the front. The first impact I felt of the war resulted from Mother's decision that I was to visit her wounded daily, after my afternoon walk. I was very shy and the necessity of thinking of something suitable to say to each patient worried me. However, when Ilya suggested that the wounded might like to be questioned about their families, the constraint lightened and eventually I found it easier to chatter to them. Tension returned during the intensely cold winter of 1916/17 when most of the patients were suffering from frostbite rather than wounds. Then the wards stank of decaying flesh and rang with the cries of the sufferers, whilst those who endured their agony in silence became angry and embittered. At the same time the laughter which in the past echoed through the house was far less frequent.

As the war dragged on and setbacks at the front multiplied, anti-German feeling increased, especially among the working classes. During the winter of 1916/17 the Empress was openly, although still only verbally, blamed for the nation's defeats. In the hope of appeasing public opinion, St Petersburg was foolishly renamed Petrograd on the assumption that its name was of German origin, whilst Peter the Great had given it the Dutch name of Peterboorgh. Nevertheless, on Sundays, Maykins returned from the English Governesses' Club, run by the vicar, the Revd North,† with faith in

---

*W. Blunt, *Lady Muriel: Lady Muriel Paget, her Husband and her Philanthropic Work in Central and Eastern Europe*, London, 1962, p. 63. The Anglo-Russian Hospital in Petrograd had been set up in 1915 on the initiative of Lady Muriel Paget, who, unable initially to go herself, had despatched Lady Sybil Grey as administrator. Launched as a gesture of goodwill towards the Russians, and staffed primarily by English surgeons and nurses, the hospital opened officially on 30 January 1916.

†The Revd F. W. North was chaplain at St Petersburg, 1905–11, then chaplain at the Moscow English Church. The Revd B. S. Lombard succeeded him at the former, where he had been Assistant Chaplain since 1908.

an Allied victory unshaken. In contrast, during that same winter, Uncle Sasha came home on leave greatly depressed because shortages of every kind prevailed in his regiment. Determined to obtain winter clothing, guns and ammunition for the men who were still in summer uniforms, he was soon disgusted at the apathy, demoralization, profiteering and shirking rampant in the capital and returned to the front before his leave was up. In Russia that winter women showed more spirit than many men, and when a Siberian peasant called Bochkareva dressed as a man and founded the Women's Battalion of Death, many educated girls joined it.

Volodia and I seemed always to have known that people in all walks of life felt greatly dissatisfied with the Tsar's political and economic policies, and also that the lives of all members of the imperial family, as well as of prominent politicians, were often threatened. For as far back as I can remember our governesses and tutors had been instructed to avoid crowds gathering round street incidents, but Volodia and I were not frightened and felt intensely curious about such events. So did Maykins who, like Mother, instinctively sympathized with the unfortunate. She and I invariably approached a crowd to see whether there was anyone whom we could help.

Volodia, six years older than me, was allowed out by himself. He was thus better informed about political disturbances and more involved in them. Although a staunch monarchist he possessed the warmest of hearts and his sympathies were always with the oppressed. When fourteen he cut school on 1 May to join a demonstration organized by some radical students. Inevitably he was among the first to be arrested. His extreme youth was recognized and a telephone call was put through to Father, telling him to collect his son immediately and exercise better control over him. But, regardless of the severest of punishments, Volodia refused to mend his ways and, from then on, annually on the last day of April, his tutor and all the servants were ordered to keep him locked in his rooms for twenty-four hours.

Even so, annually, Volodia contrived to escape and join the demonstrators. He was invariably among the first to be arrested; Father was always quickly informed and his release secured. On returning home he would be furiously scolded and locked into his rooms for another twenty-four hours. He never attempted to escape from these second incarcerations and could be heard happily playing a musical instrument, exciting his dog, and singing such songs as 'Yip-I-Addy, I-Ay, I-Ay', or 'Goodbyee Chin Chin'. He had a sunny temperament but, as the hours dragged on, he took to intoning Sobinov's* lugubrious

> The sun comes up and the sun goes down
> But it is dark in my prison cell.

As the situation worsened, Father also took to singing that song as he paced up and down. Then he became too miserable even to do so for, having lied about his age, Volodia had joined the army as a motorcycle despatch rider. Because of his youth he was posted to his unit's headquarters in Petrograd. One morning he overheard plans to murder his commanding officer. Untrained in subterfuge or self-protection, he rushed to the nearest public telephone to warn his general. He was overheard; his insignia of a non-commissioned officer were torn from his uniform and he was dragged for trial before a group of hastily summoned, hostile men. A sudden outburst of gunfire enabled him to escape, probably saving his life. He must have had a charmed existence, for he was to evade execution sixteen times in the next three years.

Maykins and I saw one of the first disturbances leading to the outbreak of the 1917 Revolution. Returning home from my piano lesson along the Nevsky Prospekt we were surprised to see mounted Cossacks and police rounding up a group of demonstrators, viciously cracking their whips (*knouts*) as they did so, occasionally lashing out on the bystanders. It was a hateful sight.

A couple of days later street fighting broke out all over the city, reaching its peak on what came to be known as Red Monday. Described as a bloodless revolution it was in reality marked from the start by considerable violence. Police stations were attacked, policemen pitilessly hounded and often beaten to death. The abolition of military ranks and insignia was interpreted by the populace as a licence for ferocity; epaulettes, swords and medals were torn from their wearers, the victims being at best manhandled, quite

---

*Leonid Sobinov was a lyric tenor with a voice of great purity, as much admired as Chaliapin, but older.

often murdered. The imperial eagles were wrenched from the buildings and shops which they adorned, courts of justice with their precious archives were set on fire, shops were looted. Machine-guns mounted on the roofs of high buildings were often fired at no one in particular. As I stood one morning looking out of my bedroom window on to sedate Mokhovaya Street, some shots were fired, and a harmless passer-by fell on his back into a pool of blood as his entrails spilled out on to the pavement with his life.

Probably because of the tenacity with which he had clung to life, Rasputin's murder in December 1916 seemed so shocking, even to a society inured to terrorism, that very little was felt of the relief which would have been well nigh universal had the death resulted from natural causes. The sense of evil which had emanated from Rasputin intensified at his death, enveloping the capital in a poisonous pall. It thickened at his secret burial. A few days later, as Maykins and I were returning from an afternoon walk along the tree-lined Sergeevskaya Street, a car with a coffin protruding from it passed us, travelling at speed. Another car racing after it managed to ram it at a short distance from us. A scuffle ensued; some eight men seemed involved; shots were fired and the first car burst into flames. Startled into immobility, Maykins and I watched the flames envelop the coffin. Later our *dvornik* (yard porter) told us that the coffin contained Rasputin's body; that, outraged by his burial at Tsarskoe Selo, some young men had disinterred the coffin and made off with it, with the intention of throwing it into the Neva but, when pursued by devotees of Rasputin, they had preferred to burn it rather than to surrender it. I have never been able to confirm this story but, at the time, it was widely accepted as true by the poorer inhabitants of Petersburg. No books that I have read other than Alex de Jonge's *The Life and Times of Grigorii Rasputin*, refer to Rasputin's burial place.*

Within days of the collapse of the tsarist regime it had become usual for bands of armed, trigger-happy youths, most wearing military uniform, to career through the town in lorries, stopping at any house that caught their fancy to insist on entering and searching it, ostensibly for arms and enemies of the people. These youths were

---

*A. de Jonge, *The Life and Times of Grigorii Rasputin*, London, 1982, p. 340.

so arrogant, so confident, so menacing that no one dared refuse –
that is to say no one but Maykins. In our house, as they passed from
one room to another, opening cupboards and drawers, removing
anything they fancied whilst commenting loudly and disparagingly
on what they saw, glorifying in their power, Maykins would station
herself outside the door leading to my rooms. She was by nature
fearless; anger made her intrepid, inflaming her cheeks until they
glowed in fierce contrast to her deep red-coloured hair. Although
there was nothing of value or importance in my rooms, she barred
their entrance, confronting the youths with a flow of Russian rendered especially telling by her atrocious accent and poor grammar.
Faced by so small, so fiery and voluble a duenna, none ever dared
defy her and my rooms were never searched.

Regardless of these and similar outrages, a feeling of hope, of
faith in the future, of a rebirth, pervaded the capital. Even children
sensed it. People felt free to express their opinions and were elated.
Ceaseless political meetings were held at street corners. Eloquent
orators electrified listeners with visions of a free, idyllic society. It
was all very exciting. Maykins had to drag me away. As at Easter,
so now strangers stopped in the streets to exchange three kisses and
to proclaim the dawn of a new, a golden age. Beguiled, I was
bewitched by the vision of a heaven on earth. Yet, without becoming conscious of the inconsistency, I remained passionately devoted
to the Tsar, passionately anxious for my country to remain loyal to
its allies.

It may have been on 5 April 1917, perhaps as an antidote to my
feeling of elation, that Maykins took me to watch, from the
Summer Gardens, the solemn, long and stirring funeral procession
of the victims of the Bloodless Revolution.* They were to be buried
in the Field of Mars, the former parade ground of the imperial
troops stationed in the capital, now a park. As the winter had been
exceptionally severe the ground was still frozen so hard that it
proved impossible to dig the communal grave and dynamite had to
be used to blast out a large hole at the centre of the unpaved, dusty

*Tamara wrote that the burial was on 5 May. However both Meriel Buchanan
in Petrograd, the City of Trouble, London, 1918, and the Hon. Albert Stopford in his
anonymous The Russian Diary of an Englishman: Petrograd 1915–1917, London, 1919,
refer to the burial of victims of the Revolution in the Champs de Mars as taking place in
April. There may, of course, have been two mass burials.

parade ground. The cavity looked enormous and untidy but the burial ceremony was dignified and sad. The coffins, and there seemed to be many of them, were covered in red cloth. They were lowered into the communal grave to the accompaniment of majestic music.

Soon after, Maykins and I went to spend a few weeks in our villa at Pavlovsk,* but the atmosphere there had undergone a startling change. The mood was one of fear. Only a few miles away, in the Alexander Palace at Tsarskoe Selo (now Pushkin), the imperial family were living under close surveillance and the few still using their villas were apprehensive. Although the peasants had become sullen and withdrawn, Maykins and I resumed our long bicycle rides, but now army deserters roamed from village to village, and our devoted gardener begged us to stop cycling. By the end of the month we were back in Petrograd and Mother persuaded Maykins to return to England with the last batch of British subjects to sail.

In Petrograd Mother's highly intelligent Lettish maid was soon to disappear without taking leave, to throw in her lot with the Bolsheviks. She was the only member of our large and devoted staff to do so, and we never heard what became of her.

About this time posters appeared in the streets of the capital alongside the traditional manifestos. I found them absorbing. During my history lessons I had already studied some of the manifestos used by Russia's past sovereigns to inform people of their decisions. I had also come to realize that experimental artists such as Jean Cocteau, Larionov and Goncharova accompanied their exhibitions with printed statements. The poet Mayakovski had done so before the outbreak of the 1914 war. When, in the twenties in Paris, I came to know some of these artists, their gentleness and consideration of others seemed to belie the reports of their earlier activities. The verbal manifestos which had been posted in the streets of Petrograd generally took the form of exhortations, sometimes of instructions and were boring, but the pictorial posters were arresting, forceful and amusing; they were an innovation which delighted me.

Mother's hospital having emptied, she closed it down and soon

---

*The grounds of the eighteenth-century imperial palace, 30 kilometres south of St Petersburg, had become a popular resort.

after Maykins's departure, she and I left for the Crimea whilst
Father stayed in town, intending insofar as it was possible, to watch
over Volodia who, with other non-commissioned officers, was
guarding the Winter Palace, taken over by the Provisional Government. Simeiz, our Crimean destination, lies west of Yalta. It was
not connected by rail with either of the two Crimean terminals of
Simferopol or Sebastopol. As Simferopol was reached first, we
generally used it as our point of arrival, continuing our journey in
carriages. That involved spending a night in a bug-ridden hotel in
Eupatoria. In 1915 we had tried covering the distance in a day,
travelling by car, but everyone had felt so ill on the road's sharp
hairpin bends that in 1916 we reverted to the use of the carriage.

In 1917 I was surprised at finding myself travelling alone with my
mother for, although a caretaker looked after the house at Simeiz,
on former occasions our head servants had always accompanied us
when we visited. Travelling alone was a new experience and we
enjoyed it. The train journey was uneventful, the drive no different
from those of former years. The weather was perfect and the familiar coastal road as beautiful as ever. As usual we spent a night at
Eupatoria and, as usual, were devoured by insects. Simeiz welcomed us as warmly as ever and soon we were joined by Aunt Malia
and her four children. Her twin sons, Jim and Alec, were my boon
companions; although they were a couple of years older than me,
we were inseparable. We had invented a language incomprehensible to others; it was to prove invaluable when the Bolsheviks came
to power for we taught it to Uncle Sasha who in his turn taught it
to his aides who often made use of it.

The days which followed seemed perfect. For the first time in my
life, I could do as I liked all day, within reason, because, apart from
my mother who was unaccustomed to looking after me, there was
no one to supervise me. My only duty was to appear punctually at
meals, looking washed and tidy. As I disliked the pebbly beach and
very deep sea I made use of my divine independence to spend hours
on my pony, Volchok, riding long distances in the company of my
dashing Tartar groom, Tair. He was young, handsome, fearless and
daring. We had similar tastes and became such close friends that
he often took me to his mountain village. I was always welcomed
and treated as an equal, a rare privilege for a Russian because
the Tartars were devout Muslims thirsting for autonomy and

determined to keep Russians at a distance. The men were fiercely jealous of their women, who were beautiful and spirited; unveiled, self-reliant and elegant, the women loved jewellery, suspending strings of gold coins along the sides of their tall, brimless, cylindrically shaped hats.

In contrast to Turkish peasants the Tartars were house-proud, their two-storeyed, whitewashed, wooden houses with brown verandas, well-kept; strings of fruit and vegetables were suspended along the sides of the verandas to dry in the hot sun. They were extremely hospitable and I enjoyed being welcomed with bowls of deliciously rich yoghurt, coarse cheese, unleavened bread and whatever fruit was in season. In those days the Crimea abounded in luscious fruit – large, sweet juicy muscat grapes, squelchy pears, succulent peaches, fragrant apples and delectable melons. Sitting on a veranda listening to the village elders laying down the law, or playing with their children in the dusty street, smelling of heat, I learnt to understand and respect an outlook which I was later to encounter among the Ottoman Turks who had once been the Tartars' suzerains.

As formerly, in 1917 we went to Alupka to shop and often to Yalta, then a very small seaside town where, as in Alupka, the shops along the sea-front sold boxes studded with shells, small looking-glasses adorned with local views, fossilized sea-horses and white bone penholders with a tiny round glass concealed amid their carved decorations; by squinting through the glass a view of Yalta could be discovered. Divorced from the outer world, blissfully contented with my surroundings, I taught myself not to think of the war and almost to forget the revolution, although letters from the north describing the first abortive Bolshevik attempt to overthrow the Provisional Government made it rather difficult, especially since Volodia had been involved in the Government's defence. It was not until September that the outer world imposed itself on my inner world, for the grown-ups had become tense and worried by reports of atrocities being committed in Sebastopol by sailors of the Black Sea Fleet. Nevertheless these horrors seemed remote and unreal until some sailors stationed in Yalta captured their officers, tore their insignia from their uniforms, tied boulders to their feet and dropped them into the sea off Yalta's pier to drown, standing upright in the very clear water, to the accompaniment of sailors' jeers.

The brutalities were too much for my mother and aunt. Ignoring their husbands' instructions they decided to hurry back to Moscow. As in the past, we chose Sebastopol as our point of departure. We drove along the coastal road, flanked by vineyards, passing the inlet of golden-coloured sand which distinguishes Balaklava from the rest of the Crimean beaches, past Inkerman to Sebastopol. At the time Sebastopol was still a small town with its nicest streets lined with small, two-storeyed, Regency-style houses. On arrival the boys and I rushed to my favourite street, with the prettiest houses, but it was empty and so unusually quiet as to seem unreal, more like a stage set than an inhabited place. We were intimidated.

A marked contrast to the muted street, the station was all frenzy. Every available place was crammed with people, some fussing over children and belongings, others crouching over bundles. We were obliged to fight our way on to the platform and into the train. There were seven of us and, to my relief, with the station-master's help, we were able to grab a compartment and keep it to ourselves. As we travelled north in a series of slow spurts we came to value our privacy for the train was not only crammed with people but festooned with them, army deserters swarming on its roof and bulging out of its doors. Everyone was bad-tempered, dishevelled and grimy, us included. It was our first experience of grime as distinct from wholesome dirt, and I hated the feeling. No food or drink could be obtained and as the journey lasted five and a half days instead of three, for the first time we experienced hunger, if only in a mild form.

We reached Moscow in the dark. Father and Uncle Mitia were waiting at the station, but seemed displeased to see us. Instead of greeting us they hurriedly bundled us into the car. On slamming the door they caught Aunt Malia's hand in it, but their attitude was so hostile that, like Mrs Disraeli, she did not cry out.* It was not until we reached the house that we discovered that she was close to fainting from pain. Before much could be done for her, the night's

---

*Disraeli, about to make an important speech in the Commons, was accompanied there by his wife, who was not to hear his speech, having vowed not to do so until he became Prime Minister. On getting out, Disraeli slammed the carriage door, crushing her hand. She made no sign of the excruciating pain she must have suffered. This and other descriptions of her physical bravery are given in F. E. Baily, *Lady Beaconsfield and her Times*, London, 1935, pp. 252–3.

curious stillness was shattered by the sound of gunfire. We had
arrived in Moscow at the outbreak of the October Revolution, at
the precise moment when the Bolsheviks were launching their
successful bid for power. The attack had been expected and
accounted for the anger of our fathers at our return to town.

The battle lasted a week. Our house stood practically at the centre
of Povarskaya Street, at each end of which was a square, with a
church at its centre. The Bolsheviks occupied one of the churches,
their opponents the other. Each had mounted a machine-gun on
the roof of their respective church. The range of each gun, with
only occasional exceptions, reached to just about the middle of
Povarskaya Street and as a result our house was often hit by both
guns. The firing was sustained and we hurried to install ourselves
in our basement where our parents soon became immersed in seemingly endless games of bridge. At each particularly long burst of
gunfire the younger maids shrieked in very much the same way as
during a thunderstorm, whilst the older ones invoked God's help,
the menservants crossing themselves as frequently as the women,
albeit more quietly, commending their souls to the Almighty. Our
inner hall porter, a Tartar, was less restrained; he prostrated
himself with such frequency in what he believed to be the direction
of Mecca that we advised him to retain the recumbent position for
the duration of the struggle. Attracted by sniper fire he promptly
did so, quickly succumbing into so deep a real or simulated sleep
that it was futile to ask him to do anything for us.

Left to our own devices we children, all of us readers of *Little
Folk* and the *Boy's Own Paper*, entertained ourselves by daring
each other to go upstairs during a cannonade to fetch some
especially heavy, fragile or awkward object such as a large and
ornate mirror for Lucie, my pretty sixteen-year-old cousin, to
admire herself in. The fun of this game carried us through the first
two or three days of the fighting, then it palled and for most of
the rest of the week we immersed ourselves in books – in my case,
at first, rather childish adventure stories, then more exciting works
until, finally, I came across Uncle Sasha's copy of Henri Barbusse's

---

*Henri Barbusse's vivid account of life in the trenches was published in Paris in 1916. An
English translation by W. Fitzwater appeared under the title *Under Fire*.

Le Feu.* I had never read anything like it. The horrors of trench warfare on the Western Front blotted out those taking place on our doorstep.

My dismay increased when Sasha Kropotkina* proceeded to pace up and down reciting Kipling, time and again choosing the poem *Tommy*, in which he describes the plight of the private soldier, wanted here, there and everywhere during a crisis, but never remembered once life had reverted to normal. Blok's poem *The Twelve*, which I was also reading at the time, although largely incomprehensible to me, filled me with dread; Anti-Christ seemed verily to have descended upon earth and the future looked bleak until Sasha Kropotkina revived my spirits by making me learn Kipling's *If*; the poem restored my nerve. Meanwhile, in Petrograd, whilst defending the Winter Palace, Volodia once again narrowly escaped death. Since his name was now on the wanted list Father decided to travel south with him where, depending on events, he could either join the troops fighting the Bolsheviks or attend a provincial university.

No. 42 Povarskaya Street had been so severely damaged in the fighting that, when the contest was over, we were obliged to move out while its roof was repaired. We settled into a small rented furnished flat in a poorish district of Moscow. Conditions throughout the town had become chaotic, for although victorious the Bolsheviks were not as yet fully in control and thieves and muggers were able to take advantage of the breakdown in law and order to plunder and murder at will. To keep them at bay the men in our new district took turns at guarding their houses at night, keeping watch in pairs with the aid of a gun; in our block they formed fours and played bridge throughout the night.

From the age of about four I had been the victim of a terrifying, recurrent dream. I would wake from it screaming, although within a year or two I had learnt to stifle my yells if not my fears. Explosions, hugely magnified versions of the ominous ear-splitting

---

*Princess Sasha Kropotkina, a family friend then living with the Abelsons, was the daughter of Prince Peter, Russian savant and revolutionary, who escaped to England in 1876. He returned to Russia after the Revolution, but was disillusioned. The Princess, who left Russia after her father's death in 1921, was often thereafter in Paris. Huddleston writes that she was among the most versatile women he knew: she wrote, lectured, designed clothes, was interested in interior decoration, and also concerned herself in politics and economics. S. Huddleston, *Bohemian Literary and Social Life in Paris*, London, 1928, p. 198.

crashes made at spring's violent advent, by huge blocks of ice colliding into each other as they careered down the Neva towards the open sea, became the accompaniment to my dream of undefinable horror. The sound resembled a dismally wailing siren, similar to that used at the Putilov Munition Works, a sound as soul-destroying as that of London's wartime alert. On waking I was unable to remember my dream or to define the cause of my terror, although I was also unable to forget its horror or the malevolent atmosphere which accompanied it. Until now nothing in the dream had seemed in any way related to my waking life. However, a cruel ordeal awaited us on our return to Povarskaya Street. Nightly, between three and five, we listened as we lay in our comfortable beds, to death sentences being carried out on young non-commissioned officers captured by the Bolsheviks and imprisoned in a neighbouring mansion. By counting the salvoes we could estimate the number of victims so prematurely encountering death. Our helplessness scarred us and left us with a passionate detestation of injustice. Talkative and outspoken though we all were, we instinctively refrained from referring to our nightly ordeal.

With the resilience of children Jim, Alec and I started collecting bullets, not all spent ones. There was a great variety littering the streets and I scored by being the first to find one with its tip sawn off, which we assumed to be a dumdum bullet. Since possession of weapons and munitions was strictly forbidden, our hobby was dangerous. That added to its charm. We savoured the risks, oblivious of the peril in which we were placing the entire household; gleefully we concealed our bullets from prying eyes by suspending them along the inner sides of the central heating gratings. They were never discovered, and were still in their hiding place when we left the house.

Whilst we were busy concealing our bullets, our parents were feverishly seeking where to hide the few pieces of jewellery which had escaped confiscation. Eventually Jim suggested the perfect place. He was a talented musician and had often examined the interior of our Bechstein piano. Cavities beneath the wooden panels at each end of the keyboard were of the correct sizes; the objects which our parents hid in these escaped detection even after our ground-floor reception rooms were handed to a theatrical company to prevent confiscation. As the actors only used the rooms in the daytime, we reoccupied them at night, challenging each other to mock duels with their fencing equipment, to Jim's accompaniment on the valuable piano of the sonorous French military march, *Sambre et Meuse*.

Hoping to benefit more from foreign protection than from the pleasure of a theatrical visit, our parents converted the billiard room into a bed-sitting room and let it with its adjoining bathroom, to Captain Maurice Barre, the military attaché to the French Embassy.* Captain Barre was tall, very thin, very reserved, very stiff and correct in appearance and of impassive mien. His behaviour remained formal and decorous throughout the year he spent with us. Although he never unbent he became an excellent companion, often inviting us to play billiards at the table which filled half his bedroom or talking to us of Paris or the war on the Western Front.

Although accustomed in the Crimea to go about by myself, I had never as yet been out alone in town and when life in Moscow returned to comparative normality I did not at first want to do so. For a glorious fortnight or so, with no one paying much attention to me, I delighted to spend my days reading. Inevitably, however, I wearied of my hothouse existence and became a nuisance to the servants. When they protested I tried to amuse myself by looking out of the window, a sterile pastime in that quiet residential street. Eventually my longing for the outer world mastered my pride and I consulted Mother. My predicament dismayed her. She could not bring herself to allow me to roam the streets unattended, yet there was no one among the younger and more agile maids whom she could trust not to panic in an emergency.

The problem was discussed endlessly; the solution struck me as delightful as it was unexpected. We had a large, devoted, highly intelligent, fierce-looking dog called Lord. With a bulldog's head and a brindled body, straight of leg, he stood almost four feet high. His name suited him, for his appearance was magnificent; his bravery equalled that of a lion; his wisdom matched his intelligence; he was indeed pre-eminent among dogs. Was he a bull mastiff? I have never seen another dog which resembled Lord. As Maykins had always maintained that I was basically sensible and

---

*Capt. Barre has not been identified as serving in either the French Army, the Navy or the French Foreign Office.

trustworthy, it was decided that a former batman of Uncle Sasha's, a hussar of many years' service, was to teach me how to take cover during an exchange of gunfire and how to reconnoitre a street. Illicitly he also taught me to handle a revolver. It was all very exciting. Once I had learnt these skills I was free to go out, if accompanied by Lord. With Lord to protect me I explored the length and breadth of Moscow, talked to strangers, when invited entering workmen's flats. Lord never left my side and his appearance and deep growl terrified any youth who dared to approach. With Lord as my sole companion my walks became thrilling.

Inevitably there came a day when Mother decided that my education had to continue. Since it was no longer possible to be taught at home I was to go to school. Mother finally settled on the nearest, Miss N. G. Brukhonenko's school. A fairly high wall separated its playground from the gymnasium which Jim and Alec attended. Sergei Konovalov, who later became Professor of Russian at Oxford, went to the same school as the boys. A couple of years older than the twins he was already an ardent politician, a close to centre radical, an inspiring orator and a passionate idealist. He was very tall for his age, strikingly handsome, with a slow, endearing smile and an engaging personality. Our morning breaks coinciding, we were often able to listen to Seriozha who scaled the dividing wall to deliver his impassioned, profoundly patriotic tirades, the boys gathered on one side of the wall, the girls on the other. Together we followed the disintegration of Russia's military resistance to the enemy with acute anguish. We felt that our country was being dishonoured by the negotiations taking place for a separate peace. Our spirits rose in February 1918 when negotiations broke down, only to turn to dejection when a fresh German thrust culminated in the peace treaty of Brest-Litovsk.

We felt humiliated and dishonoured by the arrival soon after of Count Mirbach as German ambassador to Moscow. As we were obliged to pass the ambassador's residence on our way to and from school, our anguish bit deeper every day. Often a black limousine stood outside the embassy, quite a small German flag fluttering from its bonnet. Anger and resentment raged in me. The twins shared my feelings. After much debate we decided that, if the car was unattended when we passed, we would take it in turn to break off the flag. Whatever the risk we swore on oath to carry out our self-appointed task, fully realizing that it was dangerous. To succeed we had to hide in a doorway until the ambassador's driver entered the count's house. Then a dash across the street, a quick snap of the flag's stick and a panicked flight down the street brought safety to the frightened avenger but seemed to have little effect on the ambassador for, when next sighted, a fresh flag fluttered audaciously above the car's bonnet. The process became wearisome and nerve-racking. In due course, we resorted to other tactics.

Remembering that hydrangeas were said to bring bad luck if brought indoors we decided, even though flowers had become a rarity in Moscow and were exceedingly expensive, to raise enough money to send the Mirbachs a large potful. We scraped, saved and scrounged and eventually watched as a handsome plant of the blue variety was delivered to the ambassador's residence. A few days later Count Mirbach was assassinated.* We were jubilant on hearing the news then, as its meaning sank in, we felt responsible and became gravely troubled. When the ambassador's post was promptly filled by another envoy we belatedly realized that Mirbach was not responsible for Russia's withdrawal from the war and that we had chosen the wrong victim.

Death stalked the streets. One night, just after Uncle Sasha had left our house, a man of similar build was gunned down outside it. On seeing him fall our porter hastened to report Uncle Sasha's death. All of us adored Uncle Sasha and feared for his life, but we children could not believe that he had been killed like some mad dog, more especially since Morgenstern, Petersburg's leading fortune-teller and skilled interpreter of handwriting, had years before warned Uncle Sasha that he would die an unnatural death two months after his thirty-fifth birthday. That fatal day was still six months ahead. On this occasion a few agonizing minutes sufficed for Mother to confirm that the victim was a stranger. Morgenstern's prophecy had held; would it prove correct in six months' time, we miserably wondered.

Uncle Sasha was widely loved in Moscow for his altruism, and admired as a gifted barrister, a splendid orator and quite a good

---

*Mirbach was assassinated in his embassy by a Cheka official, probably with the approval of Lenin since the murderer later reached high position in the Communist Party.

poet. His sympathies were with the oppressed, many of whom he had defended in Moscow's law courts. The poor were devoted to him and he was as popular with Moscow's intellectuals as with the beau monde. He disapproved of autocracy and detested Bolshevism and all that it stood for. He longed for a constitutional monarchy. From as early as July 1917 he worked for the establishment of a democratic, freely elected government. After the October Revolution he courted death by striving for this in secret, soon with the support of a group of equally courageous and liberal-minded men who formed themselves into a secret society no member of which, apart from himself and two of his closest associates, knew the names of more than five of their colleagues. They hoped to effect a *coup d'état* in the late spring of 1918. Meanwhile they planned and kept in touch, by means of coded messages in preference to meetings or telephone conversations.

As spring 1918 drew near Uncle Sasha was sometimes in urgent need of messengers. When very hard pressed he used one of the twins or me to deliver his instructions. We knew the danger we were in and the gravity of our task, for our uncle warned us from the start of the risks involved, making sure that we understood and were willing to face the consequences, almost encouraging us to refuse to serve him, before sending us on a mission. Knowing what was at stake we were proud to be of use. Ingenuity was sometimes required, but it was never beyond our grasp. On one occasion Uncle Sasha bestowed on me the ribbon and clasp of one of his four St George's Crosses, awarded for gallantry. I still have the ribbon which I treasure, not as a tribute to my exploit, but as the only gift of his which I still possess.

Although we children found life exciting, our parents were becoming increasingly worried and depressed. Food had become scarce but Easter was not too far off; nor was Lent, which should make hunger easier to bear. However, as the last day of Butter Week approached, determined to raise our spirits, we decided to hoard what food we could and to sit down to a family feast in Aunt Lily's house at no. 46 Povarskaya. Like most people finding themselves short of food for the first time, we talked of that luncheon party with increasing frequency and relish. We had been promised *blini* (pancakes), the traditional first course of a Butter Week meal, even if unaccompanied by caviare or followed by much else.

On the day we were all so hungry that each of us found some way of occupying the morning. I went for a walk with Lord and returned home before the others. Almost immediately the front door bell pealed in so peremptory a manner as to make any delay in answering inadvisable. A lorry-load of armed youths demanded entry. By that date would-be searchers had to produce a document to justify such demands. The leader of this band handed me a permit written on notepaper headed by a skull and crossbones. Intrigued by their crest I opened the door wide and asked them to identify themselves. They were Anarchists, bent on ousting the Bolsheviks. Confident, businesslike and not unfriendly, they were eager to expound their political creed and their aims. 'Anarchy is the Mother of Order,' they asserted, but when I expostulated and chided them for confiscating people's property their leader turned a cold stare on me and remarked, 'The people of this country have waited three hundred years for this moment.' The enormous length of that period of expectancy, aggravated perhaps by hunger, over-whelmed me and I burst into tears. My sobs distressed the Anarchists. They gathered round to comfort me and we were soon on personal terms. Eventually I was even able to show them round the house.

They commented a trifle sadly on the limited amount of gilding in the reception rooms but cheered up when we reached the kitchen and found the cold meat, our contribution to the lunch party. While eating it they spoke of commandeering our house. The prospect of being ejected, probably before luncheon, did not appeal to me. With considerable perspicacity I started telling them about the drawbacks to the house, casually remarking that there were more convenient, handsomer ones in the street. 'Do you mean the house next door?' one of them asked. 'Oh no, further up,' I answered, adding however that our outhouses, which had been converted into a pavilion, were better than most and, whilst searching for a more suitable house, they might like to use them and draw up on their crested notepaper some form of agreement.

My suggestions appealed and, on parting, they handed me their claim to the pavilion. I was not dissatisfied with my achievement for I had saved our house and acquired a sheet of that coveted notepaper, and neither was Mother displeased on hearing that I had retained possession of our house. She kissed me, and my elders were praising me for my subtlety while my contemporaries were looking at me with quizzical, jealous eyes when the doorbell pealed even more ominously than when the Anarchists had rung. It was accompanied by frantic knocking. We were still grouped in the hall and, this time heedless of danger, flung open the front door.

My Aunt Lily, who was also my godmother, stood on the threshold, shaking with fury, tears streaming down her cheeks. She was panting. Amidst gasps she explained that, acting on the advice of the young girl from no. 42, the Anarchists had commandeered her house. They were threatening her husband, they had mounted a machine-gun in her hall, opened the front door and were inviting all passers-by to enter and choose one object from the house. It was useless for me to insist that I had not told the Anarchists to seize no. 46, for no one would believe me. The praise I had enjoyed seconds earlier had turned to intense anger and, for the first time in my life, I was severely shaken. Mother in the past had always been anxious to protect me, but on this occasion she showed no desire to shield me. It was she who decided that I was to go to the house alone, without even Lord at my side, and attempt to dislodge the Anarchists; if I failed to do so I was to insist on my right to remove an object.

Feeling too angry and ill-used to be frightened I ran to no. 46. I found the front door wide open, a machine-gun occupying the centre of the hall, and a banner above it proclaiming: 'Anarchy is the Mother of Order.' There stood my uncle, red-faced, surrounded by angry, screaming youths clicking revolvers. A glance into the dining-room convinced me that our luncheon had been eaten by others. Smarting under the combined effects of hunger and injustice, I accused the Anarchists of having lied and got me into dire trouble. Startled, they turned towards me, expostulating. Whilst we screamed at each other, Uncle Jacques escaped. I asked them to leave. They laughed and refused. I demanded food: none was left. I asserted my right to remove one of my aunt's objects. My claim was carefully discussed and considered legitimate. I could make my choice from the ground-floor rooms, but not from any others.

Scores of objects stood in the longish series of reception rooms.

Although I knew them well I had never considered them before, having taken them for granted. Now, as I walked slowly from room to room carefully examining their contents, I found to my surprise that there were not many objects I really liked; my taste must differ radically from that of my uncle and aunt. That astonished me. Moreover the large size, the weight, or the fragility of many of the objects and the uselessness of most of the others rendered them all singularly unsuited to the conditions in which we were living. I could not decide what to take. Eventually my hesitation annoyed the Anarchists. Losing patience they gave me five minutes to choose an object and get out. In a flash, I remembered having the day before returned the second volume of *The Three Musketeers* to my uncle and forgotten to borrow the last. Darting into the library I seized it and ran home. There I found myself in dire disgrace. Never before or after was I to be so bitterly reproached.

Uncle Sasha had been staying with my uncle and aunt at no. 46 and was to have come to our Butter Week luncheon. On entering the house slightly late he was confronted by a very different situation from the one he expected. Unperturbed, he informed the Anarchists that he was lodging in his sister's house and since he intended to continue living in it, he expected his bedroom and its contents to remain undisturbed. His demand was considered fair and agreed to. Uncle Sasha for his part reacted philosophically to the news that the luncheon had been eaten and was soon on excellent terms with his new hosts. Indeed, some became firm friends and during the week for which they retained control of Moscow, all of them insisted on sharing their food with him. They had been obliged to fight hard to seize Moscow from the Bolsheviks and they fought even more bravely in their efforts to retain control, but the Bolsheviks were far more numerous and better armed than the Anarchists and were able to inflict such heavy losses on their opponents that few of the latter survived the contest. Those who did, accepted defeat or went into hiding.

Towards the end of the summer, as I walked home from school one afternoon, I passed a man standing in the middle of the street reading a newspaper, tears streaming down his cheeks. Surprised by his anguish I glanced at the paper and saw a headline printed at the top of the page in exceptionally large capitals:

SMERT NIKOLAYA VTOROVO it read. Assuming that the last word represented the genitive case of an unfamiliar surname, I questioned Mother. Since the word meant nothing to her she sent out for an evening paper. A glance revealed that I had failed to recognize the genitive case of the numeral, to make the heading read, not 'Death of Nicholas Vtorov' but of Nicholas the Second. There was no jubilation in Moscow; regicide preyed on most minds.

Meanwhile Uncle Sasha and his two closest associates had been denounced and were arrested a week before their planned *coup d'état*, ten weeks before my uncle's thirty-fifth birthday. To begin with they were held in the dreaded Lubianka prison and subjected to harsh and intensive examination for they were the only plotters who knew the identities of all the conspirators. Later they were transferred, first to the Butyrki prison, then to Taganka where the questioning was even harsher.

In gaol prisoners were entitled to receive a daily food parcel from their relatives. Although it was widely believed that the warders kept many of these themselves, and even though food was very short, no day passed without a queue of relatives forming at the prison gate carrying the precious tokens of their love and concern for the captives. We took it in turns to deliver Uncle Sasha's daily parcel, handing it to the warder with bated breath as we studied his expression, for it was by his refusal of a parcel or his expression when accepting it that it was sometimes possible to discover whether the arrested man was still held inside the building, or whether he had been transferred or even shot.

The prison was far from Povarskaya Street; public transport had become virtually non-existent. The weight of the food parcel often made the journey arduous, but we were helped in that exhausting and heart-searing task by one of the Anarchists who, on hearing of Uncle Sasha's arrest, emerged from hiding and insisted on taking his turn with the daily delivery. His devotion and loyalty sustained us when we were all convinced that Morgenstern's prophecy would be fulfilled.

Life fell into a new routine. At ten o'clock every morning one of us would set out for the prison carrying the precious parcel and would be lucky to be back at home by mid-afternoon, for the queue became daily ever longer and progressed ever slower towards the prison gate. It was sometimes possible to obtain permission to visit a prisoner. I was able to see my uncle twice. On the first occasion I was quite unprepared for the long, low, drab room where the grey-looking prisoners were lined up, each standing opposite a small window, along one side of a barrier, their guests opposite, along another barrier, a soldier in the passage between them to listen to all that was said. Horrified and tongue-tied as I was, it fell to my uncle to do the talking. He chided me gently for my distress, teased me a little and told me never to be daunted by force.

I did a little better on my second visit, but with the soldier listening to all we said it was impossible to do more than exchange banalities. Words of love would in any case have unmanned us both. Impudence seemed the most suitable course to follow, especially since the prisoners were neither cowed nor inactive. They somehow contrived to be photographed, to smuggle the photographs out of prison for delivery to their relations and friends, even to send letters. Uncle Sasha wrote to each of us, doing so in English. I received one photograph and a letter and cried over both in secret, chiefly in the lavatory. I treasured them. Though inevitably dealing with banalities these letters were infinitely precious and served to mould our conduct throughout life. To me he sent a postcard which read 'with love from your "convict uncle" walking with the officer with the wide stripe on his breeches so that my forehead only may be seen. Sasha 22/VII/1918 To Tommy.'

The letter was jauntier and meant to cheer me. 'My dear Tom', it read,

It was really nice of you to write that long letter and especially to send me that box of sweets in honour of your birthday. It was rather piggish of me not to come to congratulate you on that great day but you see I could not leave my present residence as the people here assure me that they could not spare me even for a few hours. Well, being popular has its drawbacks and I have to stay with 'my people' for 24 hours a day for over five weeks already and Heaven knows for how many more to come. But you must not imagine that it is so very hard in prison – by no way is it any worse than trench life, minus the shells and bombs as there are no air raids here. It is only a bit trying to stay indoors when it is fine outside, but, well, once it cannot be helped one has to comply to Fate's orders.

It is a great pleasure to see your faces through the little window when you come to see 'the convict', but when one thinks of the difficulties you have to get over, the long hours waiting for those few minutes of conversation, one realizes that it is hardly worth it and that it is a great sacrifice for people who have lots of things to do to spend in such a way a whole morning. Letters are a great pleasure too but unfortunately one cannot keep up a regular postal service so that the best way of doing it is to store the letters in anticipation of some chance to send them over.

By the way – who was it that went to Riga and wrote Lucie the letter that made all you people scream with laughter? I could not make out the name as there was a splendid ink-blot just on it. Well Tommy, if you have time to spare do write me some other time and tell your cousins that all their names might beautifully be spelt with 3 letters for each – (guessed?).

Well, ta-ta, with love from your old Uncle Sasha.

PS Give my love to your parents and Aunt Lily and Uncle Jacques.

6/VII/918

Despite repeated interrogation Uncle Sasha and his two friends and closest associates never divulged the names of their fellow conspirators. Relentlessly, the authorities used all the methods known to them to make them speak, even resorting to bribery. Although perhaps genuinely reluctant to shoot Uncle Sasha, who was much loved by Moscow's poor, on 4 July 1918 they informed him that he was to be executed that night. He had time to write to his sisters to bid them farewell. This time he wrote in Russian. This is a translation of his letter:

The OGPU   4/7/.8.918. 6 p.m.

Dear Sisters,

And so, evidently, it is all over, and in a few hours I will set out for a destination where there are neither relations nor friends, and not even an OGPU. There is nothing we can do about this and, although it is stupid and distressing, I shall have to die without even bidding you farewell.

You will, of course, realize that I am not feeling cheerful – but my spirit is firm and my last hours are not proving over painful, so you must not distress yourselves unduly in picturing my last moments. I shall remember your selfless devotion until my death, now imminent. I was fated to give you much trouble at a time in itself immeasurably hard for you, and then to depart as I might equally well have done in the early days of my arrest. But enough about this. I want you to know that the love and care with which you constantly surrounded me have been a great comfort to me. I shall remember all of you until that minute when I become incapable of thought, and I hope that you will always think of me as one who loved you all, and loved his country, perishing in floods of uselessly flowing blood . . . Prepare Father for the sad news. Perhaps it won't be published – if so, so much the better.

Would Malia give EY my last farewell and ask her to forget me if she can. Fondest love for the brothers, Gina, the children, Jacques, Henry, Boris, Mitia, also Ilia. Farewell. I shall know how to die. A last impromptu at parting –

> From the hail of bullets no refuge I sought,
> Not death, but cowardice despising.
> With a smile on my lips, life's battles I fought
> And a joke as I die from my soul is arising.

The letter took several days to reach us. We had no reason to suppose that his situation had in any way worsened; we therefore continued to deliver the daily food parcels to the guard, who continued to accept them. It was only from our Anarchist friend that we learnt that, in a fresh attempt to force my uncle to divulge the names of his associates, he had been driven to the execution ground and placed before an open grave. Disregarding his demand to die with his eyes unbound, a scarf had been tied round his head, the order to fire had been given, shots had rung out and Uncle Sasha had remained standing, unharmed. The execution had been a mock one, a trick intended to break his nerve. It failed to do so but, finally, on 16 August, the penalty was carried out. As predicted he was shot, two months after his thirty-fifth birthday. Once again he was able to send his sisters a letter of farewell; like the earlier one it was in Russian.

Taganka prison *16/8/918.*

It is now midnight.

Dearest sisters,

I have just heard that our fate will be settled tonight, and the prosecutor implied fairly clearly that the verdict will be 'either to your ancestors or to the devil'. I assume that the former is the more likely so I shall spend what time is left to me in bidding fare-well to those I shall leave behind. They will probably suffer more deeply, and certainly for longer, than we who are departing.

It would be silly of me to persuade you that I am not worth mourning or grieving over, but I do assure you, and that with absolute sincerity, that I am perfectly calm. It is not easy to die when the whole of life has not been lived, when much remains ahead and three years of war lie behind – but I do not fear death, and I shall sleep as calmly as ever tonight. If I depart without having accomplished anything important my conscience will nevertheless be at rest for I have never done anything dishonour-able, nor was I tempted, when faced with death, to purchase my life at the cost of others. If I am the first in our fine clan to be a convict and the only one to be condemned to death, it is nothing to be ashamed of since even my executioners can charge me only with loving my country too intensely. I love her more than myself, more than my family to whom I have caused such trouble and anxiety, and am now bringing this last great sorrow.

I suppose I should be thinking of my affairs, but, somehow, I can't. Broadly speaking everything is in order. My books will show that although I have nothing to leave, no one will have anything to pay for me. To my nephews and nieces I bequeath that which neither prison nor execution can take from us – the memory that we too have people who place honour and life before death. Let them never forget it for then my death will not have been in vain.

Prepare Father for the sad news – I fear it will be impossible to conceal it. And believe that I shall remember you all, whose love has lightened the sadness of my last difficult days, until my last minute.

I kiss you all.

Your loving brother.

Although my mother had for some time been longing to leave Russia, whilst Uncle Sasha was alive we had not considered doing so. Now a promise made to him by his sisters necessitated an attempt at escape. When Mother told me of that decision she warned me that Lord would not be able to accompany us. 'What would become of him?' I asked. Gently but firmly she told me that she would have him put down. That struck me as yet another murder. Profoundly shaken and distressed I called my dog and fled the house. Blinded by misery I walked the streets in a daze. Finally I found myself in the Kremlin's Alexandrovsky Gardens, walking towards the wall built along the top of the escarpment overlooking the river.

A small, white Pomeranian was sitting on the wall; his mistress stood by him holding his collar as the drop to the embankment below must measure at least fifty feet. Suddenly, unpredictably and almost completely out of character, Lord galloped towards the wall and jumped. Why had he done so? Had he intended to land on top of the wall beside the Pomeranian or, having sensed my misery, had he decided to commit suicide? If the former, that skilled judge of distances had miscalculated for he missed the wall and disappeared from view.

Within seconds he was howling in agony far below, lying in deep distress at the foot of the wall. I was about to follow when a passer-by caught me, turned me towards the gate and, holding me firmly by the hand, ran with me to the exit. We had a long way to run but Lord was still alive and in acute pain when we reached him. He still knew me. Pillowing his head on my lap I added my howls to his. A crowd gathered; people came forward to help. A cab was found; we were both lifted into it; someone got in with us, directed the cab to an animal clinic and paid the driver. There was no hope for Lord. His injuries were beyond cure and a kind vet put an end to his misery.

Shortly after, we left Moscow for Petrograd where famine raged and disease, chiefly cholera and typhus, was rife. Again I walked the streets, this time generally alone, noting the peeling stucco on the admirably proportioned houses, the silence of the streets, the beauty of those vast empty expanses. I bade each and all of them farewell.

The final parting took place in December 1918.* It was a clear and lovely winter day. St Petersburg was looking its most beautiful, infinitely more intimate and more lovable than ever before. I felt devastated at leaving. As I stood for a final moment on the little bridge separating Russia from Finland I knew that I would never again live in my homeland, that I should never again see Volgovo or Ostrogovitza, never gallop in the Crimean foothills or smell Pavlovsk's lilacs and acacias, never find myself enveloped in a murky Petersburgian fog or hear the melting ice crashing in the Neva, never again feel the bite of Moscow's breezes.

I longed to give vent to my feelings but knew that it would be ill-advised to do so and that any lack of fortitude or act of sentimentality would shock the family. Swallowing my grief I crossed the little bridge which was to confer on us the inestimable gift of freedom of speech – a gift I was even then able to appreciate without at the time feeling sufficiently grateful for it. As I did so, I also realized that memories of our homeland would prove so painful to revive that each of us was likely to recall them only in solitude, the pain of expressing them in words proving too acute to bear. The others must have had similar feelings to mine, for between ourselves we were hardly ever to talk of our past lives.

---

*In 1914 one could go to Finland from St Petersburg by train or boat. The train journey to the customs post at Terijoki, 49 kilometres, took one and a half hours. The steamer to Helsingfors, a twenty-hour journey, went four times a week. See *Baedeker's Russia*, 1914, reprinted London and Newton Abbot, 1971.

STATELESSNESS

TAMARA makes the journey from Russia to Finland seem entirely normal and matter of fact. However my cousin, Evelyn Waley, says that the party escaped from St Petersburg hidden in a cart. This would accord with reports of other refugees fleeing Russia through Finland. An account of one such escape is given in N. Stone and M. Glenny's *The Other Russia*. There Irina Yelenevskaya describes how she and her family escaped in March 1920. Leaving the train at Shuralovo they hid until nightfall. Then, burdened by rucksacks packed with underwear, washing things and extra shoes, they were guided through the forest, along tracks covered in deep snow until, hours later, they reached the river marking the border. The ice was beginning to break up; it cracked ominously, but held as they crossed. But their problems were not yet over: persuading the Finns, by then accepting no more visa-less refugees, to bend the rules was not easy.

It is unclear what, or how much, luggage Tamara and her party took. She refers to sables and diamonds, and often talked of twenty or so pairs of long white gloves. Were they hidden in the cart along with the escapees?

Tamara and her mother were joined in flight by the Ponisovsky family. Tamara mentions seven escapees. Her Aunt Malia died from typhus in Petrograd, her illness delaying and almost thwarting the flight. Apart from her mother and herself, the others were her uncle Mitia and the four Ponisovsky children. In Stockholm the exiles were befriended by Dr Morris Davidson, employed by the US Legation to enquire into conditions in Russia, where he had spent some six months until October 1918.

No records exist of disembarkations in the United Kingdom from European ports, but the exhausted party who landed at Newcastle on 10 January 1919 must have sailed on the Danish steamer *Kronberg*, the only ship from Scandinavia to berth in either the Tyne or the Wear that day. An index in the Public Record Office, Kew, records telephone conversations between Grisha Vilenkin at the Imperial Russian Embassy and the

75

Foreign Office, but I have been unable to trace any correspondence about visas. Since the Abelsons and Ponisovskys were then self-supporting, there should have been no problem of admission.

It is difficult for us, passports safely to hand, to understand the despair of suddenly finding oneself stateless, with no right of abode, no freedom of movement, no permission to earn a living. Tamara used often to say that, on leaving Russia, her mother impressed on her that henceforth she would be a guest wherever she lived, with a guest's obligations of courtesy, of compliance, and of restraint from criticism.

Between 1918 and 1922, almost two million fled Russia, nineteen thousand through Finland, others, including remnants of the White Army, through Turkey or into the Balkans, yet others eastwards into Asia. Many were destitute, hungry, often sick. They included monarchists and social democrats; leaders of finance, industry and commerce; liberals from the professions and academe; scientists, artists and high-ranking military officers. But there were also manual workers, miners, factory workers, road-makers and farm-hands. The one thing all had in common was the expectation of a speedy return to Russia, following on a Soviet defeat.

It was not until 1924/5 that the exiles began to realize that a return was not imminent. Meanwhile life was increasingly difficult as countries tightened their nationality laws; without a nation you were without documents, unprotected from unwarranted expulsion. Rules of domicile varied from country to country. In the United Kingdom, the Home Secretary could deport anyone he considered inimical to the public good, and there was no right of appeal. The French Minister of the Interior had a whole series of infringements which merited instant expulsion – non-compliance with identity paper regulations; conviction of an offence, however trivial; delay in renewing identity certificates; unauthorized employment, or not having found employment; non-payment of taxes, and so on.

Usually naturalization was limited by age; the would-be national had to have resided for a given number of years, usually five, in the country; he had to be of good character with sufficient means to support himself and family; a sponsor was necessary, as was adequate knowledge of the language of the country of adoption; and an oath of allegiance would have to be taken. Many refugees either could not meet these conditions or would not swear the necessary oath, thereby relinquishing hope of a return to Russia.

When the League of Nations accepted responsibility for the refugees, the most urgent need was to provide some form of identification to enable them to travel in search of employment. The task was given to Dr Fridtjof Nansen, appointed High Commissioner for Refugees in August 1921. Then in his sixties, Nansen had been an Arctic explorer but later obtained diplomatic experience: from 1906 to 1918 he was Norway's first ambassador to London, and he was a delegate to the League of Nations from its inception.

By 1922 Nansen had introduced a travel document which became known as a 'Nansen passport'. It consisted merely of a stamp bearing his photograph and the words 'Société des Nations'. Those able to contribute were charged five gold francs for the document, valid for twelve months, then renewable on payment of a like sum. The proceeds financed a revolving fund to cover transport costs for those without means to seek employment. Loans were repayable in instalments once an individual became self-supporting. By the end of 1929, fifty-one governments recognized this identification as a travel document, although it was not a guarantee of residence. A 'Nansen passport' was available only to Russian and Armenian exiles, not to refugees in general.

During 1920 and 1921 Tamara, by now safely installed in London, received several letters in English from her cousin Vera Vydrin, left in Moscow. Vera was enjoying school immensely and was anxious to compare curricula. Her school held a masquerade – even the teachers dressed up, and one could not recognize them. She questioned Tamara avidly about plans for the future, admitting in October 1920 that she herself had none, 'as one does not know if you won't be found frozen in bed next morning!!!' – though confessing to exaggeration. She tells Tamara not to worry about the Oxford entrance examinations: 'I am sure you will pass – Russians are much more clever than English,' she writes.

By 1921 Vera was giving English lessons after school: even so clothes had to be sold for money to buy sufficient potatoes to ward off hunger. That year, she mourned the death of her father from a heart attack. There were no more letters from Vera after 1922 although Tamara preserved a few from Vera's mother, Aunt Rosa. These make no mention of conditions in Russia, dealing purely with personal matters – congratulating Tamara on her engagement in 1927, and on the birth of her first child in 1931.

4

An English Intermission

> And I am rich in all that I have lost.
>
> Siegfried Sassoon, *Memories*

WE REACHED Stockholm shortly before Christmas 1918, and spent a month in the Hotel Royal waiting for our English visas. Our arrival did not pass unnoticed. Strangers welcomed us with tact and great generosity, materializing as if by magic to feast us at nightly banquets, which they persuaded Mother I was old enough to attend. After months of near starvation, the luscious meals seemed unreal, the product of a dream world. Although she appeared old to me, a poetic element entered our lives when we met Selma Lagerlöf.* We went skijoring† in the Skansen, we window-shopped. The town was ablaze with lights. In Russia all shop windows had been boarded up, allegedly for ideological reasons, but in reality because there were no goods to display. Without glass windows to reflect the light and seduce the eye, streets in Russia had seemed sightless, almost dead, grim and dispiriting. In Stockholm they dazzled; the narrow streets of the old town led to small squares, in each of which fantastic and immense Christmas trees sparkled with coloured lights. Yet above all, our chief delight lay in eating. We ate with pleasure, almost with abandonment, certainly with gluttony, forgetful of the plight of those left behind. When our consciences did at last stir, the twins

---

*The Swedish novelist, Selma Lagerlöf, whose adventure stories Tamara had enjoyed reading as a child, was the first woman to win the Nobel Prize for Literature (1909) and the first to be elected to the Swedish Academy (1914).
†A sport in which the skier is towed by a horse.

and I embarked on countless secret discussions about morality and social obligations, but even the fiercest of our debates failed to control our appetites.

Bergen was picturesque but provincial after Stockholm, and we were glad to board a ship bound for England. We disembarked in Newcastle after a very rough crossing and drove to the station. It seemed surprisingly quiet, but we eventually found a solitary porter who informed us that the railway was on strike. He was difficult to understand and seemed to find us equally incomprehensible. It was getting dark. We stood dejectedly discussing our predicament. We were cold and miserable. The prospect of being stranded in those bleak surroundings struck me as so frightful that my self-control snapped and I started to cry. Genia, my youngest cousin, was quick to copy, howling her loudest.

Our distress galvanized the porter into wheeling our heavy luggage into a shed. Then, distributing our overnight bags amongst us, he told us to follow, and led us into a street at a sharp pace. Trailing behind, we traversed numerous streets without knowing where we were going. Eventually we turned into a narrow road bordered by small terraced houses, each with a neat front garden. Our guide entered one of them, advanced along a narrow path and rapped on the door. A young woman opened it and stared at the seven of us with astonishment. We stared back, no less surprised than she.

Although we failed to understand her opening remarks or our porter's reply, we gradually realized that, not knowing what to do with us and mistakenly assuming that we were destitute, he had led us to his wife. She proved no less sympathetic and generous than her husband. Conducting us into her living-room she proceeded to make tea, cutting us thick slices of fresh bread. Somehow this warm-hearted couple succeeded in providing sleeping quarters for us all in their small house. Such kindness reduced Mother to tears. It was the only occasion throughout her long years of exile that I saw her cry. As we settled down for the night in our makeshift beds, each of us felt that life still had much that was good in store for us.

On the following morning, one train at any rate was leaving for London. Our porter installed us in it. We were met by Mother's eldest brother, a member of the Imperial Russian Embassy, and driven to his house at 31 Palace Gate. I believe my aunt thought us difficult guests, yet her butler was always ready to welcome us to his pantry. Nevertheless we soon moved to the neighbouring De Vere Hotel.

Within days of settling in, I became ill with whooping cough. Instead of sending me to hospital as requested by the hotel management, Mother rented the entire first floor where we lived in isolation. As I slowly regained my health, I often lay by the balcony doors looking out over Kensington Gardens where severe-looking nannies hobnobbed whilst their charges languished in capacious, gleaming prams. The hall porter, a large, immensely impressive man with a marvellous sense of humour called Charles, became a great friend and often called to cheer me up with a joke. So too did Alice, the delicious housemaid with a cockney's sense of fun. Maykins returned to us, abandoning an excellent position with an English family to look after me and my youngest cousin. I was delighted to see Maykins, but I also felt that I no longer needed a governess and bitterly resented my loss of independence. I hope I had the grace to conceal my feelings.

Meanwhile our parents were flat-hunting. Eventually they settled on a furnished flat in Albert Court Mansions, just behind the Albert Hall. The rent of twenty-five guineas a week did not seem excessive. There was, of course, no chance of Charles becoming attached to us, but Mother did not hesitate to persuade Henriette, the hotel's superb Belgian cook, and dear Alice, to come and look after us, Alice producing Agnes, an equally lovable girl, who became our parlour maid. Our days became watered-down versions of our original way of life. We did not realize our extravagance in ordering twelve cakes daily for tea from Rumpelmayer's in St James's, to avoid overworking Henriette who was managing without a kitchen maid. Although the flat was spacious it took us some time to get used to living in what seemed to us cramped quarters.

The best part of my day was my early morning ride in Hyde Park. My horse, accompanied by a middle-aged groom, came from a mews just off Palace Gate. The rides helped to reconcile me to my new surroundings.

I was given pocket money and allowed to shop, but my greatest source of pleasure was travelling on the top of an open bus, preferably in the front seat. The European towns which we had visited in the past possessed trams which scarcely differed from those of St Petersburg, although we had been forbidden to use them, for fear of catching a disease such as cholera, diphtheria or typhoid. But we had never seen buses as splendid as London's, each with an open upper deck offering an unimpeded view of terraced houses, enclosed verdant squares, an infinite variety of church steeples and curiously shaped Victorian house-tops. At dusk it was often possible to look into the lit rooms where people of my own age could be seen seated at a table, a piano or close to a fireplace, even on a rocking-horse.

Those glimpses of secure, well-regulated daily life made me long for home, for the rocking-chair in which I used to curl up with a book and for my black and tan toy terrier dog. Years later, when leaving London with my husband on an enticing trip abroad, as the train meandered through the streets of Calais, passing alongside blocks of flats lived in by the town's poorer inhabitants, the sight of a family gathered round a kitchen table for their evening meal pierced my heart, arousing a longing for as orderly and changeless a way of life, even though I was at the same time acutely aware that my love of adventure was keener than my delight in happy domesticity among the stay-at-homes. At the bombing of Calais, I grieved simultaneously for the destruction of those French flats and the disruption of their owners' lives, and for the insecurity of our future and the improbability of our ever again being able gaily to travel the world. And, indeed, although the last of these fears proved to be imaginary, travel after the Second World War never regained the intense excitement which I used to feel when the Channel steamer docked at a French port, and numerous blue-bloused French porters cheerfully swarmed on to its decks, seized one's luggage and led one to one's sleeper destined for Italy or the Levant.

At about this time it was noticed that my sight was deteriorating and that my hands shook. Mother decided to take me to Berlin to be examined by Herr Pagenstecker, perhaps the foremost eye specialist. He ascribed some of my loss of eyesight to malnutrition, some to a congenital defect, prescribed difficult exercises and advised me to postpone wearing spectacles for as long as possible. His advice proved excellent and, even for reading, I was not to need glasses for another thirty years. The specialist who examined my hands could find nothing physically wrong and, mistakenly I feel sure, ascribed my condition to nervous strain.

Mother and I travelled to Berlin in a first-class sleeper and, as in pre-war days, stayed at the Adlon, although on this occasion sharing a room. As we drove from the station I was astonished to see people carrying their paper money in laundry baskets. I assumed that they were millionaires and marvelled at the wealth of a defeated nation. The next morning I came abruptly to understand the full horror of galloping inflation.

On our return to London my education had to resume. As a first step I was to have piano lessons on Saturday mornings at nine o'clock. My master was a Belgian refugee, M. Charles Hénusse, a member of the Brussels Conservatoire. He came wearing a frock-coat and white kid gloves, looking very like Shakespeare because of his carefully trimmed, reddish beard. His formal clothes and manner had a touch of the undertaker and may therefore have been responsible for the feeling of homesickness which possessed me when playing Chopin's *Funeral March*, slowing my tempo to the funereal. One Saturday, obviously irritated beyond endurance by my rendering, Monsieur Hénusse's reserve cracked. 'Mais, voyons Mademoiselle,' he cried, 'dépêchez-vous, le cimetière ferme à cinq heures.' Deeply mortified I never again played that particular piece of music.

After various false starts I went as a day girl to Miss Spalding and Mademoiselle Griboval's Ladies School at 133 Queen's Gate.* Olga, Vladimir Nabokov's elder sister, joined me, but neither of us proved good mixers. Olga, having poor eyesight, was clumsier than me, but my ankles were apt to give way without warning and fling me face downwards on the ground. However, it was Olga who, on several occasions, collided with the houseman carrying the boarders' soup which, they maintained, was the best part of their lunch. But Olga was more docile than I. At games she tried to do what was expected whilst I rebelled and, when goaded beyond endurance to play lacrosse, hit out wildly, but intentionally, bringing the stick down on the head of a schoolmate. My action was considered unforgivable by everyone and to my delight I was barred from all games other than tennis, which we played in Battersea Park. We

---

*The school existed from 1919 to 1932.

were driven there in a brake pulled by two splendid white horses.

Nina Seafield, whom I was not destined to meet in adult life, became my only close school friend. She was short, sand-coloured and very shy, but her stammer did not damp her sense of humour. The *thé dansant* had become the rage and on Saturdays Lady Seafield often gave one for her daughter. I was one of the very few of her schoolfellows whom Nina invited. Although my partners did not amuse me, I liked these occasions; they were very grown-up affairs and I immensely enjoyed the familiar steps including dances such as the Lancers, Scottish reels and Sir Roger de Coverley which Madame Vacani had taught me. I also enjoyed sipping a weakly laced cup.

I was a misfit at school. It was no help to have been so well taught in Russia that I was put into a form with far older girls, one entitling me to use the library. This right was resented as much by my class-mates as by my contemporaries, and I was often teased as well. I retaliated as best I could, and made no effort to conceal my resent-ment. Many lessons failed to interest me, although I revelled in Miss Thornton's classes on English literature. She was an inspiring teacher and, regardless of the language difficulty, she even succeeded in enabling me to appreciate the lilt of Chaucer's words, although at a much later date it was Nevill Coghill's renderings of the poet's works which enabled me fully to savour their quality. At school I also enjoyed the weekly current events and history of art classes, subjects new to me. Nevertheless I very soon learnt to play truant. First, I took to skipping a day here and there, exploring the neighbour-hood's side-streets and junk shops. I became more daring and started to miss two consecutive days. Even then I escaped detection, but when I cut three days in succession I was found out and severely reprimanded. On promising to mend my ways, I was forgiven.

On Saturdays I visited the National Gallery and the Victoria and Albert Museum, but do not remember going to the British Museum or the Tate, or to have gone to the cinema before my Oxford days. Yet I often went to the theatre. That winter Forbes-Robertson was appearing in a series of Shakespeare plays. I saw them all, and developed a boundless admiration for the actor. I also thoroughly

---

*The French actor and playwright Sacha Guitry (1885–1957) was born in St Petersburg and first appeared on the Paris stage in 1902. In 1920 he came to London bringing a play he had written at the age of sixteen.

enjoyed the Sacha Guitry season,* but was disappointed by the aged Sarah Bernhardt's appearance in *L'Aiglon*.* In contrast, although enthralled by the beauty of Melba's voice, I felt obliged to keep my eyes shut to avoid being repelled by her ugly body and poor acting. Chaliapin, although with a failing voice, transported me into the reality of the theatre's unreal world by the mastery of his acting and the force of his personality. Pavlova possessed a magnetic quality similar to Chaliapin's and although I saw her dance only once, and then at a charity matinée, her rendering of the Dying Swan enthralled me. Mother occasionally took me to call on her in Hampstead; I found her intimidating and mannered, and felt relieved when allowed into her garden to watch some swans swimming on her pond.

The only Russian artist whom we knew in London was Roerich. It seemed to me that he was even more homesick for central Asia than for Russia proper. Both his sons shared his unhappiness. Serge Konovalov, also a frequent visitor, joined us to listen spellbound to Roerich talking affectionately and nostalgically of Uzbeks, Mongols, deserts and mountain passes. But all too soon Roerich was to leave for India where he found some contentment. I was also greatly attracted by Sir Rabindranath Tagore whom I met at much the same time at Uncle Grisha's. While won over by the poet's dignity and affability, it was the equanimity with which he regarded life that especially impressed me.

With the approach of spring, I began to long for the country, especially for rivers and forests. The others were probably experiencing the same desires, for on fine weekends, unconscious of extravagance, we often hired a chauffeur-driven Daimler, generally going to Maidenhead for lunch at Skindles followed by boating on the Thames. We took it in turns to row; although the Thames looked very different from the rivers we remembered, we were quick to respond to the charm of its willows, its slender, pencil-shaped poplars, and its outspread elms.

We made few English friends, chiefly I suppose because of lack of introductions. Most of the people we knew were members of the Imperial Russian Embassy posted to London before the start of the

---

*Bernhardt was particularly associated with *L'Aiglon*, the play written in 1900 by Edmond Rostand, in which she played the part of Napoleon's son.

war; they had their own problems to contend with, and did not introduce us to their English acquaintances. What little we saw of English life seemed very pre-war; we therefore failed to realize how much it had really changed for the English, or how their ranks had been thinned by death in the course of the war.

Our substantial sum of money – which had lain in an English bank since the summer of 1914 – started to dwindle. This was hardly surprising when our way of life, seemingly modest to us at the time, is assessed by present-day standards. Mother sought oblivion in bridge, which she played badly though for very small stakes. Normally a gallant loser, now the loss of even minute stakes distressed her, especially when she pondered our financial situation. One day she decided to sell her sables and pearls, virtually her only valuable possessions. Not knowing how, she asked an acquaintance to act as go-between and was badly swindled over the deal. Scotland Yard was called in. Its officers impressed us by their kindness and efficiency, but Mother felt unable to follow their advice to prosecute the go-between, an acquaintance of long standing. Worried and distressed, she now found herself richer by £3,000, but poorer by £7,000. Our prospects continued to deteriorate, yet Mother let herself be goaded into betting that I could pass into Oxford as easily as the daughter of a fellow bridge player. Doing so involved passing the university examination 'Responsions', and also those to a college of my choice.

Time was short and Responsions seemed beyond me, for either Greek or Latin was obligatory, as were mathematics. I had never studied either of the ancient languages and was incapable of understanding even the rudiments of mathematics. Miss Spalding felt that, in the time available, it was asking the impossible. However, the prospect of independence was a carrot which I could not resist. When Mother absent-mindedly promised that I should go to Oxford if I passed the necessary examinations, I applied myself with fervour to learning Latin and strove to master, with the help of a Cambridge senior wrangler, the small amount of geometry, algebra and arithmetic required. Difficulties about my age were settled in time for me to travel to Oxford, to stay at St Hugh's College whilst sitting my college entrance examination.

One evening, Miss Jourdain, the principal, invited me to coffee in her study. I knew nothing about her, nothing about the vision which she and Miss Moberley believed that they had seen when on a visit to Versailles,* nor did I know anything about Oxford life or the position of women in the university. I did not even know that it was only a little over a year since Convocation had admitted women to full membership of the university. Cambridge still withheld that privilege, yet in Russia women had possessed it since the latter half of the nineteenth century. But none of these subjects was mentioned that evening. Our conversation was lively, unconstrained and wide-ranging. I found it stimulating and assumed that I would enjoy collegiate life. I now felt increasingly anxious to do well in the entrance examination. Luck favoured me in the general paper, for the questions included one on the old-fashioned girl. My extensive reading in four languages provided me with models ranging from Pushkin's Tatiana to Jane Austen's heroines, and I was able to give my thoughts free rein.

The day on which I heard that I had passed into Oxford also brought news of Father's escape from Russia and the probability that Volodia would soon cross into Persia, whence he would be able to make his way back to western Europe. When Father arrived in Paris, in 1921, penury stared us in the face, so my parents decided to live in Paris, where it was easier to be poor than in London, easier for Father and Volodia to find work, and where we all had friends among the Russian exiles. We moved almost immediately, renting a modest, poorly furnished flat in the Rue Singer, just off the Place de la Muette in Passy. The flat was too small but it was cheap and we were glad to be reunited. Never having heard of temporary employment I spent my time reading, steeping myself in the works of Baudelaire, Verlaine, Rimbaud and Mallarmé as well as in Balzac's portrayals of mankind. But we did not live in perfect amity. For all our devotion to each other we were at too close quarters to be easy going.

---

*Miss Moberley was Miss Jourdain's predecessor as principal of St Hugh's College. In 1901 they had visited Versailles. Walking through the grounds they met eight people in strange attire – two gardeners, a red-faced man, an insolent footman, a woman and girl, a lady sketching, a man in a dark cloak. Subsequently the two ladies decided they had gone back in time. See their reminiscences, *An Adventure*, London, 1911, repr. 1955.

OXFORD

ALTHOUGH much has been written by or about the Oxford under-graduate of the 1920s, the 'bright young things', many of whom were Tamara's friends, the very restricted life of the undergraduette has seldom been described.

Women had been admitted to lectures at Oxford from 1873, but not until 1920 could they sit for a degree, and even then were barred from reading for a qualification in divinity. A woman had to be accepted by one of five 'Societies of Women Students', as the colleges were described in the *University Examination Statutes, 1920/21*. St Hugh's College, founded in 1886, moved to a new building in 1916. Eileen Yonge, there in the early 1920s, wrote that it was a 'happy mean between the carefully guarded gentility of Lady Margaret Hall and the cranks, freaks and spectacled scholars of Somerville'.

Passing examinations was not the only necessity for the award of a degree. Students, both male and female, were required to hold resid-ence for nine terms. This involved attending morning chapel and eating dinner in Hall forty-two times a term. On Sunday evenings, St Hugh's undergraduettes were obliged to sit in on an evening lecture by the Principal. The rules regarding behaviour were extremely strict and were described in a leaflet issued to all students:

Invitations. All students are expected to be in College for dinner unless they have had leave to be absent. Students are expected to consult the Principal before accepting invitations to lunch, dinner or evening parties; boating, garden, or picnic parties; before going to Eights or walking on the towing path . . . Students may go out alone with their brothers, but may not go alone to their college rooms or lodgings. All tea parties including men must be given in a common room or the garden by leave of the Principal . . . A student may entertain her father or brother in her room, but if she is inviting friends to meet her brother, the party must be given in a common room . . .

Students are not allowed to go to dances in Oxford during term; nor in the Vacation when staying in College . . .

The College gates are locked at 9 p.m. . . . No student is allowed for any reason to be out later than 11 p.m.

Even male students found some of these rules preposterous. The editor of the undergraduate magazine *Isis*, in the issue of 26 October 1921, compared the position of women at Oxford with that at Cambridge. Having congratulated Oxford on opening their degrees to the fair sex, he pointed out that at Cambridge, although that privilege was not as yet granted, 'the sexes see much more of one another. They dance together, walk together, tea together, are seen about together, more often and more familiarly.' The subject is returned to in the issue of 4 June 1924, which quotes from the 'disgraceful' restrictive rules. In his memoirs, Wilfrid Le Gros Clark, appointed Professor of Anatomy at Oxford in 1934, wrote that he was 'truly astonished' to find that women medical students were still segregated when dissecting cadavers.

Tamara sat her first hurdle, the college entrance examination, in March 1921. The charge for staying in college was seven shillings a day. She was instructed to wear a dark coat and skirt, white blouse, black tie, black shoes and stockings 'as some of the papers will be taken in the University Examination Schools'.

The examination consisted of an English essay; a general paper; an unseen translation from Latin, Greek, French, Italian or German. The candidate had also to sit a paper selected from languages, modern history, English literature, mathematics or natural science.

The choice in the three-hour English literature paper was wide, four questions, including one obligatory one comparing three poems, having to be answered out of twenty-five. The language paper involved a one-hour translation from each language submitted. These two papers, being printed, are doubtless those taken in the University Examination Schools. The other papers are cyclostyled. Three choices were given for the two-and-a-half-hour general essay:

> What is a classic?
> The right of the majority to rule.
> An old-fashioned girl.

whilst four to six essay-type questions had to be answered in the three-hour general paper. In another literature paper, in which it was necessary to answer four questions in three hours, Tamara seems to have concentrated on those dealing with Shakespeare.

On 23 March, Miss Jourdain wrote advising Tamara to have extra English coaching, 'to bring that language up to a higher level', yet stating that a place would be kept for her provided she surmounted the next hurdle.

Responsions, for which the candidate was to present herself in the same attire, was in mid-June. Four subjects had to be taken, at least one from each of three groups. Two languages were to be included other than English. The groupings were (a) Latin, Greek (b) English, French, German (c) Mathematics, Natural Science or Maths and Natural Science. It was necessary to satisfy the examiners in three subjects at one sitting. The fourth could be passed later.

Another hurdle, Moderations or Mods, so called because it was assessed by moderators, came at the end of one's first year. An oblig- atory paper on the Holy Scriptures – either on one of the Synoptic Gospels or on the Acts of the Apostles – could be replaced, if the candidate was of age or the parent or guardian objected on religious grounds, by a prescribed philosophical book or books. This option was taken up by Tamara who preferred Pascal's *Pensées* to the Bible. A telegram to Paris, despatched on 10 July 1922, announced the successful accomplishment of that hurdle.

Finals were conducted by public examiners. The syllabus for the new degree combination of Philosophy, Politics and Economics, as published in the 1921/2 Examination Statutes, comprised eight ele- ments, including moral and political philosophy; British political and constitutional history to 1760; British social and economic history from 1780; the history of philosophy from Descartes; polit- ical economy.

The ceremony of matriculation by which the student was admitted to the university, and which so amused Tamara, though slightly modernized, had not changed so very greatly from that described by Mr Verdant Green in 1853. Within a fortnight of arrival the student, in academic dress and accompanied by a dean in gown and hood, was presented to the Vice-Chancellor. The student was handed a copy of the University Statutes and of the Proctors' *Memorandum on the Conduct and Discipline of Junior Members of the University.*

The Vice-Chancellor then said, 'Know that you have been today entered in the Register of the University, and are bound to observe all the statutes contained in this book, as far as they concern you.' By this quaint ritual Tamara was duly enrolled.

Harold Hobson, in his autobiography *Indirect Journey*, writes that, in the twenties, between £250 and £300 was an adequate income for an Oxford undergraduate. This would cover college expenses and several society subscriptions; eating out; book-buying and the occasional theatre in London. Cecil Day Lewis gave £210 as the absolute minimum, leaving no margin for subscriptions or parties. An article in the *Morning Post* of 25 November 1921 stated that most students were allowed £300 a year, but that it was possible to make do with £275 if one wanted; ex-servicemen had to survive on grants of £225 a year. Rhodes Scholars, who had to keep themselves during the vacations as well as term, received £300 a year but, said the journalist, most had to top this up from private sources to £450 or £500. The charge for board and residence in a private family varied from two and a half to five guineas a week, the usual being three guineas. In 1995, an Oxbridge student would look on £6,000 a year as a subsistence-level allowance.

Tamara preserved her engagement books for her first two academic years, but not unfortunately that for 1923/4. From the start of her first term, she had tea engagements almost every day. In her second term, the tea dates are interspersed with occasional visits to the theatre or cinema, and to that term's OUDS (Oxford University Dramatic Society) production. The summer term is punctuated by teas on the river. During her second year, invitations multiply, dinner engagements becoming normal, and elevenses at Fuller's frequent. On returning to Paris for Christmas 1922, her first appointment was with her dressmaker, so money could not have been too tight then. Vacations were just as crammed with teas, dinners and theatre and cinema visits.

On the last day of Eights she had tea with 'Otto and David'. Could that have been David Talbot Rice whom she was later to marry, or was it his cousin David Rhys with whom she lunched later that term? Those are the only references in the diaries to either David, although she saw quite a lot of both. The majority of the events recorded in her memoirs, the lunch with Oliver Messel, the drive with John Gielgud, must have taken place in her final, diaryless, year.

The Hypocrites Club, of which many of her closest friends were members, was founded by a group of Trinity and Oriel men as a moderately serious conversation society. Gradually, pubs being out of bounds, it degenerated into a fashionable, perhaps snobbish drinking and eating club, where shove-halfpenny was played. Christopher Hollis names Richard Hughes and Robert Graves as presiding spirits, and admits to drink in abundance, but says it was mostly beer. However, Henry Yorke, writing as Henry Green in *Pack My Bag*, describes his first visit: 'Someone gave me a German mug full of what from the mug I took to be beer, but when I tasted it, found to be much stronger.' Anthony Powell, in the first volume of his memoirs, writes of the members as ranging from the aesthete Harold Acton to David Talbot Rice and Lord Elmley, both sometime secretaries, who 'with many more, could not have been less aesthete-like!' Powell thinks David Talbot Rice introduced his Eton friends, Acton and Robert Byron. Evelyn Waugh was a member, but for a period was excluded for smashing up much of the furniture with his heavy stick. A description less tinged with fallible memory, since more contemporary, came from the pen of Brian Howard, writing in the *Cherwell* in 1927:

> During the whole of this period, and half-way down St Aldate's, flourished a club. In spite of a tendency towards beeriness and elderly Sussex bards, it was, at the time, the one club which had entirely freed itself from the jejune snobberies, various and vapid, which constricted the life of every other. Hypocrites in name, they left hypocrisy to the rest. Nightly Mr Peter Ruffer extracted beauty from the most unwilling of pianos, while Mr Robert Byron, looking like some possessed Hungarian prince, added the gimlet of his voice . . . Others there were, and the pity is that I cannot remember them all. Mr Evelyn Waugh, the best of all our artists of that time, and Mr David Rice, who now unearths forgotten cities in Asia Minor.

To celebrate the demise of the club when banned by the authorities, a stupendous fancy-dress party was held at the Spreadeagle in Thame. John Fothergill, the gentleman landlord, reported that 'The dancing was terrific. I have an image as of wild goats and animals leaping in the air. It must have been a record party in Oxford's history.'

He goes on to express his gratitude to the members: 'Whatever their indiscretions and unpopularity in Oxford, they did like good furniture and a beautiful room, good food and wine and they practised conversation'

Once Tamara became a home student and escaped from corporate living she enjoyed Oxford. The 'home students' were administered by what is now St Anne's College, whose principal was Christine Burrows. They too had a set of rules, perhaps not quite so restrictive as for those in college, but certainly not lax:

1. Students may obtain permission to visit Colleges and College Gardens and to attend College Chapels provided (a) that they do not go into Colleges alone (b) that they do not go into men's rooms except with a chaperon approved by their Principal . . .

2. They may attend debates at the Union, the theatre, concerts and public meetings . . . They may go to tea at cafés approved by the Principal but not frequently or alone.

3. They are not permitted to walk on the tow path of Lower River, or to take long walks or bicycle rides, or to boat alone.

4. They may receive calls from gentlemen known to their parents and may accept invitations but may not walk, bicycle, boat or go to cafés without an approved chaperon.

5. They must get permission to accept evening invitations, or luncheon, picnic or boating parties. They may not accept invitations to dances.

6. They may not go out after dinner or supper without permission.

From the viewpoint of the authorities, Tamara's career was far from satisfactory, as we learn from a packet of letters in the archives of St Anne's College. On 3 December 1921, Miss Jourdain wrote to the Principal of St Anne's that a request would be received from Tamara to become a home student:

I expect you will like to know something about her. She came up for entrance in March 1921 & was recommended for English. She came down in June in Responsions but in September passed in 3 subjects. I kept a vacancy open for her till Jan 1922, but she was just failed again in Latin, & we cannot take her. On the other hand she cannot afford to wait, as she is not well off. She is a very nice girl, well brought up, of Jewish descent. She is pleasant to deal with & is anti-Bolshevik. I would have taken her but for our rule about Responsions . . .

Tamara is registered as a student of St Anne's from 29 January 1922, having matriculated five days earlier. The registers show her keeping eight terms, until the end of the Trinity (summer) term of 1924. When registering she gave her names as Helen Tamara, her date of birth as 2 July 1903 instead of 1904, presumably to appear to comply with Oxford's minimum entry age of eighteen.

The chaperon rules do not seem to have curbed her much. In May 1923 the Senior Proctor of Corpus Christi informed her Principal that he had caught one of his students out walking with Tamara, then living at no. 4 Museum Road. When questioned, the undergraduate had said that he had stayed with Tamara's family in Paris. Perhaps he and the Indian she befriended were one and the same? Pram Kumar Mitter went up to Corpus Christi in 1921.

Tamara changed digs frequently. In August 1923 she asked permission to lodge with a Mrs Ball because she liked dogs, but the following month she informed the authorities that she had arranged to board with a Mrs Fisher at 4 St Margaret's Road. The winter of 1923/4 was troubled. On 11 November 1923, Tamara wrote to her Principal from Chalfont Road:

I have just received your letter which has delighted me because it denotes the fact that you are giving me another chance for showing that I can appreciate being trusted. Next term you will see how I value your kindness, now I will but thank you very very much for it.

What had she been up to? Perhaps she was not getting on with her landlady, for between 4 February and 28 March 1924 there is a string of complaints to the Principal from Mrs Fricker of the same address. Admittedly Tamara was almost always in by 10.30 p.m. and up for breakfast by about 9 a.m., but she then disappeared for the day: both her main meals were eaten at Dr Counsell's (Dr Counsell, a GP and friend to many undergraduates, kept open house), and she also frequented the Moorish Café. She was, Mrs Fricker complained, 'elusive and vague at times both in speech and contact'. Although capable of looking after herself, the landlady felt that the Principal should know of her student's 'restless life'.

Was it the chaperon rules which caused yet more trouble in February 1924? Her tutor wrote to the Principal:

> I feel it hard to give a really good opinion of Tamara's case without having heard her at all (so as to judge how far her disobedience was deliberate) . . . I should suggest gating her for the rest of term, on the understanding that she will behave reasonably to Mrs Fricker, and sending her away as early as possible in the eighth week (say Thursday) . . . in any case a definite understanding that her gate book will be gone into weekly next term and that she will be sent down at once, if anything goes wrong.

Academically things were not going too well either. An undated letter (autumn 1922?) from tutor to Principal reports that Tamara was very anxious to do PPE and had promised to work hard, but it would be advisable for her to stay up until Christmas (1924); with two more years' hard work she should get a second. In June (1923?) her tutor, Miss C. V. Butler, reiterated that Tamara should stay up longer:

> She is an intelligent creature, with much confidence in her own wits and power of work . . . By working hard in this long vac she should get through. She should get a 4th next summer, or just possibly a 3rd, but it seems a pity she should not do better and grow up more, as a result of another year. By June 1924 she will have had only $2\frac{2}{3}$ years, heavily handicapped by P Mods and Responsions.

All this good advice, and an exile to Wales to work, were to no avail. On 19 July 1924 Tamara wrote to her Principal:

> I have just heard of the results of Schools & find that I have failed – this probably is partly due to my hay fever.
> As I have another term's residence to keep I wonder whether you would be so good as to allow me to come up next summer term & take Schools again if my parents wish me to.

Although a reply was sent on 20 July Tamara never acknowledged it. It is just possible the letter never reached her, for she had told the Principal that, because they had had to leave their flat, the family was travelling in Europe and letters should be addressed to her care of various postes restantes.

5

Hope Deceived

Home of lost causes, and forsaken beliefs and unpopular names, and impossible loyalties.

Matthew Arnold, *Essays in Criticism* (Preface)

I REACHED Oxford on a cold October afternoon. At St Hugh's my domain, a bed-sitting room, was very small. My fellow under-graduettes asserted that the architect who designed St Hugh's had miscalculated and as a result our rooms were a quarter of their intended sizes, a statement which I half believed but have never veri-fied. At dinner time the hum of voices led me to Hall, where I was assigned a place. I had had no experience of communal feeding and the noise, especially the sound of knives scraping on plates, set my nerves on edge, preventing me from speaking to either neighbour. As soon as possible I fled, unaware that it would have been sensible to make my way to the Junior Common Room.

I had been informed that residence was kept by being in college by eleven o'clock every night and by attending seven o'clock morning chapel on all but a very few mornings. On my first morning I woke at about seven and went in search of a bath. St Hugh's possessed very few bathrooms; all were occupied. Patiently I waited for the door of one to open but, with time running out, I returned to my room unwashed, threw on some clothes and hurried to chapel. As I reached its threshold the door closed in my face and one of my obligatory days of residence was passing unrecorded. I returned to a now vacant bathroom resolved not to be caught out again. By the time I had recovered my equanimity and entered the dining-room I had missed breakfast.

Three Russian men in their last year at Oxford were long-stand-ing family friends and Mother had made all three promise to keep

an eye on me. On that first morning of my first term, as I walked
down the Cornmarket in a disconsolate frame of mind, I met Genia
Lourie. Noting my depression he suggested having a cup of coffee
in the Cadena Café. As I unburdened myself so my spirits started
to rise. I looked around the crowded café, so different from its
French or Austrian counterparts, and noticed my college bursar
regarding me with a fixed look. I bowed to her but she continued
to stare at me; I bowed more deeply; still she gazed at me, unsmiling, ignoring my greeting. Puzzled, I bewailed the strangeness of
Oxford's customs, its noise in Hall, the seemingly malicious slamming of the chapel door as I reached it. I wondered whether I would
be able to adapt to so different a way of life, whether it might not
be wiser to return to Paris, find work and contribute to the family's
finances. Genia told me not to be silly. He spoke of the pleasant
aspects of Oxford life, of the excitement of discussing any subject
under the sun with contemporaries; of the wide differences in
taste and ideas to be met; of the beauty of the town's buildings;
the stimulus provided by one's tutors; the delights of the river.
Duly encouraged, I returned to college where I was told that
the Principal wished to see me. Delighted at the prospect of con-
versing with Miss Jourdain no less pleasantly than I had done when
taking my entrance examination, I hurried to her study.

I was received by a very different Miss Jourdain. Now her short
and stoutish figure confronted me with sternness as she portent-
ously remarked, 'I know exactly what you were doing this
morning.' Apologetically I hurried to explain that I had not
intended to cut chapel but had missed it by a couple of seconds,
that although I was up by seven o'clock I had been unable to find
anywhere to wash. 'That is not what I mean,' snapped Miss
Jourdain. In astonishment I asked whether I should not have bowed
to Miss Bullen on seeing her in the Cadena Café. A curious silence
ensued, Miss Jourdain seeming no less mystified than I. Then,
looking closely at me, controlling her irritation, she asked whether
I had studied the university's chaperon rules. I had no idea what she
meant. Had I not seen an envelope in my room containing much
essential information? Collecting my thoughts I recalled an envelope that I had forgotten to open, nor could I remember what I had
done with it. Still looking aggrieved my principal told me to find it,
read its contents and then report back. Later that evening I heard

of Miss Jourdain's habit, when learning of our misdemeanours, of implying that her knowledge stemmed from psychic powers. My spontaneous reference to Miss Bullen had prevented her from impressing me with her gift of second sight.

My room had been cleaned, my empty luggage removed and the all-important envelope propped up on my desk. It contained, among other things, a set of chaperon rules adopted, I think in 1920, on the admission of women to full membership of the university. I read them with a growing sense of outrage. What sort of society, I wondered, could object to a girl being seen *en tête-à-tête* with a man in a restaurant? What sort of society could object to girls attending a mixed party in an undergraduate's rooms unless chaperoned by a married woman, however young? What chance had I of meeting a married woman at Oxford who would not only agree to chaperon me, but whom I would also be prepared to foist on any friends I might be able to make? Bitterly I recalled that, in my determination to preserve my independence, I had refused the offer to become a maid-in-waiting to one of Europe's few remaining queens and another to serve an Indian maharanee. The chaperon rules were offensive: I could not see myself complying. There would be many occasions when I might want to rush to my Russian friends for comfort and advice.

The society in which I had grown up was not permissive, yet it was too worldly and rational not to accept the existence of sexual deviations, marital ramifications and conjugal infidelities. Nevertheless decorum was universally observed and I had never encountered what Evelyn Waugh later referred to as 'lechery'. The chaperon rules seemed to imply an acceptance of promiscuity. Would I enjoy living in a society which needed such offensive rules, I asked myself. Would I succeed in attending chapel the requisite number of times? Had I made a mistake in coming to Oxford? I could not in all honesty, I concluded, undertake to keep the chaperon rules. I hurried to inform Miss Jourdain of my decision, asking her to arrange for my luggage to be brought back so that I might pack and leave next morning for Paris.

Genuinely upset, Miss Jourdain asked me to sit down and rang for tea. I was not then aware that tea was the British panacea for all ills. Then, patiently and with deep feeling, she told me of the long struggle women had waged to gain, first admission, and then full membership of the university. She spoke passionately of the impression the first intakes of undergraduettes would make, how essential it was to ensure that no single girl fell short of the high standard of behaviour expected. She charmed me and overcame my scruples; indeed, as much as it was possible, we became friends and I have never wavered in my admiration of her. Yet there were several occasions during that winter when, like a temperamental housemaid, I rushed to Miss Jourdain clamouring for my boxes. However, she always managed to persuade me to stay. But, at the start of her last illness, she advised me to abandon college life in favour of that of a home student at what is now St Anne's, helping me to find digs. I was to owe most of my future happiness to her insistence that I should stay on at Oxford.

The ceremony of matriculation amused and pleased me, although the cap which an undergraduette was obliged to wear at lectures and tutorials was so hot and heavy that it always gave me a headache. I made little headway at St Hugh's. I loathed Hall. I felt miserable in the Common Room and I was reluctant to spend my evenings in girlish talk over cups of very sweet cocoa. In return I was heartily disliked for locking a bathroom door late at night to enter it very early in the morning for a quick bath. Even so, by the end of term, I was seven chapels short on my residence.

Financially as well as scholastically the loss of that record of residence was likely to prove disastrous to me. Deeply distressed I consulted Miss Jourdain who must, I think, have agreed that a vendetta had been waged against me. Characteristically and very endearingly, after only a short silence, she remarked on the number of churches in Oxford; the next day being a Sunday it should not prove impossible to attend seven church services on that day. Very gratefully, and with no less of an amused smile on my face than on Miss Jourdain's, I thanked her and went to consult my friend the porter. With his help I found that, by starting with communion at 6 a.m., I could fit in the six remaining services, complying with the letter if not the spirit of residence regulations. In Paris, Volodia howled with laughter, as much over the regulation itself, and its compromise, as over my failure to cheat over the number of churches I had visited on the last day of my first term.

Early in my second term my bath problem, and so also the chapel difficulty, were solved as a result of a chance meeting with the poet

W. B. Yeats. I no longer remember where I met him or how, but I must have amused him by my account of these difficulties. He was living at the time in a tall and very narrow Georgian house in The Broad. His response was instant and brooked no refusal. I was to come to his house at two o'clock on any weekday afternoon I liked, bringing my towel, soap and other essentials, and take a bath in his house. His bathroom was the oddest I had ever been in, for it had been inserted at almost first-floor level, in a gap between the house next door and the wall of its own staircase. One crawled into the bath from the staircase through a door opening outwards, and stood in the bath to undress and dress. As one lay soaking, looking out on the Martyrs' Memorial and down St Giles's, one could admire at leisure the curve of that noble street. Chiefly because of its view I made frequent use of that curious bathroom but seldom saw its owner and never came really to know him, nor did I ever meet any members of his family or household, yet I often think back with deep gratitude on his act of disinterested kindness and the delight which I experienced when looking down upon St Giles's.

At the start of my first term a succession of undergraduettes called on me to persuade me to join the diverse societies they represented. I instantly ruled out the sporting and religious, and decided that my foreign accent would prove a drawback were I to join the dramatic or debating societies. Instead, being interested in politics, and knowing little of British Conservative, Liberal and Labour policies, I decided to join all three societies to discover which I sympathized with most. It did not occur to me that this entitled each club to claim my allegiance and that my action was at all reprehensible. I had no intention of making a secret of my membership of the three societies but as the subject was never raised some weeks passed before my nefarious conduct was revealed. Then, late one evening, three very angry young women marched into my room and demanded to know whether I had indeed joined each of their societies. Astonished by their ill-suppressed fury I readily admitted that I had, but before I could explain why, they announced that I had been expelled from all three.

On finding myself debarred from politics I started going to the Union, listening to its weekly debates with delight from the gallery to which women and guests were relegated. The orators reminded me of Plato's *Republic*: 'Youngsters . . . argue for amusement, and are always contradicting and refuting others in imitation of those who refute them; like puppy-dogs, they rejoice in pulling and tearing at all those who come near them.'* Many of the speakers I heard there were splendid in their oratory and lucidity, for the undergraduates included older men who had been through the war, whilst among the younger were Quintin Hogg, now Lord Hailsham, and Edward Marjoribanks, who was to die prematurely by his own hand. It was from that gallery that, in 1922, I saw Edward Longford who soon after became a dear friend. Bravely and ostentatiously, as a passionate advocate of Irish independence, he refused to stand when the Union's members rose to pay a two-minute silent tribute to Field Marshal Sir Henry Wilson, gunned down that day by two Irish republicans as he stood outside his house in Eaton Place.

Having to be back in college by eleven o'clock made it virtually impossible to see the end of any theatrical production, even of some films. Because of that, and also owing to lack of money, I seldom went to any evening entertainment other than concerts. My social life was largely confined to the hospitality most dons extended to their students. These parties were, for the most part, exceedingly formal, rather stilted affairs which I dreaded. Notable exceptions were those given by Miss Lane Poole. Hers were enlivened by caustic remarks which gained piquancy from the length of her thin nose, where the equilibrium of her precariously balanced pince-nez was endangered by the nods which accompanied her more astringent pronouncements. Miss Rogers, whose opinions were inspired by her boundless love of France, was more robust and predictable, although far less elegant than Miss Lane Poole. In contrast Professor Forbes, who occupied the Chair of Russian, although no less devoted to Russia than Miss Rogers was to France, was of a more reserved temperament and, instead of ranging over several aspects of Russian culture, preferred to confine himself to some of its particular features. Whereas Miss Rogers was short, on the plump side, rather bent and shabbily dressed, he was tall, thin and very neatly turned out. The rooms belonging to each of them were almost equally filled with books, volumes bulging from their shelves to overflow on to window seats, chairs and tables, sometimes even reposing on the

---

*The Republic of Plato, tr. B. Jowett, 3rd edn, Vol. II, Oxford, 1908, p. 539 B.

floor. However, it was warm-hearted Professor Margoliouth and his kindly wife who invited me most often to their house.

There I made friends with a young Indian, whose father, I seem to remember, was a judge in Bombay. We were both in our first year and he was drifting in Oxford's numerous cross-currents as rudderlessly as I. He was gentle, witty, well-read and good company. As he had nowhere to spend his Christmas vacation I asked Mother whether she could find him a cheap room near us in Paris and whether she would welcome him at all times at home. She readily agreed. Meanwhile, at St Hugh's, our amicable relationship had been noted and misinterpreted. The best-intentioned of my contemporaries commented on it unfavourably and the kind Margoliouths questioned me closely about it, yet so tactfully that I failed to understand their purpose. It fell to Miss Jourdain to explain colour prejudice to me. Both amused and shocked, I had no difficulty in convincing her that I was never likely to fall in love with him but that, as we both felt equally isolated at Oxford, Mother intended helping him to spend the vacation agreeably in Paris where, regardless of our penury, we still kept open house. Miss Jourdain accepted my explanation and he and I continued to meet until we had each gained a footing of our own in two quite distinct circles of Oxford's lively and multifarious society.

I enjoyed Oxford's tutorial system which reminded me of the private lessons I had had as a child in St Petersburg. Divinity, a compulsory subject then with an obligatory examination by the end of one's second term, had a number of set books from which only one, I seem to remember, had to be studied in depth. I chose Pascal's *Pensées* and was therefore given the passionate and lively Miss Rogers as my tutor. As I had assumed that I would read English I was also obliged to include Anglo-Saxon among the subjects in which I would be examined at the end of the Lent term. I had until then known nothing of the Anglo-Saxons, not even of their existence, but I now became fascinated by their history and language as well as by the exploits of Oswald's right hand.*

---

*Oswald (AD 605–42), king of Northumbria, and Christian saint. One Easter, he ordered his meal to be given to beggars, and the silver salvers on which it was served to be broken into pieces to be used by them as money. Seizing his right hand Aidan, bishop of Lindisfarne, declared, 'May your hand never decay.'

Later, having decided not to read English, and having given in to my mother's entreaties to study something more practical than archaeology, I chose the new school of Politics, Philosophy and Economics. This included an obligatory introductory study of logic. Under the guidance of Mr Brewis, I found the course fascinating and rewarding, although he was not so much concerned with the veracity of a given premiss as with its logical presentation and development. The tutors who permanently influenced me were, first and foremost, A. J. Carlyle and to only a slightly lesser degree, the philosopher R. G. Collingwood.

A. J. Carlyle lived in Holywell. There, in his study crowded with books, I read him my weekly essay. He was a most endearing person. Tall, thin to the point of emaciation, with spectacles that seemed to travel up and down his long, pointed nose, he listened to me with semi-closed eyes. Then, after summarizing my arguments, Carlyle would discuss my text, phrasing his criticisms with kindness, constantly breaking off to raise a wide variety of subjects and ideas. It was those far-ranging conversations which proved of inestimable value to me.

Professor Collingwood, who saw me in his rooms at Pembroke, was more aloof, less inclined to digress, more incisive and far less considerate, making a habit when I was well launched in the reading of my essay, of releasing a clockwork mouse at my feet. Although I half came to expect it, it always startled me and made me forget what I had been going to say. Nevertheless the clarity of his mind, his view on the limitations of logic, the reconciliation of question and answer and the logical development of his ideas helped to train my mind almost as much as did Carlyle's wide-ranging outlook.

From the start the beauty of Oxford, still unmarred by the buildings which now distort so much of its balance, acted as a balloon to my spirits, quickly overcoming my fits of depression and homesickness. Not so its climate. The prevailing damp combined with the coldness of most interiors soon made me feel so ill that I decided to see a doctor. I did not know how to set about finding one, but on my frequent visits to Blackwell's bookshop I often passed 37 The Broad, a mellow two-storeyed Georgian house, now occupied by part of the façade of the new Bodleian Library. A large, well-polished, copper plate on its front door displayed the name of

Dr Counsell. The name inspired confidence, the house seemed welcoming and as it was also conveniently situated I decided to consult Dr Counsell.*

I could not have made a better choice. Doggins, the name by which he was known to generations of undergraduates, was a kind and experienced doctor, but he was more than that – he was witty and sensible, an excellent talker, a widely travelled man, a keen walker with a deep knowledge of botany. Above all, he had a passion for the theatre. He and his daughter Molly quickly became close friends and it was through him that I met a wide circle of my contemporaries, many of whom became friends. He, his wife and daughter kept open house; their welcome was never lacking in warmth and Doggins was always ready to treat, advise or help anyone in need. Although a dedicated doctor, he probably at times regretted not having become an actor and satisfied his craving for the stage by devoting his leisure to the Oxford University Dramatic Society and it fell to his nephew, John Counsell, the adventurous director of the theatre at Windsor, to become a professional actor.

However, the first friends I made at Oxford were not especially interested in the arts and at least one of them, an attractive and gentle undergraduate with the surname Morris, was determined to turn me into a devotee of cricket. In perfect weather we would make our way to the Parks, seat ourselves and, as I indolently watched men dressed in white standing out against the marvellous greenery of England's grass and trees slowly hit a smallish ball about, I struggled to maintain a conversation which was only remarkable for its frequent halts. After spending several afternoons in that rather desultory manner I became restless and eventually dared to ask when the real game of cricket rather than the warming-up exercises was likely to start. Our friendship survived

---

*Counsell, Dr Herbert Edward, MRCS, FRCS, BA (Doggins). After qualifying at Guy's, Counsell built up a flourishing general practice in Hampshire, simultaneously developing his interest in surgery. In 1897 he moved to Oxford, to all that he loved – music, theatre, lectures, library, congenial company. The better to understand the problems of his undergraduate patients, he matriculated at New College, graduating in modern history in 1906. His university activities included athletics and drama; for many years he was prompter for the OUDS. Undergraduates were encouraged to drop in on him, day or night, for tea or chocolate, so long as a light shone in the window and the door was unlocked. During the Great War he served as a surgeon. After losing his sight in the late twenties he was cared for by his younger daughter. His son had been killed on the Somme.

the test and although our visits to the Parks ended, we continued to see each other at increasingly longer intervals, until divergence of interests brought an end to meetings.

My friendships were not confined to members of the university. At the time Cristina Casati was living in Oxford, in rooms in the High close to Queen's College.* My mother had known her mother and that may well have been the cause of my meeting her. I found Cristina strikingly beautiful, marvellously vital, deliciously impulsive, at times haughtily reserved, at others generously outgoing. She was sophisticated, independent-minded and quite a few years older than I. Perhaps sensing that I was still feeling rather lost, she encouraged me to call on her and I was glad to do so. Once I found Marconi waiting to take her to London. That meeting was a fleeting one, but it must have been at Cristina's that I met Lady Ottoline Morrell, for meet her I must have done, since one day as I was bicycling along the High a carriage and pair drove up beside me. Lady Ottoline was driving. Bending her long body towards me and slightly inclining her head, she addressed me in her naturally sepulchral voice, inviting me to tea at Garsington on the following Sunday. Unnerved, too shy to refuse, I mumbled an acceptance but as she drove off the doubts I had felt but disregarded started to assail me. They intensified when I discovered that Garsington was not the name of an Oxford mansion but of a splendid country house situated some five miles to the south-east of the town.

It was fortunate that I discovered my mistake in good time. Starting early on the appointed day I proceeded to bicycle to Garsington. As I pedalled eastward I realized with a sinking heart that I knew nothing about my hosts, their background and interests, their occupations and friends. Tired, probably dishevelled, I eventually reached Garsington's stone boundary wall surmounted by an iron railing, turned in at an imposing gateway and was confronted by a gabled, mellow grey stone house flanked on each side by a tall hedge planted at right angles to it to give the effect of a

---

*The daughter of the notorious and fabulously beautiful Italian Marchesa Casati, Cristina married, in 1925, Lord Hastings, later the 15th Earl of Huntingdon. She later married the Hon. Wogan Philipps (Lord Milford). She died in 1953. Philipps, subsequently remarried, lived in Gloucestershire; he and his wife became close friends of Tamara.

courtyard. Controlling the impulse to ride away, I propped my bicycle against the wall and rang a bell.

Eventually the door was opened by a maid. The absence of a butler gave me a shred of confidence even though the maid was as aloof as the most officious of menservants. She led me to a pleasant garden where a number of people had assembled. My hostess was the tallest of them all, and the draperies rather than clothes which seemed to swathe her body increased her distinction. Lady Ottoline stared at me for a disconcerting moment then, perhaps recovering her memory, introduced me to her husband who was as tall as his wife, though better looking and less talkative. I knew none of their guests; the names of those to whom I was introduced meant nothing to me; in manner, if not in appearance, they seemed a race apart, in no way resembling anyone that I had ever met. With none was I able to hit on a subject of interest to them; none tried to make any contact with me. Conversation between us languished. Miserably I followed them into the house for tea. There, there were paper-thin cucumber sandwiches and asparagus rolls, both agreeable innovations as far as I was concerned.

The house appealed to me, for its contents and furnishings were immensely personal. I thought them attractive. Just as later I was to associate Gerry Wellesley (later the 7th Duke of Wellington) with obelisks, so was Garsington to become for me the evocation of the prettiest boxes imaginable, boxes of every conceivable shape and size, fashioned out of all possible materials, boxes which had been acquired either because of the excellence of their workmanship, for the beauty of their proportions or the inclusion of some unusual feature. Later I learnt some had been made by the Omega Workshop.* The paintings on the walls interested me. It was obvious that the majority were works of quality, yet their styles were unfamiliar to me and even when the artist's signature was legible it conveyed no meaning. Later I learnt that they were for the most part the works of contemporary British artists.

Faced with a long bicycle ride back to Oxford, combined with my complete inability to establish any contact with my fellow

---

*In 1913 the art critic Roger Fry gathered a group of craftsmen to make furniture, pottery and textiles. Pieces signed with the Greek letter 'Omega' were often decorated by artists connected with the Bloomsbury Group. The Workshops were not financially viable and the project collapsed in 1917.

guests, I fled from Garsington as soon as I could. I was able to appreciate my hosts' kindness in inviting so young and insignificant a foreigner as me to their house, but, much though Lady Ottoline's personal magnetism attracted me, I never felt at ease among their friends and did not visit Garsington again after the end of my first year.[*]

After my first visit to Garsington it was with considerable trepidation that I let myself be persuaded by Greville Worthington to spend a weekend with his grandparents, Lord and Lady Aylesford, at Maplehurst, their country house near Lichfield. I had been brought up in a society where platonic friendships between girls and boys, women and men, were regarded as natural, although it was also recognized that such friendships were enhanced by a touch of courtesy often lacking in unisex relationships. Since Greville and I were very fond of each other without being in the least in love, his invitation did not strike me as unusual. If his grandparents wondered, they were too wise or too nice to allow their doubts to obtrude. Nevertheless, as we neared Maplehurst, memories of Garsington assailed me, increasing my customary shyness, and I deferred the dreaded moment of meeting strangers by insisting on visiting Lichfield Cathedral. I was enchanted to come across Lady Mary Wortley Montagu's tomb,[†] for it was as a result of her introduction of the Turkish cow pox inoculation into England that Catherine the Great had invited Dr Dimsdale to Russia to vaccinate herself and her son, the future Tsar Paul, against the dreaded smallpox disease.

How different Maplehurst proved from Garsington. There I had entered an unfamiliar world. Here I was met by that delicious, rather heady, somewhat oriental smell, a compound of pot-pourri, old leather, dogs, tobacco and sweet-scented flowers, so typical both of the old Russian country house and the English, a scent

---

[*]Anthony Powell says of Garsington that 'young men from Oxford were welcome as much to be overawed as encouraged.' Although he was often invited, he nevertheless found his visits alarming, describing them as 'for a nervous undergraduate, an ordeal of the most gruelling order'. *To Keep the Ball Rolling*, Vol. I, *Infants of the Spring*, London, 1976, pp. 186–7.

[†]Lady Mary Wortley Montagu (1689–1762) accompanied her husband when, in 1716, he was appointed ambassador to the Porte. She became very interested in Turkish art and customs, and had her son vaccinated against smallpox. When they returned to England in 1718 she encouraged the embassy's doctor to vaccinate Londoners.

which I was later also to encounter in Trebizond, in the family mansion of our Turkish friends, the Nemli Zades.

My elderly hosts greeted me with a warmth and simplicity which instantly set me at ease. Clearly Greville was much loved by them and, as one of his friends, I was made very welcome. The rooms were spacious, well proportioned. Much of the furniture dated from the eighteenth century, the paintings consisted chiefly of family portraits, the silver was old and beautifully kept.

My hosts were very keen on archery. After tea I was led to the park and given a lesson in pulling the bow but proved a singularly inept pupil. On returning to my bedroom to change for dinner I found flowers on my dressing-table. Had we, I wondered, provided them for our guests in Russia? The custom is a charming one and highly civilized. My case had been unpacked. A friendly maid came to ask whether I needed her help. An airtight tin containing biscuits, presumably in order to ward off night-starvation, stood on my night table along with a number of books. There was early morning tea with paper-thin bread and butter to sustain one till breakfast time.

During the idyllic weekend I often thought that nothing could, or indeed should, disrupt so even, so considerate and kindly a way of life.

6

Widening Circles

It is beauty alone that the insolence of satiety cannot touch.

Gregory of Nyssa, *Treatise on the Soul*

WHEN I returned to Oxford as a home student, I moved into enchanting digs in Bath Place, where the chimes of Oxford's church bells resounded all around me, much as they had done in Moscow, warming my heart. Without realizing it, the magic of Oxford enslaved me. Its beauty delighted me and its roof lines, towers, spires and pinnacles remain a lasting source of fascination.

Imperceptibly, life became enjoyable. I had somehow acquired a circle of entertaining acquaintances and several cherished friends, four of them undergraduettes. Libby Crosthwaite was the closest whilst we were both at Oxford and, as a result of her admiration for Meredith, I became obsessed with words. Sadly I lost touch with her on going down. Years later I saw something of her brother, Moore. When I first met him he was still a schoolboy with an endearingly lively and well-stocked mind, exceptional good looks and an insatiable appetite for Fuller's iced walnut cake. Age and a distinguished career in the Foreign Office were to curb his craving for that cake without affecting his high spirits and intellectual curiosity.

My friendship with Jane Martin, an undergraduette at Somerville who later married Kenneth Clark, was less intellectually stimulating but more fun, yet it too ended after Oxford, to resume more casually after my marriage. Jane was beautiful but seemed unaware of her looks, possibly because she was badly off and could not afford good clothes.

I remained on close terms with Rhoda Gwynn, my third undergraduette friend, until the Second World War when our lives diverged. Rhoda had a Pre-Raphaelite face and figure, a gentle and loyal nature and a cultivated mind. A niece of Stephen Gwynn,[*] she was to marry Bill Brenan, Gerald Brenan's brother, one of the BBC's earliest recruits.[†] Rhoda described her homeland, Ireland, as a friendly and gentle place where idiosyncrasies flourished. However it was through Christine Trew, the dearest of my four friends, and her future husband Edward Longford, that I later came to know Ireland at first hand.

My friendship with Christine lasted until her death and was so close that she became godmother to my elder daughter.[‡] Although Christine's mother lived in Oxford, Christine spent her terms at Somerville reading Greats.[§] She was considered one of the college's most gifted students. She later made her mark as a novelist, but all too soon she abandoned authorship to help Edward run Dublin's Gate Theatre. However, Christine's novels continue to be read, although by a diminishing group of admirers. Their influence, together with that of John Dos Passos, seems to me to be discernible in the work of Henry Green.

Although Edward Longford was of much the same age as Christine, he gave the impression of being younger, perhaps because of a boyish impulsiveness which he retained throughout his life.[#] All too often he repelled people by his fervour and the didactic manner in which he expressed his views. The courage and persistence with which he upheld his ideals masked his extreme kindness. He taught me to drive, at a time when a car was a much treasured possession. He chose the road to Thame for my lessons

---

[*]Stephen Gwynn, writer and journalist, was Member of Parliament for Galway City 1906–18. Serving with the Connaught Rangers in the First World War, he was made Chevalier, Légion d'Honneur.

[†]A friend of the Bloomsbury Group, Gerald Brenan made his home in Spain. Best known as the author of *South from Granada*, based on the village in which he lived in the twenties, and an analysis of events leading up to the Civil War, *The Spanish Labyrinth*.

[‡]Longford, Christine Patti. Educated Wells High School; Somerville College, Oxford. Married Edward Pakenham 1925. She wrote several novels and more than twenty plays for the Gate Theatre in Dublin and for the Longford Players, continuing to manage the theatre for some years after the death of her husband.

[§]Oxford honours BA in classics and philosophy.

[#]Longford, Edward Arthur Henry Pakenham, D. Litt. Educated Eton; Christ Church, Oxford. At Eton awarded the Wilder Divinity Prize. In 1931, when the Gate Theatre ran into financial difficulties, Longford put money into it. Member of the Eire Senate 1946–8.

because it ended up at the Spreadeagle Hotel where the owner, John Fothergill, always received us with affability. If we lunched there he would honour us by drinking a generous portion of our wine to ascertain its quality; at tea he served us with honey which, he said, came from the slopes of Hymettus;* none of us dared refer to the hives which occupied quite a large area of his back garden.

I also met Nancy Lindsay, the daughter of a distinguished gardener in whose steps she was to follow, although at the time she was specializing in rare books. She was living at Sutton Courtenay in the Asquiths' home on the Thames where the garden, in which we spent much time, was the first in a long series of beautiful British gardens from which I have derived great pleasure.

It must have been at Doggins' that I first met Charles Graves. Already an established London journalist and gossip columnist he often came to Oxford, chiefly, I think, to visit two of his brothers – Robert, who was living at Islip, and John, who was in his first year. I found Charles amusing and was pleased and flattered by his frequent invitations to the large and stimulating luncheon parties he was fond of giving at the George. Defying the chaperon rules I accepted them with alacrity. After one of those parties Charles drove me to call on Robert. Almost on arrival I was handed a very new baby to bath. That experience was so unnerving that I seldom returned to the Robert Graves' household.

Through Charles I met Carl Bechhofer Roberts, a contemporary of his and a fellow journalist. He was a mysterious person who, according to some people, was of Russian origin. He knew Russian and was certainly in touch with a number of émigrés, many of whom believed that he had been connected with the Dunster Force.† Bechhofer Roberts carried himself with panache. He was expansive as well as secretive. Also through Charles I met Ford Madox Ford and his wife, of whom I was to see more, and, a year later, she persuaded me to try free-lance journalism by introducing me to the *Westminster Gazette*. After a fortnight submitting daily

---

*A Greek mountain celebrated for its honey and marble.
† The Germans nurtured hopes of penetrating into Asia. Berlin–Baku–Bokhara became a feasible possibility after the disintegration of Russia. Major-General L. C. Dunsterville, Kipling's Stalky, was despatched with a hand-picked force of two hundred to rally local opposition and prevent further Turkish or German infiltration. See Maj.-Gen. L. C. Dunsterville, *The Adventures of Dunsterforce*, London, 1920.

titbits without seeing any of them in print or getting paid I returned to Paris.

In my second year at Oxford my friends often mentioned Oliver Messel who seemed to have been endowed with many talents including irresistible charm and subtle wit. I begged to meet the paragon, and eventually did so at a lunch party at Christ Church given by either David Talbot Rice or Harold Acton. Although I arrived punctually I found everybody already seated at table. I was directed to the only vacant place, between a man whom I did not greatly like and a subfusc youth disfigured by projecting teeth. He introduced himself as Oliver Messel. Although inhibited by his dull conversation, I tried to entertain the young man I had been so anxious to meet. This was a struggle because there were frequent silences and too many eyes were watching me.

I cheered up at the appearance of the magnificent meringues for which the Christ Church kitchens were famous, meringues which figured as prominently at our luncheons as hot buttered anchovy toast and Fuller's iced walnut cake at tea. Suddenly, when my neighbour bit into his meringue, he left his hideous teeth embedded in it and revealed his attractive looks. The elaborate joke had succeeded and my momentary feeling of chagrin was soon dispelled by Oliver's blithe laughter. We became hilariously happy as he drew a series of ridiculous sketches of the disguises he could have assumed. Alas, those exquisite doodles disappeared during the Second World War when the Germans requisitioned my parents' Paris flat.

I sometimes met an undergraduate called Frederick Loveday who puzzled me by changing his Christian name to Raoul and then leaving for Sicily in order to become a member of Aleister Crowley's black magic abbey at Cefalù. He died there soon after in what many of us thought mysterious circumstances.* Several months later his widow, Betty May, came to Oxford to dissuade us from visiting Crowley. She gave horrifying descriptions of his black masses when live cockerels were sacrificed to his deities. She was still suffering from shock and misery at Loveday's untimely death

---

*Raoul's fatal illness was reputed to be enteric fever caught by drinking water from a mountain spring in the heat of the day. However Betty May hints that other causes brought about his death. Betty May, *Tiger Woman: My Story*, London, 1929, pp. 179–89.

and was not able to write her reminiscences entitled *Tiger Woman* for another six years. When I knew her there was nothing of a tiger about her. Dark-haired, gypsy-looking, tiny with a disarming smile, she was sad, restrained and courageous. Her ability to face misfortune with equanimity impressed me, and her resilience won my respect, for I felt that it was an attribute which we Russian refugees needed to acquire. However Betty May, in addition to her obsession with death by water, had much that was amusing to talk about. She had often sat as a model for Epstein and it was from her that I first heard about London's Bohemian art world. Later Nina Hamnett and Brenda Dean Paul added further colour.

It was good to be at Oxford in the early 1920s. The war to end all wars was over, and although the Russian Revolution continued, it made little impact on the Western world and almost none on most undergraduates. However, secretly, I closely followed events taking place in my homeland. At night I constantly asked myself why White resistance to the cruel Red regime was failing. Was my parents' generation of Russians so effete? Surely not, for many had fought the Germans as bravely as Uncle Sasha and had resisted the Bolsheviks just as staunchly. Was Leo Tolstoy therefore right to maintain that even man's best endeavours become futile when events acquire their own momentum? If so, was personal courage as displayed by Prince Andrei in *War and Peace*, and by Uncle Sasha, rendered pointless by its very impotence, or was it more glorious because doomed to failure? If foredoomed, was it quixotic to try and live according to one's principles: should fortitude rather than hope be one's aim? All too often I concluded that I would be wise to enjoy life while the going was good.

The maturity of those undergraduates who had served in the war highlighted the gaucheness of those who came up direct from school. Yet the lives of the latter seemed overshadowed by a feeling of shame at having escaped the trials endured by their elders. Many seemed to feel that they had not earned the pleasures which were now within their reach; others regarded them as a right; but everyone was equally determined to live life to the full.

Although very few undergraduates possessed one, the motor car had immense potential. Some of us explored only locally, but the more adventurous resolved to travel far afield, regardless of discomfort. As the cost of living was low in most European countries, many went abroad with a blithe enthusiasm which puzzled their sedate parents. However I, with no money and no passport other than a Nansen certificate of identity, could not explore so freely. Nevertheless, even for me, life was exciting; although debarred from roaming the world, there was nothing to prevent me from embarking on intellectual adventures. I was free. While my Russian friends and relations were dying of hunger, disease and oppression, I could say anything I wanted at the top of my voice wherever I was. I could make what friends I desired. I would not starve, be imprisoned or tortured. I realized that I was very lucky.

Many of my friends were members of the Hypocrites Club. The exceptions included Richard Pares,* Edward Longford, Nigel Millett and, I think, Patrick Balfour. Richard and Patrick liked wearing pastel-coloured plus-four suits made for them by the High Street tailor, Hall, his shop specializing in cerulean-coloured tweeds and delicately tinted Paisley-patterned ties and scarves which were difficult to resist. When Jane Martin or I was depressed we raised our spirits by buying yet another Hall scarf. When wearing a pastel-coloured Hall suit Richard and Patrick's fairish hair and high foreheads linked them in my eyes with the elegant young Elizabethans immortalized by Hilliard, to whom Hugh Lygon† bore an even closer resemblance.

Although not an undergraduate and somewhat older, Nigel Millett was one of my closest friends. His effete, somewhat decadent, *fin-de-siècle* manner masked an unusually alert mind. He lived with his parents in north Oxford, in a house which he quite rightly found architecturally repellent. Because of poor health and slender means he spent most of the year in Oxford, but often spoke of his intention to live in some warm and exotic country and become a writer. Some years later, following his mother's death, he achieved both ambitions. He and his father settled in Mexico and, under the name of Richard Oke, he wrote one play and several books before death robbed him of the success which lay within his grasp. The play,

---

*According to Evelyn Waugh, Pares was a member of the Hypocrites. See Evelyn Waugh, *A Little Learning*, London, 1964, p. 181.
†With Alastair Graham the inspiration of Evelyn Waugh's Sebastian Flyte.

Frolic Wind, was a much earlier work.* It was produced in 1935 and made an abiding impression on Harold Hobson, the *Sunday Times* drama critic, who wrote in his memoirs that not only did Fabia Drake, its leading lady, defy 'the convention of costume . . . by the intimate clothing in which she took a telephone call that lasted an entire scene', but that, at a time when 'comedies ended happily, with all the virtuous characters justly rewarded', Hobson here 'encountered for the first time an emotion, a habit, a taste which the characters of the play were reluctant to identify . . . For the first time that I can remember the drama was not reassuring but disturbing.' He felt that 'the ultimate consequences of this have been tremendous; they have changed the entire nature of the British theatre.'[†]

Nigel was tall, broad-shouldered, wasp-waisted and thin to the point of emaciation. The ravages which ill health had inflicted on his face were stressed by his dark hair and colourless complexion, touched up with mauve make-up. He never complained of feeling ill or lacking money. He was always good company. He had a small though pleasant singing voice and a large repertory of music-hall songs which he intoned with charm. His rendering of Gilbert the Filbert, the colonel of the Knuts, the pride of Piccadilly, the blasé roué, seemed to personify his own concept of himself and became one of my favourite tunes.[‡]

It was through Nigel that I got to know John Gielgud, who was appearing at the Playhouse, a former big game museum at the top of the Woodstock Road, then a repertory theatre run by J. B. Fagan – an imposing figure – and his wife, the actress Mary Grey.[§] Nigel

---

*It was published as a novel in 1929. Adapted as a three-act play by R. Pryce, it opened at the Royalty Theatre in March 1935 with Fabia Drake playing Miss Vulliamy.
[†]H. Hobson, *Indirect Journey*, London, 1978, pp. 191–3.
[‡]Millett, Nigel (Richard Oke). Educated Rugby; Magdalen College, Oxford. Author of a biography of Frederick II, Emperor of Germany, and of several novels, but no plays, despite Dr Counsell's expectations of him as a dramatist. Although a fine schoolboy actor, he did not act with OUDS but advised on, and designed, some of their costumes. Counsell, in his autobiography *37 The Broad*, London, 1943, p. 183, writes of Millett: 'His striking personality was not attractive to all, but I knew him well and was fully aware that beneath his somewhat exaggerated social manner there beat a warm and affectionate heart.'
[§]This was in 1924. The museum where performances took place was 'full of stuffed animals . . . The seats were bentwood chairs ranged on wooden planks so that when you moved the whole row shifted and squeaked.' J. Gielgud, *An Actor and His Time*, London, 1979, p. 58.

and I never missed an opportunity of seeing John in a new role, but those evenings all too often ended with my leaving before the end to be back in my digs by 11 p.m.

Nigel, John and I often spent our afternoons walking or in a punt. On our most memorable expedition we went to Bath in a hired open car. John could be mischievous at times. As we were leaving Nigel's house he picked up a hat belonging to Nigel's father and insisted on wearing it. The weather was radiant; the air hot and scented, the country at its loveliest. I had never been to Bath and its beauty entranced me. We went sight-seeing and on to lunch at the luxurious Pump Room Hotel where we were fascinated by several elderly ladies in clothes resembling those worn by Queen Mary. Suddenly John realized that he would be late for the theatre unless we hurried. As we drove back at speed, a gust of wind dislodged Mr Millett's hat from John's head and blew it back towards Bath. To Nigel's distress, John prevented us from trying to retrieve it. In the event he was right; we reached Oxford only minutes before he was due on stage. I was lucky because, regardless of Miss Jourdain's powers of divination, my escapade passed undetected. Had I been seen in an open car with two men and no chaperon I would at best have been rusticated, but more probably sent down.

David Talbot Rice, whom I was later to marry, was, I think, a founder member of the Hypocrites Club. He had beautiful rooms in Tom Quad, where he often gave exceedingly entertaining and delicious luncheon parties. Although giving no indication of it, he in fact worked more than most of the Hypocrites, studying daily from breakfast to lunch time and from tea to dinner time, a practice to which he kept for the rest of his life. Through David I met Robert Byron, a close friend from Eton days. Robert was vital, effervescent, and very stimulating but his frequent wild shrieks were unnerving; moreover he was a relentless and remorseless tease. However hard I tried to remain cool he always got a rise out of me within a couple of minutes. He was ambitious and mean-spirited but David greatly admired his quick mind and passionate enthusiasms; and, being himself a most generous and selfless person, never realized how much he contributed to Robert's development and interests.

At the time, Evelyn Waugh was the Hypocrite I saw most often.

He remained a lifelong friend.* Through him I met Alastair Graham who was a great friend of both David's and mine until we lost touch in the course of our different wartime duties. Alastair was immense fun to be with: while not formally handsome he was most attractive in appearance; so too was Evelyn. Alastair was comfortably off and well turned out, often in a Hall's suit, whilst Evelyn's pale mauve plus-four suit, also a Hall's product, was subjected to so much wear that it had thinned at the elbows and knees. Alastair combined extreme hardiness with an elf-like personality, a keen sense of humour and an unquenchable taste for adventure which was later to make him our favourite travelling companion. He and Evelyn were close friends although Evelyn was more pugnacious, more vulnerable and sardonic. That said, Alastair's sense of the ridiculous was marvellously apt. Evelyn's favourite book at the time was *The Diary of a Nobody*, to which he introduced me.

Whilst I was still feeling lonely in Oxford I acquired a puppy, a young, very beautiful, dark, smooth-coated Alsatian called Ghost whose large paws were an indication of his future stature. I used to walk him in the early afternoons, generally in the Meadows, often with Evelyn Waugh as my companion. Evelyn's conversation was marvellously funny, his loathing of the bogus immensely refreshing; but one afternoon he was drunk when he joined me, so drunk, truculent and mordant that he had become a different person. I thought it best to accept his presence and shorten my walk rather than attempt to get rid of him there and then. Later that afternoon I sent him a furious letter warning him that if I ever again saw him drunk I would end our friendship. He never referred to it and I was never again to see him intoxicated.

At that period of his life Evelyn's drunkenness seemed to me to be chiefly due to a feeling of self-doubt resulting from his failure to get into the college of his choice. Although he often appeared to be in good spirits, he was not happy. At Oxford, his present was marred by lack of money and his future unclear. At the time, between £250 and £300 was a fair yearly allowance for a poorish

---

*Waugh, Evelyn Arthur St John, C. Litt. Educated Lancing; Hertford College, Oxford. After an unhappy period teaching, he took up writing. His conversion to Roman Catholicism in 1930 greatly influenced both his life and his writing. His first marriage to Evelyn Gardner broke up in 1929. In 1937 he married Laura Herbert. During the Second World War he served in the Royal Marines and the Commandos.

undergraduate; anything below £225 was extremely modest. I suspect that Evelyn's allowance was substantially less than average, because he was often obliged to sell some of his cherished books. He would have liked to have entertained generously, to have a wardrobe filled with prismatic-coloured suits. Yet on our walks rather than discuss worldly possessions we muttered 'après nous le déluge' and pondered the more immediate problem of how we were to earn our living.

Evelyn was thinking of becoming an artist and often wondered whether he should not have gone to the Slade instead of Oxford. However, during visits to the Ashmolean he admitted that, despite his draughtsmanship and delight in a painting's subject-matter, his response to form and colour was perfunctory. He did not under-estimate his skill at drawing and, although unwilling to become a cartoonist, he enjoyed producing line illustrations. Although he was not thinking at the time of becoming a professional writer he already realized that artists required self-discipline of a sort he did not possess.

It may have been in 1922, but perhaps not until the following winter, that Evelyn came to Paris on what may well have been his first visit there.* He was still very short of money, still wearing his mauve plus-four suit. The strange shape of his trousers, their unusual colour and the worn knees intrigued my mother, but it was his charm, consideration, wit and unexpected erudition that endeared him to her. Although no needlewoman, she won his heart by darning his trousers.

Evelyn spent a good deal of his time with us and our friends and was much absorbed by the anomalies in the émigré life-style. He developed a taste for the Russian night-clubs in which groups of Russian gypsies performed. He was as fascinated by their harsh voices and independent characters as my parents had been when lis-tening to gypsy singers in St Petersburg. By helping the night-club owners behind the scenes, we often ended the evening listening to the gypsies' songs. When Evelyn was with us we could sit at a table to drink a bottle of wine.

Since his death much has been written about Evelyn's character,

---

*Selina Hastings says he first visited Paris in December 1925. See S. Hastings, *Evelyn Waugh, A Biography*, London, 1994, p. 142.

most of it derogatory. Yet he possessed the vital qualities on which love and friendship depend – those of generosity, loyalty and courage. I could cite many endearing actions of his, but will refer only to a letter sent soon after our marriage at the end of 1927, when David and I were as usual short of money. At the time we were all revelling in the success of Evelyn's novel, *Decline and Fall*, yet he was still quite badly off. As his wife – 'She Evelyn' – had been ill, Evelyn arranged to take her on a cruise. Remembering how much I longed for a taste of London he wrote to offer us the temporary use of his flat. As I was not at home when his letter arrived David left it with the comment, 'Let us sell Pepys and take it.' Although greatly tempted I refused the offer. At the time, having known penury, I felt we ought not to sell valuable books for a merely pleasurable purpose.

To me Evelyn seemed at his happiest at the start of his first marriage. On returning from his disastrous cruise* he felt unable to write in London and therefore accepted John Fothergill's invitation to spend the middle of the week at the Spreadeagle at Thame to write *Vile Bodies*.† When *en route* for Gloucestershire we often used to stop at Thame to lunch with Evelyn and renew our acquaintance with Fothergill.

Evelyn and I often discussed what our contemporaries would make of their lives. We thought Alastair would end up as an ambassador; instead he became a recluse in Wales. We were sure another Hypocrite, Harold Acton, would become a poet. Indeed, he was already known as one. This was hardly surprising, for when he and David met as new boys at their prep school Harold had not hesitated to climb on to a chair to read a poem he had recently written; two of the lines, 'and out of the oven he did take / a most beautiful cake' were indelibly fixed in David's memory. At Oxford, it was delightful to meet Harold as he rushed along a street, swaying slightly as he pranced, exquisitely dressed, swathed in an immensely long black and mauve striped scarf, carrying a furled umbrella. 'Darling Tamara,' he would

---

*Mrs Waugh caught double pneumonia on the way to Monte Carlo, where they were to pick up the cruise, and had to be put ashore at Port Said. She later credited the head doctor there with saving her life.

†Hastings says that *Vile Bodies* was mostly written at the Abingdon Arms in Beckley: *op. cit.*, p. 193.

murmur, 'how nice to meet you. I have just parted from that awful X.' Those amiable words lost none of their sweetness from the probability of Harold greeting his next acquaintance with the words, 'Darling Y, how nice to meet you. I have just parted from that awful Tamara.'

The friends I made at Oxford restored a sense of fun dormant since the outbreak of the October Revolution. My work suffered in consequence but I was fully conscious of my idleness and determined to spend the Easter vacation in some remote corner of England, living austerely, with my nose glued to a book. This retreat eluded me until David Talbot Rice produced a small cottage in the Gloucestershire village of Broadwell which I rented unseen. At the end of term David offered to drive me there. On reaching it I discovered that Broadwell was scarcely two miles from his home.

I was delighted at the thought of seeing him every now and then, and gladly accepted an invitation to lunch with his parents. Their house, Oddington House, near Stow-on-the-Wold, enchanted me. Its inner hall and staircase are strikingly beautiful, the staircase being ascribed to Hepplewhite, and the family portraits included two Gainsboroughs. Tea, and as I later discovered, also breakfast, were taken in that lovely inner hall which had French windows facing a wood blue with wild anemones, soon to be replaced by bluebells. Beyond the wood was the old church, quiet and withdrawn with a great Pre-Reformation fresco of the Last Judgement surviving on its north wall. The better I got to know David, the fonder I became of him. Eventually we were meeting daily, taking Ghost for long walks, discussing all sorts of subjects, and sharing our interest in archaeology. I was entranced by Cotswold village architecture, even with the drystone walls that enclosed small fields of irregular shape.

The summer term proved even gayer than the Lent and although I continued to work seriously for my two favourite tutors, A. J. Carlyle and R. G. Collingwood, the rest of my work suffered. Feeling despondent and ashamed of my idleness, I started to frequent the Moorish Tea Rooms at the top of Queen Street, near Carfax. They belonged to James Wyllie, an accomplished artist some years older than my fellow undergraduates. His catering skills later led to his employment at Portmeirion* by Clough Williams-Ellis. We became friends and I told him how hard I found it to work. I was also reluctant to return to Broadwell and mentioned my parlous finances.

Jim knew what it was to be short of money. Recently however, he had acquired a cottage in Wales, on the slopes of Beddgelert, near a cottage belonging to a close friend of his, the writer Diccon Hughes.† They had both bought their cottages for only a few pounds, with help from a Miss Jones, the uncrowned queen of the neighbouring village of Tan-lan, who traded in second-hand furniture and employed a little maid of all work. There were still several isolated cottages scattered on the slopes of Beddgelert and Jim thought that Diccon might be able to get me one. Although lacking all modern conveniences the cottages were weather-proof, stoutly built in local stone. The scenery, Jim assured me, was magnificent and some cottages stood close to a trout stream which hurtled down the mountainside through fissures in the rock. Once a week a travelling horse-drawn shop came to each cottage selling essential food supplies and providing the only distraction.

Within a fortnight, for just two pounds, I became the owner of a three-roomed cottage in Wales. At the end of term, anxious to see my domain and start working hard, I hurried to catch the Sunday train to Penrhyndeudraeth, the nearest station to Tan-lan. As it ambled slowly through beautiful landscape I discovered that on Sundays it was impossible to buy food or drink on the train or at any of the stations where we stopped. Some eight hours later I arrived at Penrhyndeudraeth, hungry, thirsty, very cross and questioning myself about the wisdom of my enterprise.

Somehow, I no longer remember how, I reached Tan-lan where I was to stay with Miss Jones until I could furnish my cottage. The village seemed deserted. After struggling along its main street I eventually noticed a flicker of light in a window. I went to it and knocked, intending to ask for directions, but it was Miss Jones in person who opened the door to me. Although rather shocked at my having travelled on a Sunday, she welcomed me kindly and led me

---

*A holiday complex on the North Wales coast built by Williams-Ellis to demonstrate the ideas expounded in his writings on architecture, landscaping and the use of colour.
†Richard Arthur Warren Hughes, novelist; author *inter alia* of *A High Wind in Jamaica* and *The Fox in the Attic*.

to a room warmed by the first peat fire I had ever seen. 'Welcome to Wales,' murmured Miss Jones in a soft, lilting voice and, as she led me to a beautiful Windsor chair, 'You will have some eggs, bacon and tea.'

She was a tall, gaunt woman of unwashed appearance with a gracious yet commanding manner. It was only gradually that I realized that the room in which I was sitting was filthy. So was the kitchen and everything in it. An unkempt little maid quickly produced some singularly unappetizing tea, bacon and eggs. For all that the sheets were damp and of carbolic smell, my bed was clean.

In the morning I looked out of the window and saw a cluster of houses – small, squat, dull, painted in the colour known to Welsh ironmongers as Chapel Grey. My heart constricted. Had I been rash to come to Wales? In the kitchen Miss Jones greeted me with a kiss. By daylight the kitchen seemed even dirtier. Breakfast was just the same as supper. So were the succession of meals that followed, each consisting of tea, bacon and eggs. Nevertheless, mastering my revulsion, I managed to swallow samples of each. That morning, when I had breakfasted, Miss Jones harnessed her pony and we drove off to inspect my property. The air was soft, the light tender and luminous as in a Richard Wilson painting, the scenery splendid.

My cottage, a small stone rectangle, stood some three miles from Tan-lan on a slope of Beddgelert in wild, uninhabited country, perched on the edge of a tiny torrent. I loved it on sight. My spirits rose. Scrambling gaily back into the trap we set out in search of furniture. Miss Jones embarked on a monologue which ranged over Welsh legends and history. To her Merlin was as real as Owen Glendower. At times Miss Jones burst into song, her elderly, quavering voice reflecting something of the grandeur and gentleness of the landscape.

We stopped at isolated cottages. Miss Jones entered them as a respected guest to emerge the satisfied purchaser of an abbreviated version of a tester bed, a chest of drawers, a table and four chairs, all of them old, all made of oak, all beautiful in their rugged simplicity. They cost me £11 17s. 6d. They suited my cottage and met my needs. In Tan-lan I bought a new horsehair mattress and a feather pillow, a kettle, teapot, saucepan, a few plates, a couple of cups, a little cutlery. I had brought my own house linen. At Miss

Jones's insistence I very reluctantly also bought two dozen glasses and several bottles of cheap port. Two days later Miss Jones drove me to my cottage, drank a cup of tea and departed after admonishing me not to miss the visit of the weekly carrier.

Miss Jones had taken me to call on most of the village's inhabitants. As her guest I was well received, but since few of them knew much English, conversation had not flowed easily. I therefore arranged to be taught Welsh but found the language too difficult to master. In the evenings by the peat fire Miss Jones brought a sense of the ridiculous to her conversation which, for all her prudery, often verged on the suggestive. On some nights there was a loud rap on the door from miners who had spent the day working in a neighbouring pit. They now gathered round the fire and broke into song. Their voices were deep with the sonorous tone which also characterizes Russian male singers. Miss Jones distributed glasses of a sweet, sickly port and the evenings ended in an atmosphere of good fellowship.

I had become fond of Miss Jones but nevertheless felt relieved to be in my own cottage at last. When exploring its surroundings I noticed a narrow-gauge railway track but did not give it much thought until, late in the afternoon of my first day, a new sound drew me to my window. I saw, advancing slowly up the mountain, along the metal track, a boat-shaped vehicle filled with men. They were my friends the miners, the two at its centre propelling the truck by working a handle back and forth. They had come to sing to me and wish me well. I now saw why Miss Jones had obliged me to buy glasses and port. Except for Sundays, the men returned almost nightly to entertain me with their singing. In the afternoons I generally joined Jim and Diccon on a long walk. The rest of the time I studied assiduously in my self-imposed solitude. Sadly realizing that I would have very few opportunities to use my adorable cottage, at the end of my vacation I gave it to Miss Jones's hard-working little maid. I sold the antique pieces of furniture in Oxford at a considerable profit.

Gypsies had always figured in my life. In the early twenties they were also sufficiently important in England for Lady Eleanor Smith* to write about them and for Dame Laura Knight to paint

---

*Society journalist and popular novelist. Of Romany descent through her paternal great-grandmother, she drew on circus and gypsy life for many of her novels.

them. At Oxford a group of Romany gypsies often camped at Bablock Hythe, near the Eight Bells. I eventually got to know some of them and thought their way of life attractive. I had already travelled from Oxford to London on a barge in the hope of discovering whether I might like to earn my living on some inland waterway but had found the journey tedious. Now I wanted to sample the Romany way of life.

When term ended I asked my gypsy friends whether I might spend a night with them. They assured me of a warm welcome. I joined them on a glorious summer evening. We sat on the steps of a caravan sipping very strong, very sweet tea. Talk flowed easily but was dull when compared with Miss Jones's magnificently extravagant account of things Welsh. As all the caravans were full I was to spend the night in a tent with a couple of gypsy girls as companions. I had never before camped out and experienced the intense cold which, at the approach of day, follows even a very warm summer night. I lay pillowless on the hard, unresponsive earth, with only a thin ground sheet and a thin blanket. I shivered throughout the night in great discomfort. Whenever I succeeded in dozing off I was instantly woken by some noise or other and the dawn chorus put an end to all further hope of sleep. Washing in cold water failed to invigorate either my mind or body. After breakfast we exchanged mementoes and parted affectionately but I had learnt that, for all my love of travel, wandering the world in a caravan would not be to my liking. So I returned to the static life of a Paris city-dweller.

PARIS AND AFTER

Paris was, in the twenties, the place to be. It scintillated, it sparkled; writers, artists, actors, dilettantes, socialites, all homed in on the French capital.

In Tamara's only surviving letter to David Talbot Rice, written on 1 December 1925, she describes Paris as 'much the same as ever, the English & Americans being as much in favour as ever. The French are also fast returning to the pre-war mode of life & throng to all fashionable places, which are those which were originally discovered by enterprising yankies, but are now claimed as being ancient gallic amusement houses.' Should he wish to visualize her circle, she advises David to read Proust 'who has brilliantly portrayed them'.

Couture ranked with steel and motor cars as France's foremost industries. Some 300,000 Parisians were employed in the business – more if one includes ancillaries such as embroiderers and lace- and button-makers. A quarter of R. F. Wilson's *Paris on Parade*, published in 1925 and describing life in the city, is devoted to the fashion industry. He conducts readers round the thirteen-floor workrooms of Drécoll whose designer had to create some 300 different new designs each year. That however was a mere trifle: Mme Jeanne Lanvin had to design 1,000 outfits a year.

The February and August dress shows were gala occasions 'with music, tea and champagne, fine catering, awninged entrances, and everything which goes to make a notable social function'. Wilson described the couturier Poiret, who on a pre-war occasion had given Tamara a box of doll's clothes similar to the outfits he made for her mother, as 'a rotund little man with a bullet head, a face full of cropped whiskers that the owner's fifty or more years keep from being jet black, hair carefully brushed to conceal the bald area on the scalp and small grey eyes set wide apart and unusually high in that queerly shaped cranium'. One of the leading avant-garde dress designers, Poiret had commissioned, in 1908, an album of fashion drawings, *Les Robes de Paul Poiret*, in which the illustrator, Paul

Tribe, revolutionized the art of fashion illustration, ignoring detail in favour of expressing the spirit.

Describing the scene in the mid-twenties Sisley Huddleston, in *Bohemian Literary and Social Life in Paris*, refers to 'hordes of Russian exiles, some with talent and some without. They open Russian restaurants, Russian tearooms, Russian cabarets.' Of western European countries France was the Russians' most popular destination, an estimated seventy thousand having settled there by January 1922, about a fifth of whom were in Paris: the city could absorb so many because of a great demand for labour, war-time casualties having been so severe. By 1936, according to a survey of the refugee problem carried out for the Royal Institute of International Affairs, the estimated number of Russian émigrés in Paris was said to be between one hundred and one hundred and twenty thousand. Comparatively few Russians came to Great Britain – between eight and ten thousand were present in 1922, a figure which had dropped, by 1936, to two thousand.

Many of the refugees were destitute, most very poor. They came, often in shock, having experienced serious deprivation and danger, having seen relatives and friends killed and tortured; they came, to a country with different customs and conventions, and, for many, an unknown language. So they naturally tended to herd together and to set up 'a nation without a country', planning and training to restore their customs, laws and traditions and the Orthodox rites, once they returned, as surely they would, to Russia. Making no call on charity, they struggled to support themselves. Then, the daily grind over, they crammed uncomfortably into the small desks of an infant school lent by the government, to study. Elsewhere, former lawyers taught the legal texts. Commercial, scientific and financial courses were offered by the Institute of Higher Studies, the teachers being former professors and scientists. There was even a course for senior army officers; in groups of ten they attended twice-weekly lectures to cover a three-year study of warfare. The scientists and the artists were the most fortunate, the former often finding positions in French scientific institutions, the latter saved from penury by their talents.

Two Russian newspapers were published, one left wing edited by the democratic republican M. Milioukoff, the other, *Renaissance*, right wing. Nor were the old, the young or the war-wounded forgotten: a large house, a gift, was turned into a home for the aged. The rooms were sparse, as were those of two orphanages, but the fare was healthy. By 1927, a Federation of Russian War-Wounded had been set up, with a headquarters in Paris. Most surprising of all, perhaps, was a building near the Gare de l'Est. A regiment was employed at the station, the officers working alongside the men, loading and unloading railway wagons. The ground floor of an adjoining building had been converted into dormitories. The walls of the corridors were brightened with displays of uniforms and medals. A ladder led up to the officers' mess, hung with portraits of the Tsar and of Grand Duke Nicholas.

A 1946 study into the extent to which Russians and Ukrainians had been assimilated into the French way of life found that they preferred living in colonies and that, although most could now speak French, their children were often bilingual but thought of themselves as Russian rather than French. Of those interviewed in one district, ninety-seven had been naturalized, thirty-four were considering the step, but 312 had no such intention. Few had any hopes of a speedy return to Russia but most were uninterested in French society.

The refugees were not the only community examined by sociologists and economists. Professor Carlton Hayes of Columbia University was the general editor of a seven-volume study into how the French had maintained their national unity despite the stresses of the war and of the economic reconstruction which followed. Three of the volumes concentrate on economics, but his own – *France, A Nation of Patriots*, on morale, published in 1930 – examines the role of the establishment in upholding patriotism. A chapter headed 'Symbols and Ceremonies' considers such concepts as 'La France', 'La Patrie', Joan of Arc, the cock which appears on many stamps, emotive buildings such as Versailles or Fontainebleau, all contributing to French faith in the future. Tamara's researches were used in this chapter: in his preface, Carlton Hayes writes that she 'collected a good deal of useful information about French symbols and ceremonies and she, together with William C. Buthnan and a group of French secretaries, made a digest of national comments in the French press from 1919 to 1927.'

What was perhaps Tamara's most congenial job, as a member of Hayes' editorial staff, ended with her engagement in the autumn of 1927.

7

Émigré Life

What needest thou? – a few brief hours of rest
Wherein to seek thyself in thine own breast;
A transient silence wherein truth could say
Such was thine constant hope, and this thy way?

Walter de la Mare, *Vain Questioning*

IN PARIS our future looked unattractive. Financially we were almost destitute with Volodia struggling to regain his health before looking for work. Our two-bedroomed furnished flat was near the Bois de Boulogne, where Father went each evening to refresh his spirit. At bedtime, Volodia was obliged to move from the bedroom we shared to the living-room. Ghost did not simplify our lives for he needed a fairly long walk every day and his food cost more than ours. If only we had known of pet foods! However, with the exception of Father, we all loved the dog; he was a comfort, a diversion and a token of confidence in the future. Most of our relations and friends were as badly off as ourselves but some had also acquired a dog to cheer them in their misery.

Passy had become a Russian village with almost as much Russian spoken in its streets as French. Several of my girl-friends became mannequins, an occupation for which I was unfitted because of an inability to stand for long periods without fainting. A fellow countryman more astute than the rest of us had had some visiting cards printed on which he described himself as a *marchand d'idées*. With these he went from house to house offering his services in return for a modest fee. Although he failed to provide me with any ideas, he appeared to have solved his own problem, however modestly, and that in itself seemed encouraging.

It was not until Mother fell ill from exhaustion and undernourishment whilst Father was job-hunting in the Balkans that I became profoundly depressed. I had ten francs a day on which to feed

Ghost and the three of us. Although food was astonishingly cheap and plentiful, that was inadequate. I felt that the time had come to sell something. The only suitable object I owned was a much loved eighteenth-century rectangular gold ring, with the silhouetted head of an ancestress at its centre. The extra money did not solve my difficulties. I knew nothing about cookery, not even of the existence of cookery books. When the doctor prescribed chicken broth for Mother I had no idea how to make it.

Pocketing my pride I consulted our surly concierge. Placing her hands on her hips, she stared at me in amazement. 'Comment!' she shrieked, 'une grande jeune fille comme vous qui ne sait pas?' Then, perhaps appreciating my distress, she told me to buy a kilo of chicken bones. I did so but I was puzzled. I had to admit to myself that I had no idea how to convert bones into liquid. Had the concierge made a fool of me, I wondered. Had she made me waste my precious money. Buoyantly, I walked past her cubicle towards the lift. Then, necessity conquering shame, I retraced my steps, knocked on her door and timidly asked what I should do with the bones. For a moment my ignorance petrified her. Then, seizing my arm, she propelled me into the lift, pushed me into our kitchen, snatched a saucepan, tipped the bones into it, poured water over them, threw in pepper and salt, placed the lot on a gas flame and stumped out, still without speaking. I felt humiliated for us. When she reappeared bringing a sliced onion and carrot I felt mortified. Fortunately some kind friends were quick to supply me with a copy of Tante Marie's invaluable cookery book.

The affair of the chicken bones seriously undermined my self-confidence and I pursued my search for gainful employment with growing trepidation. In the mid-twenties it was not easy for an unqualified girl to find work in Paris. I answered countless advertisements and obtained a number of interviews. To begin with, when questioned concerning my qualifications, I murmured that I had studied at Oxford University. These words invariably reduced my interviewer to uncontrollable laughter. Realizing that I had nothing in my favour I often felt desperate.

One day, whilst queuing for a modest job, a pretty girl told me that, when destitute, she could always earn ten francs a day as a *figurante* on a film set. Generously she gave me the studio's address. I hurried there, asked to be taken on and was told to report to a studio near the Bastille by seven the following morning, bringing a ball dress and long white kid gloves. Rising at five, I crept out of the flat and reached the studio well before seven. I was taken on to appear in a ballroom scene. I have forgotten the name of the film, yet I spent three long days dancing a waltz which would be on the screen for barely two minutes.

The studio was lit by acetylene lamps which dripped particles of flame. We stood about for hours, repeatedly performed the waltz sequence, with my partner and I leading the dancers. Nightly I returned home, the richer by ten francs. On my fourth day I was offered fifteen francs a day for dancing a minuet in an eighteenth-century dress, an offer which delighted me. Time and again we performed the stately dance wearing tall, powdered wigs surmounted by two ostrich feathers. The wigs were hot and heavy, tempers became frayed yet, at long last, all seemed set for the final take. Then, suddenly, there was a blaze of blinding, bluish light, wild shrieks, screams of fire. One couple had moved too close to an acetylene lamp and an ostrich feather had caught alight. Its unfortunate wearer stood motionless, paralysed by terror yet screaming at the top of her voice. Her partner fled; her neighbours stampeded. Then a man tore her wig off her head, threw it on the floor, and, with the help of others, extinguished the flames. Filming was resumed.

I returned home with my fifteen francs, went to bed exhausted and instantly fell asleep. I woke in pitch dark, my eyes agonizingly painful. Groping for my bedside lamp I pressed its switch and remained engulfed in impenetrable darkness. I tried to read my clock but could not see its luminous dial. I must be blind, I thought. Would I be a permanent drain on my unfortunate family? What time could it be? Was it dawn yet? The silence in the street made that unlikely. If it were still night, it would be selfish to waken the family.

I stayed in bed thinking bitter thoughts, bitter tears increasing the soreness of my eyes. The darkness seemed impenetrable. Yet as time dragged by, the dark did seem to lighten, until my inflamed and streaming eyes could discern the outlines of my clock. Once again I tried in vain to turn on my bedside lamp. Crawling from my bed I felt for the wall switch, and light, glorious light, shone from the chandelier. I had not after all gone blind. It was my bed light which had failed me. I had panicked. Yet my eyes were so inflamed that I had to give up filming.

An uncle persuaded a local bank manager to employ me as a clerk. I knew that venture was doomed to failure but agreed to work unpaid for a trial week. My complete inability to count was quickly revealed and proved incurable. The experiment was abandoned. Shortly afterwards I noticed an advertisement in the *Figaro* for a temporary assistant to a Madame de Mirepoix whose secretary had fallen ill. Her address inspired confidence: a flat in a fashionable street just off the Rond Point des Champs-Élysées. Determined to get the job, I rushed down the Champs-Élysées without pausing at a single shop window.

Madame de Mirepoix's flat was on the first floor of an expensive-looking house. Its front door was solid and handsome, its brass plate well polished. I rang nervously. After a seemingly long inter-val the door opened hesitantly and I was hit by the pungent smell of stale cigar smoke and cat. In the hall stood a short, stout, heavily made-up elderly woman with peroxided hair and clothes that matched the mauve of her cosmetics. It was Madame de Mirepoix in person. Eighteen Siamese cats pranced, scrambled and miaowed round her. Controlling my revulsion, I stated that I wished to become her temporary secretary. My request was granted with surprising ease.

I was led into a room darkened by heavy, deep red velvet curtains impregnated with cigar smoke. The mahogany furniture was massive. Knick-knacks and photographs abounded. Apart from the vacancy on her staff there was nothing inviting about either Madame de Mirepoix, or her flat, or her cats. What could I do, she asked, quickly adding that all that she needed from me would be common sense and tact. Did I know anything about fashion, she queried, explaining that she was a fashion journalist. I admitted I did not, but added that I knew about clothes as my mother had been dressed by some of Paris's leading *grands couturiers*. Sighing at my ignorance, Madame de Mirepoix emphasized that I would have to leave her employment when her secretary was well enough to return. I was told to be at work by nine the following morning. Nothing was said about wages, and I was too shy and inexperi-enced to ask how often and how much I would be paid. I returned home elated.

Volodia was quick to notice that payment had not been discussed. Although I said virtually nothing about my employer, my parents did not take kindly to her. Mother wondered whether she might not be engaged in the white slave trade. Father, who had returned from the Balkans poorer than when he had set out, grieving at his inability to provide for us, was especially upset by my decision to earn a living. Now he suddenly refused to allow me to work for the only person willing to employ me. A family council was held. No one had any confidence in my employer but an uncle suggested that my parents should call on Madame de Mirepoix to assess her suitability. Clearly foreseeing their verdict and determined to hold on to the job, I objected so fiercely that the family gave way.

I never got used to the smell of Madame de Mirepoix's cats, nor to that of her guests' cigar smoke, but the relationship was nevertheless quite amicable. Slowly and painstakingly I typed the very few articles she wrote, listened avidly to her gossip about the *grands couturiers* and their notorious clients, carefully noting any advice she cared to give. Often I went with growing reluctance to the leading fashion houses to borrow the furs and wraps she intended wearing that evening. A very young soldier on leave from a Zouave regiment stationed in North Africa was staying with Madame de Mirepoix. She called him her *toutou*, referred to him as an adopted godson but their relationship seemed ambivalent. Much of my time was spent walking, for want of a bus fare, to the grocer opposite the Gare St-Lazare to buy delicious *crustacés* and other delectable snacks with which to regale him.

At home I was assailed every evening by a barrage of questions. In the privacy of our shared bedroom Volodia kept asking about my wages. Now that I had worked for a full month, why had I not been paid? Would I bet that I would not? Why would I not discuss the matter with my employer? Tired, worried, close to tears, I eventually admitted that I had tried to do so on several occasions but had always been side-tracked. Eventually, after having worked for six weeks, Madame de Mirepoix informed me that her secretary would be returning the following day. My request for payment was firmly rejected. Had I not come to her knowing nothing, she asked, and whilst with her had I not gained valuable experience as well as an excellent reference? Recognizing that I had indeed learnt more from her than she realized, too sick at heart to stand up to her, I abandoned my demand. Whilst genuinely sympathizing with me, Volodia could not refrain from teasing me about my innocence, but my parents were so relieved that little was made of my failure to get paid.

I confided my misery and humiliation to my closest friends, Tulia and her husband Munia Craemer. In years but not in spirits both were rather older than me, Tulia especially so. Both were gallant and endowed with dissimilar yet equally keen senses of humour. Tulia had been an adored only child. In St Petersburg her parents were famously hospitable in a society where hospitality was the rule. Their house had always been filled with people of all ages. When her mother died Tulia was only fourteen. Her father, General Danilov, expected her to run his house and act as his hostess. Her zest for life, her enthusiasms, her love of the arts and her gaiety endeared her to all his friends. She took advantage of her new position to insist on studying painting at the Academy of Fine Arts and wearing dresses made of tulle. The young men who hovered round their even younger hostess admired her paintings and nicknamed her Tulia after her dresses.

My mother had known her since her childhood but because of the difference in our ages I only got to know Tulia in Paris. She was short, on the plump side, yet elegant. Some months after escaping to Paris she had married a tall, thin Russian solicitor, rather younger than herself, a man of acute sensibility, considerable erudition and a basic serenity. They both adored Biche, a small French bulldog which Tulia had acquired after helping to dress Diaghilev's ballet *Les Biches*.* The three were inseparable and, regardless of the disparity in their heights, they had somehow come to resemble each other. When I met them they were desperately short of money but Tulia's effervescent spirit kept depression at bay. They had acquired an enchanting, unfurnished ground-floor flat in the Rue de la Tour. The french windows of their living-room opened on to a large and neglected back garden with daisy-studded grass, tall trees, and fat lilac bushes – a veritable wilderness of repose.

Following my fiasco at Madame de Mirepoix I turned to Tulia

---

*The ballet, to music by Francis Poulenc, choreographed by Nijinska, was first performed by the Diaghilev Ballet Company at Monte Carlo in 1924.

and Munia for comfort and advice. It was a Saturday morning. We sat in the garden taking stock of our situation. We had just over eighteen francs between us, with enough bread, butter and coffee to last the weekend: beyond that – nothing. 'We must invent something, invent,' Tulia exclaimed. 'Tamara,' she ordered, 'call a number.' 'Seventeen,' I muttered. 'Very well,' said Tulia, 'we will eat now. Then we will go into the Rue de Passy and walk along the left pavement because it is the closer to Balzac's house. We will stop at the seventeenth shop window and look through it till we find something we can afford to buy and transform into something we can sell.'

It had seemed a good idea until we found ourselves standing in front of a chemist's shop. Abashed by the goods in the window we were tempted to cheat and move somewhere more stimulating but, like true fatalists, we quickly abandoned that idea. Eventually we agreed that the only thing we might conceivably be able to use was a pack of almost transparent, ochre-coloured oilcloth presumably used when applying a hot or cold compress to the body. Twelve francs bought a lot of the hideous stuff.

In recent years considerable attention has been devoted to a movement which a group of Petersburgians, largely inspired by Alexander Benois, launched during the closing decade of the nineteenth century. Adopting the slogan of 'Art for Art's Sake' they formed themselves into the World of Art Society (*Mir Iskusstva*). As most of them lived in one of Europe's loveliest eighteenth-century towns they were especially responsive to that century's art and culture. At the same time, rather than ape eighteenth-century styles, they aimed at creating beautiful contemporary works. They were influenced by Russia's religious and folk arts as well as by the graphic arts of William Morris and of such contemporary innovators as Rennie MacIntosh. The society's members included, in addition to artists and architects, art historians, antiquarians, craftsmen and some exquisite needlewomen, foremost among the latter being the sister of the painter Somov. She excelled at producing dress trimmings that displayed flowers worked in minute petit-point. These were greatly admired and snapped up by Petersburgians as costume jewellery.

In 1924 as we sat in Tulia's Parisian garden on a lovely summer afternoon disconsolately looking at our ugly oilcloth, Tulia reminded us of Miss Somova and her *art appliqué*. 'This stuff is so hideous it will have to be painted,' I said in despair as we absent-mindedly fingered the horrible cloth. 'No one is to leave the table', Tulia quickly retorted, 'until we have made it into something.' 'A flower,' one of us shouted.

Frantically, working in silence, we hacked and pulled at the oil-cloth, cutting it into strips, shaping it until we found that we had made some flat, open roses and tiny rose-buds. They looked repulsive so we started colouring them navy blue, with silver and gold highlights. Our creations were transformed into surprisingly attractive trimmings. They had style. Our spirits rose. 'They are saleable,' Tulia mused. 'But to succeed we must start at the top, where decisions are made.'

Having worked for Madame de Mirepoix I knew how difficult it was to enter the establishment of a *grand couturier*, let alone to obtain an interview with a buyer or director. 'How can we?' I asked. Munia suddenly thought of Vera Soudeikina, a beautiful friend who had acted at the Kamerny Theatre in Moscow. She was married at the time to the distinguished artist Serge Soudeikin, but was later to become Stravinsky's second wife. Tulia was quick to persuade Vera to try to sell our creations. On the Monday morning, wearing a plain, well-cut black dress – the elegant *petite robe* of the period – with one of our flowers pinned at her shoulder and another at her waist, Vera entered Jean Patou's office, sold him our entire stock and got orders for more. She proved so adept a saleswoman that in a relatively short time she and Tulia were able to open a shop near the Champs-Élysées, aptly called Tulavera.*

Although we were doing astonishingly well with our flowers we realized that the fashion for them would pass and that we had to find work of a more stable kind. Mother started making necklaces from beads imported from Czechoslovakia. They sold well, among other outlets to Jay's of Regent Street in London. I was employed to decorate two flats. That proved immensely enjoyable work. However, I had to pay for all the materials straight away and then

---

*In his preface to *Dearest Babushka: The Correspondence of Vera and Igor Stravinsky 1921–1954*, tr. Lucia Davidovna, London, 1985, the editor, Robert Craft, dates the establishment of Tulavera to 1922.

wait until the flats were ready for occupation before presenting my own bill. As this involved borrowing money for months on end I soon abandoned that agreeable form of livelihood.

On reflection the fashion industry seemed my only hope and, as was to happen to me more than once when my situation seemed grim, I was suddenly offered work by a leading fashion editor. The pay was meagre but at least it was regular. The problem of being reasonably well dressed could easily have been solved had I been willing to use those fashion houses ready to propitiate a journalist by the gift or loan of an occasional garment, but my somewhat idealistic concept of journalistic integrity encouraged me to reject that solution. However I made the most of end-of-season sales. I could seldom afford to buy more than one garment at a time, but the mannequins frequently gave me good advice and one generously provided me with the address of a little dressmaker in Montmartre.

Like many small Parisian dressmakers, this one was a genius with her needle. She also had access, possibly due to a *midinette*'s (sewing girl's) help, to the coveted *toiles* (dress materials) of various couturiers' models. She had been widowed at the end of the First World War and had a young son to bring up. Her flat was tiny but it had a magnificent view over roof-tops. Her small rooms were spotlessly clean, very neat, furnished only with essentials, yet the prices she charged were ridiculously low. She loved her work as did most of those I met who depended on fashion for their livelihood. In the 1920s, insofar as Paris was concerned, they formed a considerable section of the town's artisan population. Many were embroideresses, whether working in silk, pearls, beads or metal threads, others were lace-makers, others specialized in flower and feather trimmings, still others produced costume jewellery, but the majority were needlewomen. Although they and the grandest couturiers were highly dependent upon each other, they never exploited this situation.

My work put me in touch with the free-lance designers who drew illustrations for home dressmaking patterns featured by magazines such as *Vogue*. These designers possessed an uncanny flair for forecasting what would be in fashion months later. They earned fifteen francs for a detailed drawing, whilst artists with an equally acute feeling for fashion but little experience of dressmaking were paid between five and ten francs.

Great textile manufacturers such as Rodier for woollens or Bianchini for silks possessed equally sensitive antennae. These enabled them to produce textiles so that leading couturiers could keep at least two years ahead of the calendar. Then there were the hat makers; great houses such as Reboux, where the current season's models were reworked on the head of the client to ensure that each creation, whilst keeping in the forefront of the current trend, suited its wearer. Peggy Guggenheim's mother, Florette, whose husband changed from his dinner jacket into tails in order to meet his death on the *Titanic*, was in the habit of repeating key words in her conversations three times. As a result, she once told Madame Reboux, who was modelling a hat on her head, that she wanted it trimmed with 'aigrettes, aigrettes, aigrettes'. When the hat was delivered it was smothered in aigrettes, the cost of which seemed astronomic even to Florette, yet the feathers had been so cleverly placed that, whilst grumbling at their price, Mrs Guggenheim kept the hat and enjoyed wearing it.

Whilst well aware of the transience of fashion, the creators of these ephemera were firmly convinced of its significance. And, indeed, just as Brillat-Savarin had some justification in treating pastry as a branch of architecture, so too can dressmaking be described as a branch of the fine arts by representing a blend of sculpture and painting. Poiret was one of the first to link his models to the stage, both by finding inspiration in certain of Diaghilev's productions such as *Shéhérazade*, but also himself sometimes influencing stage designs. However, until the outbreak of the Second World War, the wealthy ladies who were in the habit of buying their clothes from leading designers were for the most part sufficiently sophisticated and discerning to insist on the current fashions being adapted to their own figures. In England that wise precept was largely abandoned in the swinging sixties. British fashion is still suffering from the damage caused by this inattention to fundamental principles.

In the 1920s the two major annual press fashion shows were splendid events. The relatively small number of journalists invited were personally known to the fashion houses and welcomed as valued guests. Buyers came the day after the press view. In contrast were the mid-season shows featuring garments intended for winter and summer. Journalists were often obliged to attend three shows

a day and file their reports immediately. After morning and afternoon viewings my energy was apt to flag, but it was always resus-
citated by the more festive evening shows with their orchestras and
champagne. Lucien Lelong's evening launches were especially
sparkling, putting journalists on their mettle.

Inevitably fashion invaded my private life, obliging me to note
the clothes worn at social gatherings, race meetings and the like.
Doing so made me feel something of an outsider. At the same time
I was also finding myself out of sympathy with some of the tsarist
émigré circles. I preferred the art world to which I was gaining entry.
Largely owing to Tulia's friendship, I was getting to know such distinguished Russian artists as Larionov, Goncharova, Maliavine,
Serebriakova, Eugene Berman and Lanskoy. André Lanskoy was so
poor, shy and withdrawn that he worked in solitude and chaos,
living on the verge of destitution. However, the respect with which
Parisians regarded the arts was an encouragement to the Russians,
especially to those disorientated by the severance of contact with
their native land. Filipp Maliavine suffered from this more acutely
than many, perhaps because he and his wife were incapable of
learning French. Savel Sorin and Eugene Berman were more fortunate for, by moving to the United States, their talents were to be
suitably rewarded. I also met many artists at the home of the
Alexander Benois where I could always count on a warm welcome.*

By the time I joined my parents in Paris the Benois had moved
from Versailles to a spacious flat in Auteuil. It had a splendid view
over the Seine and a piano which Alexander Nicholaevich was fond
of playing. Books were everywhere. Some were antiquarian
volumes, others contemporary. Paintings by friends and earlier
artists hung on his walls. At the insistence of his guests, Benois
would open a folder and display some of his rather large watercolours of Petersburg, Versailles, Brittany or Switzerland as well as
his more recent stage designs. A variety of small objects also
charmed the eye and stimulated the mind. They ranged in date

---

*Benois, Alexander Nicholaevich (1870–1960). Studied at St Petersburg Academy of Art
1887–8. Prime mover in the idea that the World of Art Society should revive European
interest in Russian arts. From 1918–26 Senior Curator and Director of Painting, the
Hermitage, Leningrad. He then moved to Paris. Intimately connected with Diaghilev and
the Ballets Russes, his career as a ballet designer had started in St Petersburg in 1901 with
Sylvia. Great-uncle of Peter Ustinov.

from miniature eighteenth-century stage sets through Renaissance bronzes to works by contemporary Russians such as Von Klodt and Trubetskoy.

It was not so much these visual delights as our hosts' personalities that drew artists, writers and musicians to their flat. Anna Karlovna's endearing gentleness concealed a firm will. Her elongated face with small eyes, slightly fleshy cheeks, radiated kindness. His was a more complex personality, yet it was her forbearance and serenity which curbed the occasional outbursts of impatience and anger sparked off by the acuteness of his judgement and strict artistic integrity. His sense of taste was as sensitive as Diaghilev's and his erudition even wider but, in contrast to Diaghilev, whose first reactions were analytical, Benois' were intuitive: although his response to another's talent was as warm as Diaghilev's, it often took longer to emerge.

Benois was cautious by temperament and also superstitious. One day I was alone with him in his flat when the front door bell rang. He was not expecting a caller and froze. When the bell sounded for a second time I offered to open the front door. 'No, no,' he gasped, 'it may be something unpleasant.' We sat in silence as the bell rang a third time. At the fourth I started towards the hall but Benois told me not to open the door. A few minutes later we heard the lift descend. Benois hurried to the window hoping to discover his visitor's identity. He was too late, the street was empty. 'Who knows?' he murmured sadly. 'I may perhaps have missed something pleasant. One should trust fate.'

Like Diaghilev, Benois feared the sea. His dread of it had even prevented him from coming to London in June 1936 when Hilda Cochrane, a cousin of David Talbot Rice, presented the first one man show of his works to be held in England. Yet, years later, in 1947, Benois decided to come to Gloucestershire to visit his niece, the artist Nadia Benois, and us. I was surprised to find that he had arranged to travel on Friday the 13th, but assumed that the war had cured him of his fear of superstitions. Petrol still being rationed, Nadia and I decided that it would be pleasanter for the Benois to stay in Cirencester rather than with either of us so we booked rooms for them in the Stratton House Hotel. To save petrol, I was to meet them at Cirencester instead of Kemble, which was another five miles away although on the direct railway line from London.

They looked harassed as they stepped out of the little shunting train which connected both stations, and were worried about their trunk. It had been put in the van at Paddington; they had not seen it when changing trains at Kemble. Was it lost, they asked. I laughed at their fears as I led them to the guard's van but the van was empty and I was obliged to admit that their trunk was not on the train. My guests became despondent. The station-master assured them that their trunk would soon be found. What did it look like, he asked. What did it contain? 'My palette, my palette, the one I brought with me from Russia,' moaned Benois. Meanwhile Anna Karlovna was trying to remember what clothes she had packed. Was it nine or twelve pairs of his socks, she wondered.

Hoping to divert them, I drove them to visit the church. There was then a very good tailor close to its west porch. Alexander Nicholaevich rushed to examine its window display. 'I should like a tie, an English tie,' he announced. With clothes still being rationed, very few clothing coupons and three growing children to dress, I muttered that you needed two coupons for a tie.* 'Surely', my guest remarked, 'you would not grudge me that small number after so distressing a journey.'

The Benois liked their hotel. Next day their trunk reached them unharmed, having been wrongly addressed. They liked Cirencester and they liked Gloucestershire but they did not like the climate which was unseasonably cold, sunless and wet throughout their visit. Alexander Nicholaevich felt disinclined to paint and produced only one watercolour, a sketch of our house, to give us as a goodbye present. He never returned to England and never again travelled on a Friday or on the thirteenth of the month.

In Paris in the early 1920s Diaghilev occasionally sent Mother a couple of tickets for one of his productions. My parents' memories of the Mariinsky were still so bitter-sweet that they could not bring themselves to use the tickets and gave them to Volodia and me. At the time Tulia worked in Diaghilev's wardrobe department. I was

*For much of the war the annual allocation of clothing coupons was thirty-six per person; this was increased to forty-four in August 1946. A woman's coat and skirt was eighteen coupons, a man's suit twenty-six, a jersey five, shoes for women five, for men seven since they took more leather. For four pairs of stockings six coupons had to be surrendered, and three for a pair of men's socks.

sometimes able to act as her assistant and as a result could attend the occasional rehearsal. Today it has become fashionable to disparage Diaghilev's *corps de ballet*. Having myself seen the care with which his ballets were rehearsed, having witnessed the precision and dedication with which his *corps de ballet* learnt steps and studied the choreography, having recently read anew the ecstatic reviews written at the time by some of Europe's most experienced and exacting critics and remembering also my own delight when watching a Diaghilev production, such criticism astonishes me. No performance for which Diaghilev and Grigoriev, nor indeed Massine, was responsible could have evoked such enthusiasm from the critics and won the acclaim from their audiences, had the standard maintained by the *corps de ballet* clashed with that set by the soloists. Any shortfall would have impaired the unity and excellence of the whole. To suggest that an imbalance was permitted is ridiculous. Such criticisms are quite unfounded and, significantly, usually voiced by people who are unlikely to be speaking from experience, Diaghilev having died in 1929.

To begin with in Paris, borrowing and contriving provided the framework for our lives. Towards the end of each month there was always an émigré household which had run out of money. Those in that predicament often telephoned close friends to enquire about the state of their finances and ask whether it would be possible to join them for a bread and ham supper. Prospective hosts were promised a similar supper at the end of the next month. One day, when we were feeling very poor, an exceptionally large box of Marquise de Sévigné chocolates, the best in Paris, was delivered to us. Our spirits rose. We were all gluttons for sweets. We watched avidly as Mother's hands moved towards the satin ribbon tying the box. Then she stilled her hands, looked at us tentatively and murmured, 'We should perhaps give this to the Xs; they have had such a run of bad luck lately.' Morosely we agreed. Several weeks later some friends called on us with a large parcel. It contained a huge box of Marquise de Sévigné chocolates – our box, slightly bedraggled but, clearly, never as yet opened. It had come home to roost, having enjoyed the hospitality of several households. We traced its hosts, gave a party for them and devoured all the chocolates in one evening.

Slowly our financial position improved. Father and Volodia having both found work, we were able to rent a large unfurnished flat at 7 Rue Benjamin Godard, near the Bois de Boulogne. We furnished it with very plain, cheap yet well-designed deal furniture, adding some Empire pieces bought at junk stalls and in the Flea Market. Volodia regained his innate gaiety and could often be heard singing 'I want to be happy', 'Take your happiness while you may' and other Layton and Johnstone songs.* Mother heard of a young Slovak peasant girl who wanted to leave her native village near Bratislava to seek her fortune abroad. She came to us as a cook-general. She was called Marisha and arrived looking dazed and tired, still wearing national dress very like a Russian peasant's. After spending five years with us she replaced herself with a young cousin and married an émigré Russian artisan. We set them up in a tiny flat. They were blissfully happy living on his small earnings until the Germans occupied Paris when they disappeared without trace. They were probably worked to death in some Nazi concentration camp.

Although food was incredibly cheap in France, Mother felt compelled to spend much time searching for bargains. Once or twice a week she went to Les Halles soon after dawn, carrying home heavy loads of fruit and vegetables. After a short rest she would take Ghost for a walk in the Bois. Doing so probably tired her as much as her shopping expedition but it also cheered and relaxed her. My parents started seeing friends of their own again, meeting them regularly for bridge and renewing the French contacts they had found so agreeable in pre-war days. But, to Mother's distress, I found the French girls of my own age had too rigid an outlook. Their concern for convention formed a barrier between us, their interests were not mine. I was embarrassed at having to travel by public transport in evening clothes to their receptions. I preferred less formal circles.

It was at this stage that Maurice Barre, the French officer who had lodged with us in Moscow, traced us. Although he must have been in his thirties, he seemed old and staid to me, for he still wore the high, stiff collars later associated with General de Gaulle. His

---

*Turner Layton (1894–1978) and Clarence Tandy Johnstone (d. 1953) were a piano/singing duo whose partnership ended in 1935.

narrow trousers and close-fitting, tightly buttoned jackets helped accentuate his height. Having always liked him I was delighted when he invited me to dine *en tête-à-tête* at Maxim's. At first Mother demurred, but realizing that I intended to accept the invitation she agreed not to tell Father.

Soon dining with Barre every ten days or so became a regular and very pleasant event in my life. Now that I was no longer a child he always addressed me as Mademoiselle and I, as he was older, invariably called him Monsieur. Mother never knew that, for convenience sake, after work I called for my generous host at his *garçonnière* – a vastly improper thing to have done then. However, within minutes of my arrival we were in a taxi, heading for a renowned Parisian restaurant, most often Foyot, close to the Panthéon, where we ended up with a glass of calvados. Barre's behaviour was always impeccably formal yet it was only with him that I talked of Russia, Moscow and my still greatly missed dog, Lord. As I ranked Barre among my closest friends I was hurt and astonished by his reaction to the news of my engagement in 1927. His resentment, soon to turn to hatred, stemmed from the fact that I was to marry an Englishman; he even refused to meet my fiancé. His attitude severed a friendship by which I had set much store.

My pleasure in *haute cuisine* was encouraged by my dentist, M. Maurice Sennac, a Corsican, who was a member of the famous gourmets' Club des Cents.* Like most Petersburgians who had suffered from underfeeding I had teeth and gums that needed prolonged treatment. Sennac was short, round and very unpunctual. Until the day on which he was carried into his surgery on a stretcher, having been severely peppered whilst pheasant-shooting, I had resented his unpunctuality, but that mishap so amused me that I ceased fretting when kept waiting. For his part he tried to atone by showing me his library. When he opened some rare Japanese pornographic books I was deeply embarrassed but managed to conceal this by feigning boredom. He then desisted

---

*Membership, limited to one hundred, was much envied. Each member had a secret number and undertook when dining out to complete a pro forma assessing the meal. Completed returns were collated, indexed and circulated to members monthly. At one time a small coterie led by the couturier Paul Poiret broke apart to establish its own hundred members, the Club des Purs Cents (see R. F. Wilson, *Paris on Parade*, Indianapolis, 1924, p. 140ff.).

and, instead, often asked me to lunches; these meals were held by the Club des Cents in country restaurants unaware that they were being tested for the club's highly coveted gastronomic seal of approval. The dishes served at these elaborate meals were always excellent, often memorable, the wines delectable, the conversation scintillating, the outing great fun.

Peggy Guggenheim had recently married Laurence Vail and was living in Paris. I saw a good deal of her and her sister Hazel, then married to the writer Milton Waldman, but I got on better with Laurence's sister Clotilde. She was elegant, witty, cultivated and, although older than me, she treated me as a contemporary. Together we went to the Vieux Colombier to see plays by Eugene O'Neill, Pirandello and Ben Jonson, to Montmartre to see surrealist films. We also went to commercial art galleries such as Bernheim Jeune's. Here I coveted a delicately coloured Picasso lithograph of musical instruments grouped on a balcony in the South of France; this cost thirty pounds – so little, but far more than I could afford to spend at one go on an indulgence.

It was Clotilde who, on several occasions, drove me to Giverny to call on her friend, Claude Monet. She warned me that he was old and frail, at times seemingly withdrawn but at others stimulating. I had recently got to know the magnificent series of his paintings of water-lilies exhibited in the Jeu de Paume and was thrilled at the thought of meeting him and seeing his garden. At the time I was not a knowledgeable gardener and my first glimpse disappointed. Its beauty revealed itself only gradually. The initial difficulty resulted from its division into two sections. The part I saw first, that nearer to the house, was laid out in rectilinear lines, in accordance with French tradition, some paths intersecting others at right angles. The beds of irises and lupins near the house were smothered in wild flowers, mostly poppies. To reach the pond which had inspired the water-lily paintings it was necessary to cross a railway line and follow a lane leading to a glade smothered in forget-me-nots and fringed with Judas trees. Their outlines were mirrored in places where water was left clear by the lilies. There, in its privacy and quiet, beauty seemed ageless, transcendental.

Monet's house was modest in size, the furniture elegantly simple. We sat in the dining-room at a table with a large bowl of fruit at its centre. We sipped honey-coloured tea. Monet and Clotilde talked of colour and light, sunshine and shadow, clarity of eye and perception. Monet spoke slowly, choosing his words with care, occasionally smiling gently as if in answer to a half-remembered memory.

It must have been Clotilde who introduced me to René le Bourg and his wife. The Le Bourgs were intellectuals belonging to a set equivalent to the Bloomsbury Group. At the time René was personal assistant to Tristan Bernard – then the most Parisian of Parisian men of letters. Through them I met such writers as Mauriac whose extreme catholicism and right-wing views repelled me, and Gertrude Stein, whose ugliness and self-assurance deterred me from responding to her invitations, a decision I regretted after reading *The Autobiography of Alice B. Toklas*. Sylvia Beach's bookshop, Shakespeare & Co., near the Odeon, was almost as unappealing as the Gertrude Stein household. On the other hand, I found the Jean Cocteau–Madame (Marie) de Noailles set diverting and astringent but hardly endearing. The outcry raised by the film *L'Âge d'or* surprised me, perhaps because I enjoyed a sequence in which a beautifully groomed cow scrambled between the turned-down silk sheets of a large and luxurious bed.* With the Le Bourgs I regularly went to see such memorable films as *The Cabinet of Dr Caligari* and *Storm over Asia*.

It was either through Peggy or Hazel Guggenheim that I got to know Isadora Duncan. She had grown fat and ungainly, and was often sozzled and sad. She still moved beautifully and retained the innocence which she, perhaps mistakenly, associated with children. Although very badly off, her vitality and warmth of heart kept her buoyant. Rather than listen to her rambling theories on dance I encouraged her to talk about Russia and Esenin.† She did so with affection and compassion, without a trace of bitterness. She was lovable and splendidly Junoesque when handling the long, flowing scarf which was so soon to kill her.‡

L'Âge d'or, produced by Louis Buñuel and Salvador Dali, tells of two lovers who declare war on the bourgeoisie. Noted for its often violent surrealist scenes, the film was banned on 13 December 1930 after the cinema showing it had been wrecked by protesters.

†Sergei Aleksandrovich Esenin, her first husband, a Russian poet, committed suicide soon after their marriage.

‡She was strangled when her scarf was accidentally caught up in the wheels of her car.

In Paris, in spite of our financial difficulties, life was often interesting and always busy. Father deplored my independence, Mother longed for me to accept any proposal of marriage whilst Volodia, believing that only gaiety made life bearable, annoyed me by shouting, 'Smile, smile', whenever my gravity galled him beyond endurance. Yet I was often depressed with my inability to integrate with any set. Neither Russian émigré society with its devotion to a defunct outlook, nor Barre and Sennac's gourmet circles, nor the intellectuals of the Le Bourg or the Stein clans really suited me. The same went for musical contacts such as Koussevitsky and Stravinsky, and for the fashionable Parisian and international sets. I felt happiest with Tulia and Munia, the Benois, Larionov, Goncharova and their friends, but even there my amateur status made me feel an interloper.

Fashion epitomizes actuality and is therefore essentially transient by nature. I soon tired of it and in 1926 I abandoned fashion journalism to join the staff of Professor Carlton Hayes of Columbia University, New York, later United States ambassador to Spain. He was employed by the Rockefeller Foundation to study conditions in countries which had fought during the Great War. It was hoped that their findings, once published, would help to avert future wars. Once again I was extremely lucky for my assignment obliged me to visit practically every village in France to analyse the sentiments underlying the inscription on its war memorial. I was blissfully happy, delighting in the beauty of the countryside, the splendour of French architecture, the enchantment of its villages, the delicious regional food. Above all it was glorious to feel free, free to drive at will along empty roads, to stop in a village café, to converse with the locals whose innate intelligence had been so cleverly developed by the Third Republic's excellent educational system. Only in Brittany were the peasants bigoted and narrow-minded.

Back in the Paris office I often lunched with a colleague, Alexander Werth, an economist who had been a near neighbour in St Petersburg. He was later to become widely known and respected as a journalist specializing in Russian, and more especially Soviet, affairs. His despatches from Moscow during the Second World War attracted much attention. In Paris, when lunching together, we often marvelled at the size of our salaries, the generosity and kind-

1. Tamara, in her freshly laundered white frock, with a wide blue satin ribbon tied round her hips, is ready for a visit to her parents' drawing-room

2. Her Ponisovsky cousins: Lucie with Genia, flanked by the twins Jim and Alec

3. Tamara's favourite uncle was imprisoned in Taganka Jail, Moscow, in 1918, and then murdered by the Bolsheviks. He is reading a copy of the *Daily Mirror*

4. Tamara at Oxford in 1921: the obligatory undergraduette cap gave her headaches

5. Her future husband, David Talbot Rice. A photograph taken *c.* 1925

THE TRAGICAL DEATH OF Mr WILL. HUSKISSON SEPT. MDCCCXXX.

6. 'An unfortunate and melancholy event': at the opening of the railway between Liverpool and Manchester in 1830, the MP for Liverpool, the Rt. Hon. W. Huskisson, was accidentally run over and killed. In this drawing, executed as a birthday gift for John Sutro, President of the Oxford University Railway Club, Evelyn Waugh depicted their friends. Tamara is the swooning 'lady of quality', on the right. The copy of the line drawing given to Tamara was signed and dated, Tamara from Evelyn, July 1924. 27×31cm

7. David and Tamara at Oddington soon after their engagement in 1927

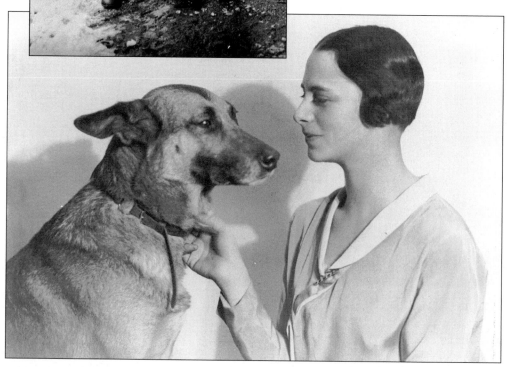

8. Tamara, with her dog Ghost, *c.* 1927, by Emile Marcovitch, Paris

9. Sumela – the precarious steps leading up to the monastery some fifty feet above ground level

10. Kurds help get the car across the bridgeless stream but, despite obvious poverty, refuse any payment

11. A pencil and crayon portrait of Tamara, signed and dated Maliavine 1927. 45×34.5cm.

Filipp Andreevich Maliavine (1869–1940), a genre and portrait painter, studied in an icon studio in Greece, then at the St Petersburg Academy of Arts. He emigrated to France in 1924

12. Pigeon House, a pencil drawing for his hosts executed by Basil Spence when he stayed there on his way to Coventry to submit the designs which were to win the award for the new cathedral. Signed and dated Basil Spence 19 June '50. 26×36.5cm

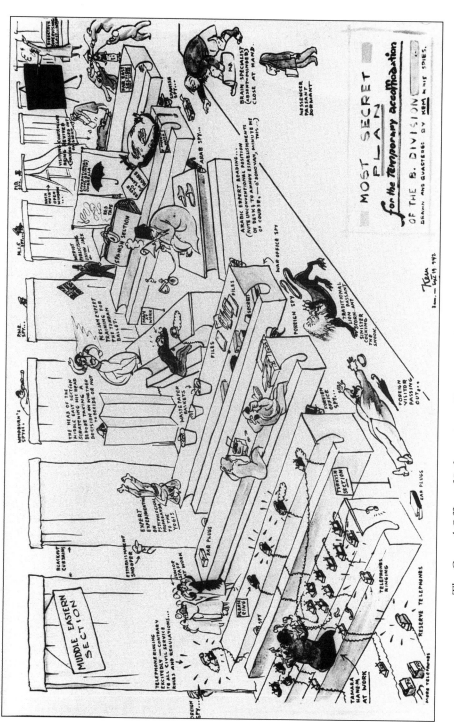

13. The Central Office of Information – Tamara, on the telephones, does not keep 'her cool'

14. David and Tamara in Poland in the 1960s

ness of our employers, the pleasantness of our work, but we could not help laughing heartily over its unrealistic glitz. We felt in our bones that we would have to endure another war.

The close friendships which I had made at Oxford did not end with my departure from England. Whenever David Talbot Rice, Edward and Christine Longford or Evelyn Waugh passed through Paris we met, celebrated our reunions and spent as much time as possible together. Mother loved these visits, especially the sight and sound of Edward, looking not unlike the Fat Boy in *The Pickwick Papers*, singing Protestant hymns with immense gusto. He and Christine were excellent company and the kindest of friends. They either assumed or discovered that I was entitled to a holiday but could not afford one. When back in Dublin, they arranged for a Paris–Dublin–Paris railway ticket to be sent to me – an easy enough undertaking today but far from usual in the Dublin of the mid-twenties.

I set out on my first visit to Ireland in high spirits, crossing on a night boat. Edward had told me to breakfast at the Jammet Hotel before taking a train to Mullingar. It was still very early when we docked. Haze obscured the sky. Here and there I caught glimpses of lovely eighteenth-century façades and enticing junk-shop windows. Only the night porter was visible at Jammet's. I asked for a bath, then breakfast. Failing to understand a single word of his voluble reply, I went upstairs, found a bathroom and had a bath in deliciously soft water. As it was still too early for breakfast I went for a walk.

Dublin was beautiful, rather decayed, clearly far from prosperous. There were beggars about. A tall, emaciated, filthy crone followed me asking for alms. I gave her sixpence, a quite substantial sum at the time. Yet, instead of thanking me, or falling back in silence, she pursued me, loudly cursing my meanness. Later I was told that tuppence would probably have pleased her but that my gift of sixpence had led her to assume that I was rich. At the time her reaction struck me as so novel, her flow of words so prolific, her vocabulary so picturesque that I was immensely amused. On hearing me laugh the creature cackled with delight, gave me a friendly pat on the back and moved away, leaving me convinced that I would delight in Ireland.

After breakfast at the hotel I noticed my bill did not include the cost of my bath. When I drew his attention to the omission the waiter fled, reappearing with the night porter and an elderly woman, who questioned me minutely about my bath. It transpired that a strike was in progress and coal supplies were running very low. My bath had deprived the hotel residents of hot water. Chastened, I drove to the station and settled into a train to Mullingar where Edward and Christine were waiting to drive me to Pakenham. Their car was full of lemons. Remembering that the Gulf Stream skirts Ireland, I wondered whether they grew locally. They did not, Christine replied, adding with a touch of embarrassment that the cook had asked for them.

Pakenham Hall is an exceedingly long, fairly low house built in a blend of late Georgian and Victorian Gothic with some crenellation. Its interior doors are set in massive Gothic-shaped surrounds. At the time my hosts were enamoured of Chinese art and had collected a number of Chinese objects including some large naturalistic animal bronzes and had painted the Gothic-styled wood and plaster decoration in their reception rooms either bright Chinese red or royal blue. The effect was startling.

Andrews, Edward's butler, was a Welshman, the only Protestant among a large staff of Catholics. His services had been pressed on Edward at his marriage by his aunt, Lady Dynevor, Andrews having worked his way up from hallboy to footman, then to under-butler in her household. With the assistance of two mischievous-looking young hallboys, he waited on us at luncheon. Later tea was brought to us in one of Pakenham's numerous sitting-rooms. Six uncut lemons lay on the tea tray; both hallboys were hovering around looking inquisitive. My hosts were ill at ease. I heard Christine mumbling and realized that she was asking whether I would like some lemon in my tea. Slightly surprised I answered that a slice would be nice. 'Are you sure that you would not like more than a slice?' Christine insisted. Her question astonished me, for we had often had tea together. 'Quite sure,' I declared. When the servants had left the room Christine admitted that she had thought it unlikely that I could consume vast quantities of lemons but her cook had maintained that Russians did so and Christine had to undertake to get as many lemons as she could in Mullingar. 'Tell her', I insisted, 'that I have become Anglicized.'

After dinner that night I was faced with an even greater ordeal.

Once again Andrews entered the sitting-room followed by the two impish boys. Setting down the coffee tray he asked Edward for the key to the cigar cupboard. 'I won't smoke a cigar tonight, Andrews,' Edward replied. 'The key, please, my lord,' Andrews insisted. 'Oh, very well then,' Edward muttered, fiddling among rolls of flesh for his waistcoat pocket. Andrews took the key and left the room majestically.

I felt apprehensive and not without reason for, re-entering, Andrews approached me and said, 'I understand, Miss, that Russian ladies smoke cigars. I hope this very light brand will be to your taste.' I was appalled. About to refuse, I noticed a look of fascinated astonishment on the faces of both hallboys. Realizing that Andrews' authority depended on my answer I thanked him and bravely asked him to prepare a cigar for me. He did so. I put it between my lips. He lit it. I inhaled. It lighted. The combination of far more and far richer food than I was used to, and the disgusting taste of pungent smoke, was almost too much. I managed to contain my nausea until Andrews and his myrmidons had left the room. Then I fled to mine.

Later Christine came to wish me goodnight and to warn me that I would probably be woken in the morning at an unreasonably early hour. 'Why?' I moaned. She explained that they were holding the school treat on the two following days, the Catholic children, who greatly outnumbered the Protestants, coming on the first day and the Protestants on the second. Both lots were invited for two-thirty, but the Catholics liked making the most of the swings and roundabouts, probably trying them out before eight in the morning.

On coming down to breakfast the next morning I found that it was the delightful custom of the house for the gardener to provide everyone with a buttonhole. As in Tantivy Towers,* breakfast at Pakenham was a feast. There were several egg dishes, kidneys, sausages, bacon, kedgeree, a choice of cold ham and whatever game happened to be in season, and the most delicious peaches I have ever tasted. Surfeited, I went out to meet the Catholic school children. They were gay, uninhibited, inventive. In the afternoon

---

*A popular operetta of this name, on a hunting theme, composed by Thomas Dunhill to words by A. P. Herbert, opened at the Lyric, Hammersmith, in June 1931 and ran for 170 performances.

they played games with zest. They ate enormous teas and, on leaving, they knew precisely which of their hosts' parting gifts each preferred. On the following day a small group of sedate, neatly dressed young Protestants arrived at three-thirty. They were not easy to amuse. At tea-time cakes had to be pressed on them and when, at parting, they were asked to choose a present it was difficult to discover which object appealed to them for their answer to each suggestion at first evoked the enigmatic answer of 'I don't mind which, Miss.'

On the whole the villagers were friendly; whatever they did behind your back, they were charming to your face. However, during my visit, I made only one friend among them, an old man living in a very small, dark hut who collected porcelain. True, the collection consisted mainly of fragments, for the most part breakages from the Hall, but he derived quite as much pleasure from his pieces as did dear Eumorfopoulos* from his finest Chinese vessels. When you come down to it, everything in life is relative.

Each day Edward and Christine took me to another splendid Georgian mansion. Most contained beautiful examples of eighteenth-century Irish silver and furniture but very few books. In one of the finest houses, the ballroom was being used as a hen house but an impressive Piranesi-like oil painting still adorned one wall. In another house, the only book, buried under an immense pile of ancient sporting magazines, turned out to be a valuable copy of the Gutenberg Bible. Yet another mansion belonged to an elderly gentleman who collected clocks. There were scores of these in every room, all ticking merrily away but no two showing the same time. Reduced to a state of imbecility by their ticking I heard myself idiotically asking my host why he collected clocks. 'To be sure, to know the time,' he sweetly replied.

Edward and Christine were already involved both in the theatre and in reviving Ireland's woollen industry. These activities, espe-

---

*Born in Liverpool, the art collector George Eumorfopoulos started collecting Chinese porcelain in his youth. Expanded to include bronzes and jade, his collection grew into the largest and most important in private hands, but was sold in the Depression for well under half its market value to the British Museum and the Victoria and Albert Museum. Eumorfopoulos however continued collecting, Islamic antiquities and European art augmenting his Chinese acquisitions. At his death it took a five-day sale by Sotheby's to dispose of his remaining collections. By then Vice-President of the mercantile firm, Ralli Brothers, he had once been its representative in southern Russia.

cially the theatre, made great demands on their time and talents for the rest of their lives. They acquired the Gate Theatre and, assembling a distinguished group of actors headed by Micheál MacLíammoír and Hilton Edwards, applied themselves to widening the existing repertory. Although the generation of intellectuals who had brought lustre to Dublin's reputation was disappearing from the scene, it was to some extent due to the Longfords' influence that the intellectual life in the capital still remained vital and amusing. Somehow they found time simultaneously, by encouraging weaving in Ireland and personally showing the products at the Dublin Horse Show, to transform a cottage industry into a profitable enterprise, thus laying the foundations of Ireland's fashion industry, an achievement for which they have not been given the credit they so richly deserve.

8

Marriage

Best trust the happy moments. What they gave
Makes man less fearful of the certain grave.

John Masefield, *Biography*

Dᴀᴠɪᴅ Tᴀʟʙᴏᴛ Rɪᴄᴇ came to Paris more often than any other
Oxford friend. He had become a senior scholar of Christ
Church in 1926 and, as a prehistoric archaeologist, he had been
assisting Professor Watelin in excavating the ancient site of Kish,
situated in Iraq, not far from Ur. It was not until David visited
Constantinople in 1925, on one of his return journeys from Iraq,
that, on seeing the great cathedral of Haghia Sophia, he became so
enthralled by Byzantine art that he decided to devote himself to
making its contribution to European civilization better known in
England. On his return he was able to inspire a similar passion in
Robert Byron whom he persuaded to accompany him on a visit to
Mount Athos. They aimed to produce a joint book tracing the
influence of Byzantine art on El Greco, whose works were almost
as little known to the general public in England as were the glories
of Byzantine art. Nowadays people frequently credit Robert Byron
rather than David for stimulating those interests in England. In
fact, the movement was launched by David who was too modest
and too loyal a friend ever to assert his own role. Their joint book,
The Birth of Western Painting, was not published until 1930. Their
adventures on Mount Athos had already been amusingly described
in Robert's travel book published in 1928 – called *The Station*,
because time had stopped on the holy peninsula long before their
visit.

David's enthusiasm for Byzantine art was noted by Stanley
Casson, lecturer in classical archaeology and a fellow of New

College, Oxford. Casson had fought in the First World War and supervised the burial of Rupert Brooke in Greece.* He had returned to Oxford to devote himself to the study of Greek sculpture. While archaeologists are not noted for generosity he possessed that attribute in the highest possible degree. Not only did he treat his students and assistants with great consideration but he also did his utmost to further their careers, insisting that those who worked on his excavations should sign their own contributions in reports of the season's dig.

In 1927 Stanley Casson invited David to join the team he was assembling to excavate Constantinople's hippodrome. During four months there they all became enamoured of Byzantium, David irrevocably, so he was especially delighted when Casson offered him the post of field director for the following season's work, to uncover the Baths of Zeuxippus close to the hippodrome, noted in their day for Greek and Roman sculptures. At the time it was customary for young British archaeologists on foreign excavations to have their travelling expenses refunded, to live free of charge whilst working on the site and to have unavoidable expenses covered. As field director David would be paid £30 monthly during the season of three to four months. After the season there was no payment for writing reports, or other work carried out on the finds.

Now, with this small addition to his personal income of £500 a year, David felt he could ask me to marry him. I had not expected him to do so and was overwhelmed by happiness. However, knowing his devotion to his parents and theirs to him, I feared that a marriage to a penniless foreigner would distress them.

David's middle brother, Arthur, his senior by eleven years, was a professional soldier who had fought on the Western Front throughout the First World War. He received minor wounds, and was mortally wounded on the eve of Armistice Day. He had been adored by his parents who saw him reflected in David. After graduating from Oxford in 1912 Harry, their eldest son, fifteen years older than

---

*Brooke, then serving with the RNVR, died on 23 April 1915, from pneumonia and septicaemia. He was buried the next day on Skyros, 'one of the loveliest places on this earth'. Two wooden crosses were planted on the grave. In April 1920 Casson, then Deputy Director of the British School of Archaeology in Athens, installed a monument approved by Brooke's mother, over the grave. See J. Lehmann, *Rupert Brooke: His Life and his Legend*, London, 1980, and S. Casson, *Rupert Brooke at Skyros*, London, 1921.

David, had gone on to read for the Bar, at the same time joining the East Riding of Yorkshire Yeomanry. Promoted full lieutenant in September 1914, he transferred to the Welsh Guards in July 1915, soon after it was raised. Although wounded eleven times on the Western Front he survived. He stayed on in the army and shortly before David proposed to me, married Blanche Devereux. I felt she had a double advantage over me; she was British and very comfortably off. David's parents could hardly fail to regard our intended marriage as a misalliance.

Although always courteous, they appeared reserved when I met them whilst in Broadwell. Would they, I wondered, regard me as an adventuress who had set her cap at their son? David assured me that, once they got used to the idea, I could count on their good will. And, indeed, within a surprisingly short space of time, we became extremely fond of each other, my relationship with my delightful father-in-law being particularly close. They begged us to stay at Oddington when in England, converting the butler's wing into a flat for us, but expecting us to join them for all meals. We were glad to fall in with their wishes since we were to spend most of the next three winters in Paris, David having decided to work for a doctorate at the École des Hautes Études in Paris under the supervision of Professor Gabriel Millet, western Europe's leading Byzantinist. During spring and early summer we would be in Constantinople.

Ghost, my beloved Ghost, presented our only serious obstacle. He was too old, too highly strung, to endure quarantine.* Since Mother adored him, it was agreed that he would stay with her when we were in England, and the rest of the year with us. Although the decision complicated our journeys, it enriched our lives by providing much amusement and, in Turkey, further security.

In October I set off with a quaking heart for Oddington, not as a casual visitor but as a future daughter-in-law. My nervousness increased as I neared my destination, nor were my fears set at rest by the kindness with which I was greeted for, on the following day, I was to meet my future father-in-law's Aunt Georgie. She lived almost next door, in a small dower house, and was adored by the

---

*Restrictions on the importation of dogs had been introduced in September 1897 but it was not until 1928 that a six-month quarantine was made mandatory.

family. She had never married and her terse and outspoken pronouncements had gained her a reputation for eccentricity and aggressiveness. She was one of the Dean of Gloucester's nine children and, when very young, it was her job to walk through the cathedral during evensong to feed her father's hens in the cloisters. She was noted as much for her common sense as for her habit of talking to herself and her dislike of staying away from home. Once, having been persuaded to spend a few days with close friends, she was heard to mutter, as she paced her bedroom floor, 'This is dreadful, this is dreadful, fortunately, it can't last long.'

Having been warned by David that much depended on the impression I made on Aunt Georgie I felt very nervous when I entered her small, rather dark sitting-room. Here I was confronted by a tiny, very thin, very upright, shabbily dressed figure with hair pulled back into a very tight bun. Tea was ready. Beautiful, handleless porcelain cups and a silver teapot, milk jug and sugar basin – all eighteenth century – stood on a magnificent tray. In the middle of the table was a large silver basket containing roundels resembling sliced candles.

We sat down. Aunt Georgie poured the tea. After a pause she said, 'Aren't you going to eat anything?' I could see nothing to eat, only the curious roundels. I glanced at David. He seemed puzzled. I looked at the basket: were they marzipan? Aunt Georgie's unblinking eyes were fixed on me as I tentatively took a piece, bit into it and spat it out. It was indeed candle, not marzipan. Biting back my tears I shouted angrily, 'It is uneatable, it's candle.' 'But surely Russians eat candles,' stated Aunt Georgie, 'I was always told that is what they eat.' Deeply offended, I wondered whether she was joking. We stared at each other. She blushed and looked embarrassed. Once again, I glanced at the table. The contrast between the beautiful silver and porcelain and the disgusting bit of candle on my plate struck me as so ludicrous that I dissolved into helpless laughter. My anger vanished as I struggled to regain my gravity.

On attempting to apologize I saw that Aunt Georgie was profoundly distressed. She adored David and would never have done anything to upset him. Indeed much time and effort must have gone into slicing the candles. She had genuinely believed that Russians ate them. Now she could not do enough for me. She produced delicious home-made bread, butter and jam, and some excellent cakes. When I laughed again she and David joined in. We had a happy tea party and became great friends. Indeed she was to prove a source of endless amusement, for she had inherited the common sense which prompted her father to advise a parishioner who complained that his wife turned her back on him when he got into bed with her, to get out of it and get in the other side.

When Volodia, stimulated by his love of France, applied for French naturalization, he persuaded Father to follow suit. Mother and I refused. All the same Father still kept a packed suitcase under his bed ready for the overthrow of the Bolsheviks and an immediate return to Russia. A man of unswerving honesty and uprightness, when interviewed for naturalization he said he longed to go back to his homeland. Unsurprisingly his application was refused but Volodia's was granted. That left three of us without documents, birth certificates or identity papers. It took my poor father three months to complete the formalities needed to enable David and me to marry. Volodia could not understand why I accepted British nationality when I had just refused to apply for French citizenship. Time and again I explained that, although I had not wanted to change my nationality for convenience, had I been marrying David in tsarist Russia I would have acted in the same way as now. Thirteen years later Volodia demonstrated devotion to his adopted country by joining the Maquis rather than escaping from occupied France.

During Father's struggle for the documents for my civil marriage, I was doing much the same for Ghost. Determined to save David as much trouble as possible, I went to the consulates of all the countries we were likely to visit when motoring to Constantinople on our honeymoon. At each I presented a veterinary health certificate and paid a large sum to have it stamped with impressive entry permits.

Meanwhile, having sold her last valuable brooch, Mother busied herself to provide me with a trousseau sufficiently large and varied to make it unnecessary for David to spend any money on my clothes for at least two years. I still have some of the crêpe-de-Chine lingerie and fine linen handkerchiefs exquisitely embroidered by the nuns of a neighbouring convent.

On hearing of my engagement some of the *grands couturiers* I had known when working as a fashion reporter offered me clothes as wedding presents, an offer I accepted with gratitude. Jeanne Regny decided to give me a thick wool suit for winter wear in England. Others suggested clothes for Constantinople. At the time I knew nothing about the climate there, but expected it to be like that of the Crimea. I was given only a few dresses for France and England; the rest were suitable for a hot, dry climate. All were extremely elegant.

We were bitterly disappointed when the weather became too vile for David's parents to come to Paris for my wedding on the morning of Saturday 31 December 1927. We were married by the Maire of the 16th arrondissement. He wore a tricolour sash across his chest and described our wedding as the embodiment on French soil of the triple alliance which had once united our three countries. He charged us two francs seventy-five for a *carnet de mariage* containing spaces on which to record the births of twelve children, and promised a free replacement on the birth of our thirteenth. We then rushed to collect my British passport from the embassy before it closed for the weekend. Marisha excelled herself at a family luncheon party.

David had longed for a religious wedding in a Russian church but my in-laws had set their hearts on a Church of England ceremony. I felt unable to face three weddings to the same man, so the idea of an Orthodox service was abandoned. David, however, gave me a platinum ring for the English ceremony as well as the gold ring used in Paris.

Our religious wedding took place a few days later at St Ethelburga's, the City of London's smallest church, recently destroyed by an IRA bomb. We celebrated at a very large, very delicious and lively luncheon party given by my in-laws at Brown's Hotel. We returned to Oddington with them to spend a couple of weeks there.

My engagement had delighted Miss Jones of Tan-lan. She wrote in a state of euphoria, congratulating me on grubby notepaper, tracing David's descent to the union of Owen Glendower and a fairy, I think Morgan le Fay, with the participation of Merlin. She also sent me a generous length of beautiful navy and white cloth woven by her mother years before. I had it made into a suit during the Second World War, and still treasure the skirt.

She begged me to bring David to stay. I was reluctant to accept the invitation fearing that the squalor in which she lived would disgust David. However, he was so touched that he insisted on going, maintaining that nothing in Britain could equal conditions in the Balkans, in Turkey and on Mount Athos. So before leaving England we went for a couple of days to Tan-lan.

Miss Jones smothered us with kisses. She had assembled a choir to welcome us and some old crones to dissert on David's Welsh ancestry. Unfortunately she had not cleaned either her house or her cooking utensils. Regardless of David's experiences in the Levant the dirt, the smell of stale grease, above all, the state of her frying pan were almost more than he could endure. However, his innate courtesy and warmth of heart saw him through the visit. Although determined never again to stay with Miss Jones, he became as fond of her as I.

On the way to Constantinople we drove first to Paris to stay with my parents and pick up Ghost. Whilst there we called on Professor Watelin, the director of the Kish excavations who had trained David in field work. He was benign, courteous and amusing. As we were leaving he ventured to give me a piece of advice. 'Always,' he admonished, 'always, when running an excavation, on Saturday relax and celebrate. On that evening give your team the best possible dinner and always accompany it with champagne.' I resolved to follow his advice.

Driving across France with one's ideal companion was sheer delight. David shared my love of France and our happiness was so evident that we were warmly welcomed everywhere. Sometimes we stayed in modestly priced hotels; at others in luxurious ones. Generally we had a picnic lunch but we dined in the finest regional restaurants where we were regaled with succulent dishes; so too was Ghost. We drove along the Riviera in blissful happiness. Life seemed perfect. I had not been to Italy since my childhood and remembered it as idyllic. To go again with David would only add to its enchantment.

The guards at the Italian frontier were pleasant and petted Ghost, waving aside the certificates I had purchased for the dog from the Italian consulate in Paris. We reached Genoa in good time for dinner, found a hotel, unpacked, had a bath and, with Ghost on a lead, set out to explore the town and find somewhere to dine. The main street was thronged with people. We had only taken a few steps when our elbows were gripped from behind by four *cara-binieri* who frogmarched us without a word of explanation to the police station. There they gave us the choice of having Ghost put down or paying a fine of five hundred lire for not muzzling him. They refused to read the Italian consulate's certificate or to take into account the frontier guards' failure to tell us that the dog had to be muzzled.

Rage possessed me. I yelled insults and defiance, announced that I preferred to die with my dog than pay the fine. David had never seen me in a rage and was visibly distressed; even the police were impressed. Since it was now too late to buy a muzzle they would allow me to take Ghost back to the hotel after stopping to dine on the way. I assured them that, apart from buying the muzzle and paying the hotel bill, I had no intention of spending a farthing in their town and would not dream of dining in it. They implored me to eat and so did David but I refused to be swayed so I went to bed hungry and David dined alone. Italy's spell over me was broken.

In Rome we were made much of by David's two cousins then at the embassy there.* I was able to leave Ghost in their garden when we went sightseeing. Almost the first time we did so I again came close to arrest, this time for following an officer on to a bus, not knowing that only senior military personnel could mount buses from the front, others having to use the back entrance. These unfortunate encounters with Fascist authority so unnerved me that, later that morning, when touched on the arm while engrossed in a painting, I spun round to defend myself against yet another arrest, only to be confronted by an equally startled, very frail old museum attendant who, doubtless hoping for a tip, was offering me a magnifying glass.

We disliked the atmosphere of Fascist Italy and, regardless of the imaginative way in which we were being entertained, were glad to leave Rome. We did a lot of sightseeing as we drove southward to embark at Brindisi on a small Lloyd Triestino ship destined for Constantinople via a number of ports on the way. Alastair Graham was to meet us in Athens. By then he had started on a printing course with Bernard Newdigate at Stratford-upon-Avon and had

---

*C. J. F. R. Wingfield was Counsellor and A. F. H. Wiggin First Secretary.

already produced an essay by Evelyn Waugh, quite beautifully, although with numerous misprints.* Now he had lost his heart to Greece, had learnt the language and was sharing a flat in Athens. We docked at Piraeus on a cold, grey February morning. Alastair was waiting, but before we could leave the dock we became involved in a lengthy argument with a customs official who, refusing to look at Ghost's Greek certificate, seemed determined to extract a large entrance fee from us. Alastair's excellent Greek resulted in our leaving a deposit for return on our departure.

At the time Athens was still separated from Piraeus by a long broad strip of undeveloped land cut into two by the main road. Both sections had recently been covered by miserable shanties for Greeks expelled from Turkey in 1922. Apart from Russian émigrés who, like my family, had voluntarily chosen political exile, the unfortunate Turcosized Greeks, like the equally unfortunate Hellenized Turks, were the first of many groups of unlucky people evicted from their homes in the course of our supposedly civilized century. With the Acropolis silhouetted above them against an ominous grey sky, it seemed that the miserable inhabitants of those hovels heralded the advent of another dark age, but the idea seemed so preposterous that I promptly dismissed it from my mind. With hindsight it has assumed the character of a premonition.

The sun came out as we reached the Acropolis. We had it to ourselves and the sight of that marvellously serene and self-assured group of buildings presented me with a new, entirely unexpected type of beauty which became for me a yardstick of architectural excellence. In the 1920s Athens was still an enchanting early nineteenth-century town. Most of its houses were only two-storeyed, their stucco façades often painted ochre. They stood in large gardens shaded by ancient fruit trees which provided so much fruit that their owners could make enough jam to last the winter, jam, together with a glass of ouzo and a small cup of Turkish coffee, being standard fare for even the most casual visitor. Although the town's water supply was inadequate, large private roof gardens were rife with heavily scented carnations and roses; the Zapeion Park was shaded by splendid trees.

---

*E. Waugh, *An Essay on the Pre-Raphaelite Brotherhood 1847–1853*, printed by Alastair Graham, 1926.

At Daphne, the immense oak under which Socrates was said to have sat, still stood in the middle of the road, propped up by iron supports, its trunk encircled by tables occupied by old men sipping drinks as they smoked their hubble-bubbles. The country's political situation was unstable but the attempts of various parties to overthrow whatever government happened to be in power were droll rather than sinister. The comic element in these upheavals was epitomized for us as we sat in a fashionable café in Constitution Square: a man who was relieving himself was so frightened by a sporadic exchange of fire that he wrenched away some of the protective metalwork of the pissoir for use as a shield as he ran for cover, enclosed within its protective framework.

Few foreigners other than diplomats, archaeologists and a handful of businessmen were living in Athens. The resident foreigners and native Athenians followed a similar way of life. There was impromptu dancing and singing in the tavernas at night and the gaiety was general and spontaneous. It was the Athens immortalized in the nostalgic film *Never on Sunday*, a way of life and an outlook which have ceased to exist. In the country districts there was widespread poverty yet seldom misery. The women were wise and thrifty, the men indolent, much of the lighter work being done by boys, some scarcely twelve years old. There was profound piety and an almost universal love of life. Every village seemed to have its skilled peasant potter as well as its weavers and spinners.

As we sailed away from Athens the weather rapidly worsened. When we reached the Marmara so fierce a blizzard was raging that the captain dropped anchor in order to ride out the storm. We were the only passengers and were on excellent terms with the Italian ship's officers, especially with Miro Cerno, the purser. They had arranged to celebrate the first day of Carnival that night and invited us to join them. We sat drinking sickly strega late into the night. There was much talk about their families, Italy's troubled past and nebulous future, their hopes for a renaissance under the Fascists. Whilst not altogether believing in them, they were nevertheless anxious to back the regime.

When we were finally able to sail into Constantinople's harbour, the town lay swathed in three feet of snow. From the ship's deck the view over Stamboul was breathtakingly beautiful with its large yet flattish domes and pencil-slim minarets, surely the most elegant of all minarets, rising above the white carpet against a vivid, cobalt-coloured sky. But a bitterly cold wind blew down the Bosphorus from across the Black Sea. My clothes, chosen with a warm climate in mind, were clearly inappropriate.

The certificate for Ghost issued by the Turkish consulate in Paris was accepted as valid. John Codrington, one of David's close friends, was waiting at the hotel to greet us. A Coldstreamer, he had fought through the First World War and then spent a year at Oxford before serving as ADC to the Viceroy of India. Now he was acting as liaison officer to the French Army Headquarters in Syria and had travelled from Beirut especially to meet us.* It was not until the 1930s, when we were living in Paris, that I really got to know him. By that time he had married the artist Primrose Harley and was working in the British Embassy. We often dined together, occasionally ending the evening at a satirical theatre such as the Deux Ânes or the Théâtre de Dix Bourses or, if Volodia were with us, at a night-club where Piaf was the main attraction. Already an excellent gardener John was to become later in life a professional landscape designer. During the Second World War he was in charge of British Intelligence in Gibraltar.

I was amused to notice that John's lightweight suit was as unsuited to Constantinople as my own clothes. Our hotel, like so many buildings in countries with allegedly temperate climates, was inadequately heated and John and I suffered acutely from the cold. David spent the days visiting the authorities on whose goodwill our excavation permit depended, conferring with the Ottoman Bank concerning the expedition's finance and accompanying me on house-hunting excursions. In the evenings the three of us sought the warmth of Pera's westernized night-clubs or its nicest restaur-

---

*Codrington, Lt-Col. John. Educated Harrow; Royal Military College, Sandhurst; Christ Church, Oxford. Commissioned in 1917, Codrington served in France with the 3rd Battalion Coldstream Guards. Awarded the Greek Military Cross when a liaison officer during the Greco-Turkish War. As ADC to Sir Philip Chetwode, Commander-in-Chief, India, Codrington helped design the residency gardens. Seconded to MI6 in 1936, he was recalled to the colours in 1942 and posted as Assistant Chief of Staff to Lord Gort, Governor of Gibraltar, where he was responsible for the evacuation of escapees from Vichy France. After the war he worked for Sir Alexander Korda at London Films, moving to BOAC in 1956, before finally setting himself up as a garden designer. His fees financed incessant travels and the expansion of a collection of rare plants. He was awarded a Royal Horticultural Society Gold Medal.

ant, the Turquoise, which was founded, staffed and run by Russian émigrés. Most of the girls employed in the night-clubs came from central or eastern Europe, the prettiest from Vienna or Budapest. Few possessed much talent and the atmosphere in all those establishments was seedy, the gaiety and sophistication scarcely even skin deep, the patrons chiefly fat, middle-aged Levantines with an occasional Turk taking advantage of Atatürk's westernizing reforms. However, all the night-clubs were well heated. Basil Gray, the first of David's assistants to join us, had arrived from Vienna suitably dressed in a warm, very long overcoat that almost reached his ankles. As he toiled up Stamboul's steep hills bent double, he was apt to trip over its hem. All the same it kept him warm by day and I suppose by night, whilst the three of us were obliged to thaw out in a shoddy but snug dive.

9

Constantinople

Seen from the Bosphorus at sunset, Stamboul rises like a
great cloud, silhouetted against pure gold . . . its edges are
cut into patterns of domes and minarets and cypresses,
above luminous banks of cloud.

Arthur Symons, *Cities*

AFTER signing our names in the embassy's visitors' book, we had
hurried to call both on Halil Bey, co-founder with his brother
and now director of Constantinople's Archaeological Museum,
and on Macridi Bey, the sub-director. Halil Bey was a tall, thin and
very grand elderly gentleman who dressed with the neatness of a
courtier. He was very much an autocrat, reserved and proud, with
paternalist instincts and impeccable manners but, owing perhaps
to his country's recent defeat, patriotic to the point of touchiness.
His handshake was at once elegant and an accomplished feat of
dismissal, for when he rose from his chair to take leave of a caller
he would, as he grasped his guest's hand, gently yet firmly propel
him through the door.

Although brought up at the Ottoman court, his loyalty to
Atatürk was so complete that, regardless of his wife's reluctance,
he persuaded her to discard the veil and appear in society. She too
was very much the aristocrat and almost as well educated as her
husband. Both suffered when she felt compelled to undertake official duties. As president of the Red Crescent, the Turkish equivalent of the Red Cross, she sometimes felt obliged to board the large
luxury tourist ships calling at Constantinople, to raise sorely
needed funds by selling flags. One day she and her lady-in-waiting
tried to get on to an Italian ship, but were rudely turned away.
Deeply offended, she telephoned her husband. Without a second's
hesitation, Halil ordered the immediate closure of the museum.
Astonished, we watched his instructions being carried out. More

and more cars conveying the ship's passengers converged upon the museum. Even after one hundred and fifty tourists had uttered entreaties, apologies, threats or imprecations Halil Bey was unmoved. His wife had been insulted; his museum was therefore closed to those who, if unwittingly, were associated with the offenders. Sadly and bitterly disappointed, the tourists departed, leaving us feeling profoundly grateful that Halil Bey had warmed to both David and me. In the summer, when living in his villa on the Asiatic shore of the Bosphorus, he often invited us to spend a Sunday afternoon there, proudly showing us his garden laid out in the early Ottoman tradition.

However, it was in Macridi Bey, the museum's deputy director, that we found a lifelong friend. As a Constantinopolitan Greek the senior post in the museum was closed to him, but during Halil's directorship he was happy in his work. Macridi was an experienced and clever archaeologist with a marvellous gift for improvisation, able, like the early Egyptians, to move enormous pieces of masonry with the help of little more than ropes, rollers and a pulley. He was also adept at handling men, knowing when to jolly them along and when to give orders. He was ever ready to help us and his advice was always sound.

Macridi was of average height, rotund, the possessor of a quick tongue, a keen wit and a warm heart. He loved gaiety, parties, good food and wine, and had an impish, often ribald sense of humour. He had a vast fund of anecdotes, few of them decorous but none of them lewd. Every morning and evening Macridi greeted us with naughty stories that became increasingly suggestive. Conducting the Earl and Countess of Athlone round the Serai he pointed out several ancient eunuchs, sole survivors of the sultanate, who liked to sit outside the second gate to the palace, on a very precarious high bench facing the former sultan's divan. Glancing severely at the slumped figures the countess asked, 'Mais ne font-ils rien pendant toute la journée?' 'Même pas la nuit,' Macridi heard himself answering.

Macridi's hospitality was boundless, combining the Greek gift for gaiety with the Turkish sense of the decorous. Keenly responsive to nature, he savoured a fine landscape, delighting as intensely as a Turk in the beauty of a single, perfectly formed flower or in the pure water of an unpolluted upland stream. After Halil Bey's death, life became difficult for the Macridis in Turkey and they reluctantly decided to migrate to Athens where Macridi gladly and gratefully accepted the curatorship of the newly founded Benaki Museum.

At the start of our first season's work in Constantinople, we rented a house for all eight of us* at Ortakoy, a village on the European shore of the Bosphorus some fifteen miles from our site. The house had a splendid view across the water to Asia and a back garden leading to a barren, rocky hillside where Ghost could have his daily run. Never having kept house before I engaged two Russian émigré ex-officers, one as cook, the other as houseman. I told them to serve breakfast and luncheon punctually, explaining that we had to reach our excavations by seven-thirty and had only one hour off for lunch. Dinner could be more flexible in its timing.

All too soon I ran into difficulties. I had never before catered for more than four; now, including our ex-officers, there were ten to feed on a daily allowance of two Turkish lire a head. The more we spent on food the less we had for excavating. David was determined that I should keep inside my allowance. As I struggled to shop in a language I hardly knew, I thought bitterly of Watelin's menu for Saturday's champagne dinners. The most I could manage was an austere Sunday picnic.

Yet I had an even greater problem; the inability of our ex-officers to produce breakfast and luncheon on time. Our cook always had an excuse for being late, one which sounded improbable yet seemed convincing. When I was shopping or working on the dig or exploring Stamboul by myself I ruminated over those excuses and began increasingly to doubt our cook's Munchausen-like experiences. Finally, in desperation, I consulted Macridi. Surprised by my innocence and also much amused he asked whether I could not recognize a hashish addict when I met one. Nicholas's excuses were his hallucinations. At the time I knew nothing about drug addiction, nor had I ever before given anyone notice. Now David insisted that I should do so. Summoning both ex-officers I once again asked if

---

*In addition to David and Tamara the staff included G. F. Hudson, Fellow of All Souls College; Basil Gray; and C. Beazley who was responsible for the archaeological drawings. Stanley Casson arrived towards the end of the four-month season. See *2nd Report upon the Excavations carried out in and near the Hippodrome at Constantinople in 1928 on behalf of the Royal Academy*, London, 1929.

they really could not contrive to serve two meals a day on time. No, they answered, and we parted with great sadness.

Macridi replaced our Russians with two Turkish women. Both lived in. The cook was elderly, wore baggy trousers which had been traditional in Ottoman times and, although forbidden by law to wear the yashmak, refused to allow any man to enter her kitchen when she was unveiled. She was also imbued with the Turkish aversion to dogs and hated Ghost. Probably sensing her dislike, Ghost developed the habit of entering the kitchen, seating himself upright in a corner and fixing his eyes unblinkingly on her. His behaviour upset her but she endured it whilst ceaselessly muttering imprecations against him. The maid, Fatma, was fat, young and indolent, but she was amiable and not unbearably slovenly. Somehow we managed to rub along and life became easier.

Domestic calm was only slightly ruffled when Basil Gray, back from an interview with the British Museum Appointments Board, found that his cherished Russian silver cigarette case had vanished from his bedroom. Suspicion rested on Fatma but I refused to allow her to be questioned and blamed Basil for leaving the cigarette case lying about. He behaved admirably; accepted my decision and never mentioned the loss again. A fortnight later, on pay day, whilst driving us to work, David realized that he had forgotten his letter of credit. After dropping us at the dig he hurried back to collect it. Flinging open the door to our bedroom, he found Fatma shaving her armpits with his razor. It was more than he could endure. He sacked her on the spot. The other woman walked out and by dinner I once again had no staff.

Next morning Macridi contrived to provide me with a Greek couple who were to prove more satisfactory. However they had a three-year-old child who, unconsciously aping Ghost, quickly developed the habit of quietly sidling into whichever room we were all sitting in. She then stood in a corner sucking her thumb whilst staring intently at us. This enraged us as much as Ghost's stare had infuriated our Turkish cook. However, we managed to control our feelings and the Greek couple stayed until our season ended.

We employed four hundred men on our dig. At the request of the governor of Istanbul's prison some were convicts serving life sentences for murders, generally committed in the heat of passion. We never had the slightest difficulty with any of them. They seemed to work even harder than their very hard-working colleagues. They were released on day parole and, as they were under oath not to attempt an escape, none ever did. They were touchingly grateful for their few hours of liberty and the chance to earn money to buy tobacco and other small luxuries. Furthermore, in the Turkish style, every morning one of them would offer me the most perfect single flower they could find.

All our workmen wanted to please but the work was new to them, and some were much slower in acquiring the knack than were the Arabs whom David was used to directing. Although Turkey had recently become a secular state most of our men were practising Muslims and strict observers of the Ramadan fast. Then they won our admiration by working as hard as ever, without even moistening their lips, although their thirst usually kept our water carriers busy.

In accordance with Turkish regulations a commissar, always a local minor government official, was attached to our dig, chiefly to ensure that we did not walk off with any of the finds. All our commissars were friendly and helpful. They spent most of the day dozing in a deck-chair, a newspaper covering their faces, but eventually on David's advice the post went to one of the museum's younger restorers. Macridi dropped in several times a day, as did Mamboury, a Swiss who taught at the French Lycée and was a keen amateur archaeologist and author of an enlightening if disorganized guidebook on Constantinople.* Some ten years later one of his pupils, then a schoolboy, Cyril Mango, now an eminent Byzantine scholar, became a regular visitor.

Turkish humour did not always coincide with ours. The disparity was especially marked when one of our barrow boys thought it would be funny to tip a load of rubble over a little Armenian hunchback working below him at the bottom of a trench seven metres deep. The victim seemed badly hurt, with a deep cut on one side of his face yet he refused to let us drive him to a doctor. Our workmen sided with him but were genuinely concerned at his condition. They busily pooled their tobacco while I was trying to disinfect his gash, but before I was ready to bandage him they had applied a tobacco poultice, assuring me the treatment would prove satisfactory. When I drove the victim back to his house, two workmen accompanied me to ensure that I did not stop at a doctor. To our

---

*E. Mamboury, *Constantinople: Tourists' Guide*, Constantinople, 1925.

astonishment the man was back at work the next morning, with the wound looking clean and almost healed.

In 1927 Stanley Casson had been given his excavation permit on condition that he would at the end of the season fill in the excavated areas to their present-day level. In 1928 the same condition was imposed on David. The ruins we uncovered there with their sculptured columns and architectural fragments were so impressive that David tried to persuade the authorities to designate the area an archaeological park. This was to stretch from the entrance to Haghia Sophia to the Blue Mosque. He pointed out that the area could become as much of a tourist attraction as the Forum at Rome, but even Atatürk turned down the suggestion. David persisted, but it was not until 1938 that he got a five-year concession to excavate the whole site. The Second World War intervened and when Allied prospects of winning seemed, to foreign observers, remote, the concession was disregarded and several small houses rose on the site. Their concrete foundations penetrate to the Byzantine levels; this makes it impossible ever fully to excavate an area which had formed part of the Great Palace of the Byzantine Emperors. The importance of that lost opportunity can to some extent be assessed by studying the exquisite floor mosaic at the base of the hill on which the Sultan Ahmed mosque stands.

When helping to uncover it I was touched to find that the earth at the centre of a peristyle consists, to the depth of a metre, of fine loam brought there to make a garden, a small, seemingly unimportant detail which illuminates the humanism of the Justinian age. I scraped away at the hard pink cement spread over the mosaic in the eighth century to form a base for a pavement of white marble slabs. It thrilled me to think that the brave and beautiful Theodora* could have walked on the pavement we were so laboriously uncovering, indeed she could even have commissioned it.

In the fifties,† when excavating near the mosaic pavement, we

---

*Wife of Justinian (AD 482–565), the Roman emperor and builder of Haghia Sophia.
† In 1951 David and Tamara went to Istanbul for a reconnoitre. Excavations were carried out over the next three years directed, when David was absent, by J. B. Ward Perkins from the British School in Rome. Work stopped when nothing further could be done without the destruction of the streets and houses now covering the site. Nevertheless a large part of the mosaic pavement had been uncovered. See D. T. Rice (ed.), *The Great Palace of the Byzantine Emperors*, 2nd Report of the Walker Trust, Edinburgh, 1958.

uncovered some impressive late Roman-early Byzantine sub-structures. The earlier ones were built of large blocks of beautifully dressed stone. The later ones, of brick, still retained beautifully vaulted ceilings and one undamaged, admirably proportioned chamber was filled with jars containing apricots perfectly preserved in syrup. The discovery thrilled our men. 'Byzantine apricots,' they yelled, 'Byzantine apricots'; but, alas, the jars were modern.

Whilst we were trying to curb the men's excitement, an elderly gentleman appeared looking embarrassed. He explained that he owned the garden with its prolific fruit-trees. His father had sold his surplus fruit to Hadji Bakir, the Sultan's sweetmeat maker, and stored the remainder in his cellars. Our man also used the cellars in this way, and as they connected with our chamber, he had been in the habit of using it for overflow. He laid no claim to it and would vacate it instantly. We assured him that he could go on using it because we would soon be re-burying it. Relieved, he persuaded us and our children to visit his garden. His father's body lay interred in a mausoleum in a corner of his house. Our host led us past it and across his large, slightly neglected garden, heavily scented with large, flower-laden rose bushes, to a semi-derelict, exquisite six-teenth-century kiosk with a magnificent view of Leander's Tower, the Marmara and Turkey's Asiatic shore.

When we were seated he clapped his hands and a maiden appeared. She was told to bring some apricot juice. She returned carrying a tray with a jug of juice and five glasses ranging from very large to minute. We thought of Goldilocks and the three bears as our host handed David the largest, and gave the rest of us each a glass of appropriate size. The apricot juice tasted delicious but was very filling. However, we had to accept a second round, although it tasted oversweet. The third round, pressed on us regardless of refusals, proved difficult to swallow. Our hospitable neighbour became a fast friend, and when we left Istanbul at an inconveniently early hour, he was waiting at the airport to bid us farewell and present us with an enormous, oozing jar of apricot juice and a huge bouquet of fragrant, overblown roses.

To return to 1928: after dismissing our workmen at five every evening and completing the entries in our log-books, David and I used to hurry to the covered bazaar to visit dealers in certain antique and junk shops. We chatted with them, examined their more recent acquisitions and were offered a glass of coffee or tea. David was assembling a study collection of Byzantine pottery which, because of our financial limitations, consisted mostly of fragments. However, when examined in conjunction with the pottery found during our excavations, our collection enabled him to compile the first book on the subject.[*]

Occasionally I could afford one of the many icons which had been acquired by Turkish dealers when Turkey and Greece exchanged their minority populations. Bill Allen, an Eton friend of David's, who had been so anxious to meet me that he had travelled out from England to stay with us, bought many more icons than I could.[†] Although he was later obliged to sell some of them, he presented the finest to the National Gallery of Ireland in memory of his Russian wife, Natasha Muratova.[‡]

Bill was to become one of our dearest friends but, to begin with, I was disconcerted by the mischievous twinkle in his eyes and his almost inaudible mutter delivered in an Irish accent. I very soon discovered that he was the most accomplished practical joker of our generation. Some of his pranks were very funny, some rather unkind. He was asked to leave Eton at the age of sixteen not because of a misdemeanour but because his housemaster had been riled beyond endurance by his latest joke, the sending to *The Times* of a letter in his housemaster's name asking whether cows ate partridges. A great many replies awaited the unfortunate man on his return to Eton for the start of the new half. Within three months of being expelled Bill had written a small book, *The Turks in Europe*,[§] which can still be read with advantage. However, his *History of the Georgian People*[#] assures him a permanent place amongst the foremost scholars of Trans Caucasia.

---

[*]D. T. Rice, *Byzantine Glazed Pottery*, Oxford, 1930.
[†]Allen, William Edward David, OBE, FSA. Educated Eton. Chairman, David Allen & Sons Ltd 1925–70. Served in the Life Guards in the Middle East and Africa 1940–2 (mentioned in despatches). Press Attaché Beirut 1943–4, Ankara 1945. Member of the Institute of Archaeology, Ankara 1951–67.
[‡]She died in 1966. David and Tamara catalogued the icons presented to Dublin, see *Icons: The Natasha Allen Collection Catalogue*, Dublin, 1968.
[§]W. E. D. Allen, *The Turks in Europe: A Sketch-Study*, London, 1919.
[#]W. E. D. Allen, *History of the Georgian People: from the Beginning down to the Russian Conquest in the Nineteenth Century*, London, 1932.

From 1928 until the depression of the early 1930s our work in Constantinople was financed jointly by Sir Philip Sassoon and Lord Duveen. During those years the British ambassador to Turkey still spent most of the year in Constantinople, visiting Ankara, the country's new capital, only at intervals. His embassy was admirably sited in the heart of the Pera; the Golden Horn and much of old Stamboul spread out behind, and its grounds stretched down the hill almost to Galata. The house had been built early in the nineteenth century by members of the Levant Company, descendants of the Ancient Company of Turkey Merchants, in a splendid early Victorian architecture. Its main staircase was sufficiently broad and well-proportioned to endow its entrance with an air of magnificence. Its ballroom was palatial, its main dining-room stately, its architectural decorations graceful but also dignified. Today, the once-splendid winter embassy has lost most of its glory, its interior having been divided into two flats and several offices.

Sir George Clerk became ambassador to Turkey in 1926. He met Stanley Casson and David in the following year and, taking to both of them, was quick to welcome David and me and to add us to his list of regular guests. His wife, the ambassadress, born Muriel Whitwell but insisting on being called Jane, became a close friend.* She was tall and elegant. The bone structure of her face was beautiful, but her lovely, deep-set eyes often reflected unhappiness. She disliked the diplomat's social round which was particularly circumscribed in Turkey where it consisted almost entirely of fellow diplomats and Turkish civil servants and officials. The wives of the latter were so unaccustomed to public life that they sat in silence, either ranged along the drawing-room walls or congregating in small, self-contained groups.

Jane was a talented – I believe largely self-taught – painter and sculptress. When the Clerks were transferred to Paris she aroused

---

*Clerk, Rt. Hon. Sir George Russell, PC, GCMG, CB. Educated Eton; New College, Oxford. Entered the Foreign Office 1899. Special Delegate of Supreme Council of Peace Conference on Missions to Bucharest and Budapest 1919. Appointed Ambassador in Turkey in 1926, a country to which he had been posted in 1910, as First Secretary. Subsequently Ambassador at Brussels and at Paris. In 1908 he married Janet Muriel (Jane) Whitwell, later, particularly in Paris, a successful artist who exhibited at the Jeu de Paume alongside Bonnard and Derain. An exhibition of her paintings at the Lefèvre Gallery in London in April 1937 included portraits of the Prince of Wales and the French prime minister, Léon Blum, and designs for the ballet *Spirit of Youth*, executed in 1933.

considerable resentment among the British community by renting a studio for herself on the left bank of the Seine, escaping there whenever possible both to paint and to entertain her friends, amongst them Chagall.

Some of Sir George's colleagues underestimated his achievements in Turkey, perhaps basing their views on his physical resemblance to a stage diplomat. Yet in the difficult post-war years it was largely due to the respect Atatürk felt for Sir George that the anti-British feeling, so intense in Turkey in the early 1920s, had almost dissipated by the end of the decade. When visiting Ankara, Sir George was frequently obliged to spend an evening with the Ghazi. He came to dread those sessions, for each of Atatürk's guests was expected to consume at least one bottle of whisky as they sat and conversed. Small wonder the occasions gave him agonizing headaches.

Jane discovered she had curative powers almost by chance. One such evening she tried to ease her husband's pain by massaging his head. To their mutual astonishment within minutes his headache lifted. As her treatment never failed to cure him they gradually came to think that others should have access to her healing powers. Her first attempts to help friends were tentative. Success soon spread and she seldom dared reject appeals for help, but she resented the time devoted to them. Both Clerks are unfairly criticized in *The Paris Embassy** by Lady Gladwyn. She states that Lady Clerk sometimes enlivened embassy evenings by playing games such as musical chairs. Although we never saw this happen she might well have done so, not only to relieve her boredom but also to conceal the fact that her relations with her husband were by then very strained.

Sir George was good-looking but short, dapper in a stagy way, aloof and impatient. He entertained on a large scale, seemingly more out of a sense of duty than by inclination. Although very conventional, he was irritated when long lunches delayed him from afternoon cruises on the *Makook*, the embassy's aged yet seaworthy launch so, at all but the most formal of luncheons, he had the first two courses served simultaneously, a footman handing an

---

*Cynthia Gladwyn, *The Paris Embassy*, London, 1976. Her husband was Ambassador in Paris 1954–60.

egg dish from the left, while a bowl of consommé appeared on the right. When lunching at the embassy for the first time I surprised my host by refusing the soup. He insisted I had both and promised to take me up the Bosphorus on the *Makook* as soon as the other guests had left. That was the first of many delightful excursions on the dear old launch. On Sundays we went further afield, often to Chalki, where William Bulwer, when ambassador to the Porte, had built an amazing dressed-stone mansion in the Victorian castellated style; here, according to local tradition, he kept his *houris*.

The Clerks seldom gave a ball, but when they did, it was superb. The grandest was held in honour of the King's birthday. Then the embassy was seen in all its splendour, the magnificent ballroom ablaze with lights, the majesty of the great staircase enhanced by footmen in picturesque Albanian costume. The band was made up of Russian émigrés and central European musicians who delighted in playing the Viennese waltzes to which Sir George, David and I enjoyed dancing. Both Sir George and David waltzed marvellously at a very quick tempo. Sir George held his partner well away from himself in the nineteenth-century style while David held his partner close, reversing no less skilfully but occupying more than his fair share of the centre of the ballroom. Their pleasure in the waltz reminded me of the zest with which, back in Russia, my young uncles had danced the mazurka and *krakoviak*, and Mother the tango. As I whirled round the Constantinopolitan ballroom, the past blended so easily into the present that there were giddy moments when I hardly knew where I was.

During my first and David's second season in Constantinople we formed closer ties of friendship with Geoffrey Knox than with the Clerks.* As councillor to the embassy Geoffrey was obliged to live in Ankara, the country's new capital, visiting Constantinople only

---

*Knox, Sir Geoffrey George, KCMG. Educated Malvern College; Trinity College, Cambridge. A natural linguist, at university Knox studied oriental languages. His first Foreign Service posting was to Persia. In 1915 he was seconded to Salonika to assist with the increased volume of work at the consulate resulting from the war. An amusing newspaper cutting headed 'Epicure of the Saar', probably printed when he was Chairman of the Saar Governing Commission, reports the complaints of a German newspaper that Knox 'liked French cooking better than German and had a library of French books', and must therefore be pro-French. The books were, the readers are told, a collection of Voltaire first editions. And the Germans are reassured that, even if he preferred French food, he appreciated German wines!

to report to the ambassador. At this time his residence in Ankara consisted of a small villa in the grounds where Britain's future embassy was being built. We met him soon after our arrival in Constantinople, and got on so well that he invited us to stay in Ankara where he proved to be a perfect host. Although our first visit lasted only a few days, he had transformed his store-room into a delightful private sitting-room for us, distributing his vintage wines, delicious Fauchon goodies and Androuet cheeses among his cupboards and outbuildings. More than that, he introduced us to the Turkish archaeologists and officials most likely to help us, and also to the most delightful members of Atatürk's circle, men such as Edip Bey, deputy for Constantinople, or Rushen Eshref, the poet who was later to become Turkey's ambassador to London.

Rushen was handsome, amusing and cultivated, a talented poet and distinguished scholar, the first Turk to translate Virgil into Turkish, and prime originator of his country's Latin alphabet, the introduction of which virtually banished illiteracy within a matter of months. I shall never forget the pride with which a previously illiterate Istanbul cobbler wrote out an order form only a few weeks after the launch of the new alphabet. Rushen's wife was as attractive and as sophisticated, cultivated and amusing as her husband. Both took immense delight in Geoffrey Knox's wonderful cuisine and in his erudition.

Edip Bey was lively and more outgoing than Rushen. Although no scholar he was well educated and fully versed in all aspects of Ottoman culture. He too savoured the good life and possessed an unusually keen sense of humour. Although short and fat he was surprisingly active. Like some mountain goat, he used to scale steep hills to reach remote villages in which peasant musicians and elderly, illiterate bards would entertain us for several hours. Edip saw nothing admirable in his efforts to ensure the survival of this rich heritage of folklore; he took more pride in inventing a cocktail consisting of ¼ whisky, ¼ brandy and ¼ raki, finished off with cointreau and orange juice.

As he thought nothing of drinking a bottle of whisky in one evening he was dismayed when Atatürk decided to send him to Mecca. He found the prospect so awful that he tried several times to cajole the Ghazi into changing his mind, a thing which Atatürk was seldom prepared to do. Finally, tiring of Edip's efforts, the

Ghazi resorted as so often to a parable, reminding Edip of the good sense shown by the Nazreddin Hodça's donkey when, the load on its back having caught fire, the beast saved itself by plunging into a village pond.* The analogy was not lost on Edip. A few weeks later he set out sadly for Mecca wearing his bowler hat.

---

*Nazreddin Hodça, a character in Turkish folklore, was usually accompanied by his grey donkey. Hodça was mouthpiece for many wise sayings such as 'Listen a hundred times, ponder a thousand times, speak once.'

10

In the Turkish Interior

There are few spots on earth richer in picturesque beauty, or
abounding in a more luxuriant vegetation.

G. Finlay, of Trebizond

THE economic crisis of the late twenties and early thirties forced
Sir Philip Sassoon and Lord Duveen to stop financing our
excavations. However, Rudolph Messel, an Oxford friend and a
cousin of Oliver, offered to replace them on a more modest scale.
His generosity enabled us over several seasons to tackle some small
trial excavations in Constantinople on Byzantine sites such as the
Church of the Murelion. He also offered to defray a more ambitious expedition in eastern Turkey which, following the Latin conquest of Constantinople in 1204 in the wake of the Fourth Crusade,
became the independent kingdom of Trebizond. It survived as such
until 1461, eight years after the fall of Byzantium to the Ottoman
Turks.

In 1929, we travelled with Ghost to Constantinople in that most
delectable and romantic of trains, the Orient Express. At the time
no one dreamt of changing for dinner, let alone dressing up for a
journey which became increasingly informal the further east it
went. Nevertheless wagon-lit passengers luxuriated under the care
of sleeping-car attendants in distinctive brown uniforms. Stops at
major stations allowed Ghost the exercise he needed. Dining-car
meals were enjoyable, especially in France where they were of five-
star quality. On arrival in Paris we were torn between leaving the
train for a memorable farewell party at the Gare de Lyon or staying
on board for a Lucullan meal as the train circled the capital. Food
was excellent in Austria and palatable in Hungary but after
Budapest it steadily deteriorated – but that too was fun. The scene

from the train's windows was always more fascinating than even the most exciting book. Throughout central Europe most country people still wore national costume. In Hungary gaily dressed women and children drove about in carts harnessed to splendidly caparisoned galloping horses. Even when natural vegetation was replaced in central Europe by tract after tract of maize, the flat expanses and distant horizons still fascinated me.

At Nish in then Yugoslavia the train divided; part for Turkey, part for Greece. When the Cassons first went to Constantinople Joan had been unaware of this. Early one morning, the lavatory at the end of their compartment being occupied, she crossed into the next car. The train stopped just as she was about to pull the plug. So Joan decided to stay put until the train moved on. Meanwhile Stan and David, both of whom shared Volodia's passion for pacing station platforms, proceeded to explore Nish station. When they returned to their compartments Joan was missing. Just in time Stan realized what had happened. With only minutes to spare they found her patiently waiting in a carriage earmarked for Athens.

After spending only a few days in Constantinople we embarked for Trebizond on the loveliest ship in Turkey's Black Sea merchant fleet. Our cabin was pleasant, the food good, the stewards friendly – especially towards Ghost whose appearance intrigued them, Alsatians being as yet unknown in Turkey. Trebizond was then off the tourist route: the odd traveller disembarked there for a day or two before proceeding to Erzerum by the then difficult road through the Zigana Pass; a tortuous and steep route which, even though engineered by Swiss technicians, was often partly washed away by melting snows. However, hazel-nut buyers for Cadbury stayed several weeks. Unattracted by living conditions in the town's hotel, they preferred to lodge at the Pension Suisse, a small establishment run by a Mrs Polycandriotis, a Swiss lady married to a Greek who, because of her nationality, had been allowed to stay on in the Pontus when other Greek families were deported. At her death her son moved to Athens where he opened a small pension still patronized by many archaeologists.

The Trebizond Pension Suisse had no bath but it was clean, well run and the plain food carefully cooked. Since Mrs Polycandriotis was glad to welcome Ghost, we took a front bedroom facing a large, barren enclosure. At dawn on our first morning we were woken by an unfamiliar noise. As in Robert Curzon's day, the empty space became a caravanserai for the camel trains which had for centuries plied over many a weary Asiatic mile, with goods for shipment from Trebizond's once busy port.* This particular caravan, one of the last to travel the route, had arrived during the night.

The only other long-term resident in the Pension Suisse was a former German U-boat commander engaged in building a hydraulic electricity station in Trebizond's outskirts. He had torpedoed several British ships in the course of the First World War before being sunk himself. He was now very sad and disillusioned. A kind and industrious man, he was so patriotic that he incessantly grieved over Germany's defeat. At night he sustained his spirit by contemplating his commander's cap, sword and Iron Cross – the sole adornments of his bedroom. A few days before our arrival he had adopted an orphaned baby bear which he put in a cage in the garden. He fed it on honey, which was easy to buy, and milk, which was much scarcer. Our efforts to keep him supplied with milk broke down his enmity, and he began to take an interest in our work and the region's antiquities. Ghost and the little brown bear became quite fond of one another, but Ghost caught so many repulsive ticks from him that we had to keep them apart.

Ghost's wolf-like appearance astonished the town's inhabitants who constantly asked us whether he was wolf or dog. Possibly owing to Ghost's presence, news of our arrival quickly spread through the town. On our very first day Ihsan Nemli Zade, the son of the local grandee, called with an invitation to meet his father. The Nemli Zades were such an ancient Turkish family that they were among the very few Osmanlis to possess a surname, a convenience which Atatürk was soon to impose on all his subjects, giving them the fun of inventing their surnames. In a street bearing their name, the Nemli Zades lived in a handsome stone mansion with a garden noted for magnificent trees and exuberantly abundant, gloriously scented roses. Following Ottoman custom the mansion was in two identical sections, the *selamlik* or men's quarters, and the *haremlik* or ladies' wing. The air in both was scented with a

---

*Described in the Hon. Robert Curzon, *Armenia: A Year at Erzeroom and on the Frontiers of Russia, Turkey and Persia*, London, 1854.

delicious compound of sweet-smelling flowers, dogs, guns and old leather typical of old country houses in both Russia and England.

Ihsan lived with his widower father and young sister. He had completed his education at the universities of Stamboul and Zurich; spoke fluent English, French and German; and was so ardent an Anglophile that he delighted in reading *The Times*. He became a close friend. In contrast his father belonged to the old Islamic culture and spoke only Turkish, Arabic and Persian. The old gentleman was very much a patrician, reserved to the point of haughtiness, strong-willed to the point of obstinacy, yet his affability and kindliness were heart-warming and courtesy and hospitality boundless. Even during our first visit he suggested that I should meet his daughter. Atatürk having by then insisted on the emancipation of women, I was surprised when a maid appeared to conduct me to the *haremlik*. Ihsan's sister was young, beautiful and cultivated. She spoke French almost as fluently as her brother, was widely read, yet she complied willingly with her father's insistence that she should lead a secluded life, veiled in the presence of men, seldom leaving the house and never doing so unaccompanied. I visited her only rarely, fearing to complicate her life by the importance I attached to personal independence.

The port of Trebizond was still important enough to warrant the presence throughout the summer of several Western consulates. When we arrived the British consul had yet to return to his winter duties at Mersin. However, our presence was of little interest to him; he offered us tea, but not the hospitality of his bathroom. The local authorities were much more helpful, especially the police and shopkeepers. The population was predominantly of Lazi origin. However, the Greeks had been there almost as long. From the eleventh century onwards the inhabitants had been augmented by Armenians and Georgians. During the fifteenth century, Turks settled on the coast, pushing the earlier Christian residents into the hinterland. In our day the Muslim population had been increased by refugees from the Caucasus and southern Russia who had abandoned their homelands because of the Soviet Government's anti-religious policy.

We quickly made friends with a carpet dealer from the bazaar who had fled to Turkey to practise his Muslim faith. He too was a man of the old school, devout, imbued with a fair measure of

Islamic philosophy, hospitable, contemplative, yet astute, equally ready to haggle and strike a good deal. His large stock included two lovely carpets. We argued amicably over their price whilst sipping their owner's tea and discussing world affairs. It was a pleasant way to make a purchase and it became a regular evening occupation, almost a game, with the financial gap between us narrowing daily.

The conquering Ottomans had converted the most ancient and finest of Trebizond's churches into mosques, although the surviving Christians had continued to worship in the smaller of the churches. In 1923, in accordance with clauses in the Treaty of Lausanne, the minority population of Greek Christians was expelled from its ancient Turkish homeland.* Most of the churches were still standing at the time of our first visit to Trebizond, many pressed into service as barns, storehouses, carpenters' shops and the like. The finest, those converted into mosques, still flourished. The most important, originally the Byzantine church of the Golden-headed Virgin (the Chrysokephalos), standing in the centre of the old town, ranked as the town's cathedral mosque. It was therefore difficult for infidels to visit, and even today no one knows whether the glass mosaic panel, its chief glory in Byzantine times, survives under Ottoman plaster.

Before the Second World War its Muslim congregation took good care of the former Byzantine cathedral of St Demetrios but its interior walls had begun to fall, exposing the fine quality of its masonry, and this showed that its original mural decoration had completely disappeared.

Original frescos seemed more likely to have survived in the former cathedral of St Sophia at the western extremity of the town. It was converted into a mosque at the conquest and was still used as such by the local fishermen. When he visited Trebizond in the nineteenth century, Finlay had noticed traces of Byzantine murals exposed by fallen plaster. After the Russians took the town in 1916 Professor Uspensky noted damage to the floor and the loss of some

---

*One of the provisions of the Treaty of Lausanne, 1923, which settled post-war European arrangements with Turkey, was the exchange of the large Greek population of eastern Thrace and western Anatolia with the Turkish population in northern Greece and Greek Macedonia. This involved the compulsory uprooting of 1¼ million Greeks and almost as many Turks. The Greeks involved were Christian but their language was Turkish, though written in a Greek script. The repatriated Turks spoke Greek, written in a Turco-Arabic script, but were Muslims by belief.

of the murals seen by Finlay. For this, local residents, probably unfairly, blamed the conquering Russians, claiming they had used the cathedral as a stable. By the time we arrived, the portrait of the founder had disappeared but, on scouting, there was enough evidence of surviving paintings – and especially of the building's magnificent *opus sectile* mosaic floor* which remained *in situ* – for us to long to uncover them. However, in 1929, there was no hope of our obtaining permission, and it was not until 1957 that we were able to get to work on them. The restoration of these thirteenth-century paintings has put Trebizond on the tourist map.†

Rose Macaulay was among the first to visit Turkey for its art.‡ She arrived in Istanbul in 1954 when we were uncovering the mosaic pavement in the Great Palace of the Byzantine Emperors. Currency restrictions were still in force in England§ and although Rose Macaulay's standing as a writer should have secured her an adequate allowance, her innate modesty and frugality had led her to ask for only £250 – which even for her was not enough.

On reaching Istanbul Rose Macaulay had asked the embassy to name a modest hotel. She was recommended to the Alp where I was staying, having come out ahead of David to prepare for our excavations. The embassy telephoned to ask me to look after her. I admired her books and welcomed the thought of meeting her, yet the request made me uneasy for two reasons: first I was very busy, second I felt slightly embarrassed at meeting her because her latest book, *Pleasure of Ruins*, contained a chapter on Justinian's house.#

---

*The figural patterns of the mosaic are made of stones cut to the required shape instead of being built up by many small cubes.

† The project was financed by the Russell Trust. Work continued for the next five years. The results are described in D. T. Rice (ed.), *The Church of Hagia Sophia at Trebizond*, Edinburgh, 1968.

‡ Her impressions of Turkey were mixed: 'It was cruelly hot . . . as a woman she was forbidden to bathe in the Black Sea; she stayed in a room "not fit for a goat".' But she was 'fascinated' by the old city of Trebizond. See J. Emery, *Rose Macaulay: A Writer's Life*, London, 1991, p. 313.

§Allowances, imposed in 1945, fluctuated between £25 and £100 per annum, although for fifteen months from the autumn of 1947 no foreign currency was permitted. For the twelve months from November 1953 the allowance was £25.

#The House of Justinian, a Byzantine building overlooking the sea, had originally been part of a large palace complex. About half the brick façade of the loggia is preserved, with marble door frames opening on to a narrow balcony overhanging the sea. It was excavated in 1953 by J. B. Ward Perkins and G. V. Spencer Corbett. See D. T. Rice (ed.), *The Great Palace of the Byzantine Emperors*, 2nd Report, Edinburgh, 1958.

Although we had examined the house the year before and I had had every intention of reading the book, I had yet to do so.

When we met for dinner that evening conversation did not flow. After a time I muttered that I was glad that she had included Justinian's house in her last book. Silence followed. Annoyed, I looked up and was appalled to find her face turning a deep crimson. I too started to blush. I was about to confess that I had not read the book when Rose Macaulay began tremulously to explain that she had never done such a thing before, had never, never until now, written about a place she had not first visited. The enormity of her pretence in this one instance had haunted her so much that she had come to Turkey chiefly in order to see Justinian's house. Would I take her to it, first thing in the morning, she asked. It was the last thing I wanted, as I wished David to arrive before meeting the fishermen living at the foot of the cliff, under the building whose ruins they had helped us to survey. However it was impossible to refuse, and after I too had confessed to my deception we felt at ease.

Rose Macaulay was a keen, very fast walker, but she came to detest walking in Istanbul where the pavements are narrow, uneven and encumbered with slow pedestrians of all ages, and by camels laden with anything from a box to a grand piano. Nor could she understand that the buses followed a circular route, so that even when she entered one bearing the right number, she often found herself miles from her destination. However we had no difficulty in reaching Justinian's house. The fishermen immediately scaled the cliff and surrounded me in an excited throng. Suddenly the headman pointed seaward, finger to his lips, imposing silence. There, poised on top of a tall, fragile column on one side of a large window embrasure which had lost its lace-like capital, sat Rose Macaulay happily looking across the Marmara into Asia. We knew the façade was unsafe. I was terrified. 'Go on talking,' hissed the village elder. He then crept towards the column and, flinging his arms round Miss Macaulay's waist, pulled her backward on to the ground. She was furious; so was I. Glasses of tea from the fisher-folk soon restored peace, and Rose apologized and expressed a desire to bathe. Here was another set-back. Although she had her bathing suit in her bag, I was obliged to point out that she could only bathe in an enclosure reserved for that purpose. She was profoundly disappointed.

When travelling in country buses the locals asked many personal questions which she much resented. I assured her that she would have to answer them with a good grace. Some weeks later I could not resist asking whether there had been any that had especially irritated her. Yes, she said, three. One man wanted to know whether her teeth were her own. Another enquired whether she was married. When she said no, he asked why. I had to admit that although the last two questions were common enough, as far as I knew the first was rare indeed.

To revert to 1929 and Trebizond, Ihsan often accompanied us on excursions into the town's outskirts, including the ruined Armenian monastery of Kaimakli perched on a steep crag over-looking the Degirmendere valley, a picturesque and evocative ruin – now a wreck. So little survives of its dressed-stone walls that it is well nigh impossible to appreciate the quality of its masonry or the daring of its architect.

Deeper into the interior stands the great monastery of Sumela, an imperial Byzantine foundation renowned for its piety. From the twelfth century onwards the industry and devotion of its monks, its architecture and the magnificence of its church furnishings had attracted pilgrims from the entire Orthodox world. However at the exchange of the minority populations its inmates had been deported to Greece, treasure hunters had made off with most of its fittings, its chapels had been desecrated, its buildings sacked and left to collapse.

In the 1970s the Turkish Tourist Board regretted its destruction and rebuilt as much of Sumela's outer walls as possible, turning into a road the track linking it to the Trebizond–Erzerum highway. In 1929 we had been obliged to leave our car at the junction of the two and walk seven kilometres along a stony path, trodden since Byzantine times by countless monks and pilgrims. We then reached the bottom of a great cliff with the monastery towering over us on a man-made ledge some fifty feet above ground level. A steep and narrow staircase led up to the monastery's entrance. To my horror I saw that many steps were missing, the surviving ones damaged and, even where the handrail existed, its support failed to inspire confidence. However, I was not to be defeated at the final lap. Controlling my terror and ignoring my dizziness, I followed David up the stairs and through a low, very thick oak door at the summit.

We staggered into a small, irregularly shaped courtyard, with a well at one end and a tiny chapel at the other. The large main church, hollowed out of the mountain, formed the courtyard's inner wall and was frescoed inside and out. However the inscriptions and paintings within human reach had been defaced, and the eyes of all the faces gouged out. That final desecration had probably been carried out by Greek women in the hope that eating them would induce pregnancy, rather than by the Turkish vandals who had damaged the other paintings.

In that beautiful if sad setting, surrounded by the glories of the landscape, untroubled by discordant sounds, the uninhabited church still seemed numinous, at peace with its injuries and overgrown vegetation. The abbot's quarters, the monks' cells, the refectory, library, hospital and guest rooms, as in many of Mount Athos's monasteries, formed the front of the building, overlooking the abyss, their verandas still supported here and there by long stilts. In one cell we found the remains of a large, badly damaged, rather splendid although fairly late icon, the Dormition. It lay face down, having served as a base for a bonfire. We picnicked on one of the more steady-looking balconies, gazing across thickly wooded valleys to the mountain ranges stretching eastward to Trans-Caucasia.*

To survey the former empire of Trebizond we had to travel deep into the hinterland on horseback. As our friends had always said that Ghost was under-exercised, we assumed that by accompanying us he would get all the walking he needed. Ihsan helped us hire two riding horses and two pack animals, but he forgot to warn the grooms that Ghost was coming with us, or to tell us that hot stony uplands might be too much for the dog. Having bought some camping equipment in the bazaar, we neglected to tell our friend the carpet merchant of our plans, and ignored a warning from the local police that brigands were operating in the hinterland.

Ihsan drove us to meet the grooms. On seeing Ghost they passionately protested at having to travel with so unclean a creature.

---

*For further information on Kaimakli and Sumela see G. Millet and D. T. Rice, *Byzantine Painting at Trebizond*, London, 1936.

Our determination and their poverty eventually broke their resistance, and we belatedly set out on our journey. The weather was perfect: the scenery increasingly magnificent as we negotiated tortuous paths into the belt of woodland. The air was deliciously scented, yellow azaleas attracting an immense number of wild bees. The honey from their forebears had reduced Xenophon's troops to 'madness' when they reached Trebizond after the battle of Cunaxa in 401 BC.* Centuries later, in 1916, the region's wild honey had the same effect on the Russian soldiers advancing on Trebizond. Forewarned, we avoided eating it. We found a magnificent site on which to pitch camp. As the sun set, the temperature dropped dramatically. Apart from the night with the gypsies at Bablock Hythe, I had never slept out. Once again I had a sleepless night, what with the cold, the baying of jackals, and then the twittering of birds. While I thrilled to the idea of nomadic life, I never got used to the facts of it, such as having to shake my shoes to make sure that there were no scorpions residing in them.

We woke to perfect weather. The scenery was as beautiful as the day before, even when luscious vegetation gave way to outcrops of rock, and the paths got stonier. Towards mid-morning we reached a village, the last inhabited one we saw for a fortnight. A group of elders sat under a huge plane tree. We exchanged greetings, answered numerous questions and sipped a glass of tea. Beyond the village the path got steeper and stonier. A couple of miles on, Ghost collapsed in exhaustion, his pads lacerated. He seemed to be dying. I was in tears, and David hardly less upset. We laid Ghost in the shade, applied wet towels to his head and massaged his heart. He gradually came to and tried to wag his tail, but was too weak to do so.

We considered the situation. Our two pack-horses could not be expected to carry much more. We decided to retrace our steps and seek help. David assumed the role of good shepherd and slung Ghost across his shoulders, whilst I walked behind sheltering their

---

*'The number of beehives was extraordinary, and all the soldiers that ate of their combs, lost their senses, vomited and . . . none of them were able to stand upright; such men who had eaten only a little were like men greatly intoxicated, and such as had eaten more were like mad men, and some like persons at the point of death.' Xenophon, *The Anabasis, or Expedition of Cyrus*, tr. Revd J. S. Watson, Book IV, Chapter 8, section 20, London, 1883.

heads with gigantic leaves. Back in the village, the old men were still drinking tea when we laid Ghost at the foot of their huge tree. They pondered our problem and concluded that Ghost would have to go by horse – which the village could not provide. Could we have a donkey? After another long silence a venerable patriarch agreed, and after a further delay he reappeared with a diminutive creature, scarcely taller than Ghost.

Our many delays had irritated David. He ordered the grooms to distribute our equipment between a horse and the tiny donkey and to prepare the second horse for carrying Ghost. Their protests reverberated through the village square, but the tea drinkers were on our side and persuaded the grooms to distribute the loads. But how was Ghost to be carried by the remaining horse? As he could not lie in a Y-shaped pannier, another venerable figure offered us his *sunduk* provided we swore on the Koran to return it; a *sunduk* being anything from a packing-case to a trunk, in this instance it was a tea-chest abandoned by the Russians in 1916.

For two days Ghost travelled, inert. On the third day, recovered, he sat up. Seeing us in the distance he concluded that riding was delightful provided it enabled him to keep up. Emitting disconsolate howls he leant forward, bit his mount's back until it broke into a trot and caught us up. We tried, but failed to break him of the habit and, at the cost of further delay, we continued at the same pace as our pack animals.

Ghost puzzled everyone. One day, early in our travels, we met our first shepherd, who asked whether Ghost was dog or wolf. A bit of both, we assured him. 'How so?' he persisted. 'Oh,' said David, 'his mother was a wolf, his father a dog.' We rode on through countryside drained of all its inhabitants at the exchange of populations; it was only on the following day that we met another shepherd. Like all his colleagues he was accompanied by extremely large and ferocious sheepdogs, wearing dangerously spiked iron collars as a defence against wolves. Those sheepdogs are so fierce that they are a real menace to strangers who, when in danger of attack, are advised to stand still, strip and face the animals nude, since the sight of a naked person is said to terrify them.

Fortunately, on seeing our cavalcade, the generally hostile shepherds were quick to call their dogs and hurry towards us. This man was the first to do so, and he approached us gingerly, enquired whether Ghost was a dog, a wolf or some other creature. Half dog, half wolf, we assured him. 'How so?' he asked, noting Ghost's pricked ears and alert look. 'Oh, his mother was a dog and his father a wolf,' we replied. Angrily he pointed out that we had said the opposite to yesterday's shepherd. It was impossible for the two men to have met since our first encounter. We were astonished that the second knew what we had said to the first. However, disliking the appearance of both, we decided to go on baffling unsympathetic individuals by varying our answers. We later learnt that local shepherds were convinced that we were accompanied by a tame wolf – hence probably the respect with which they greeted us, and that we were not attacked by some brigands who we later heard had been in the region.

We went through many abandoned villages. Usually the houses were still in good condition, their windows and doors intact, their furniture still in place. The roofs of most of the unbaked brick houses had fallen into the rooms below. In one house a table was laid for a meal still awaiting people long since herded down to the coast for shipment to Greece. Riding through these villages was eerie: our grooms felt the places were haunted by the spirits of their former owners, so although David and I often spent the night in an abandoned house, they always set up their camp well beyond the villages.

One day we entered a large and particularly attractive village, once surrounded by fertile, well-tended fields. To our astonishment a robust patriarch emerged from one of its largest and best-preserved houses. He told us that he was living in it with his wives and bachelor sons, his married sons occupying neighbouring houses. About three years previously, when seeking fresh pasture for his sheep, he had found the village and had been quick to appreciate the beauty of its setting. So he had hurried back to his native village, assembled his family and swept them off with their possessions to the deserted village. Untroubled by ghosts or pangs of conscience, they had installed themselves in the nicest house and were so happy they intended ending their lives there. They asked us to join them – there was a wide choice of excellent houses, they would give us a couple of sheep and goats so we could breed flocks of our own.

As they spoke, a Theocratic existence seemed quite tempting.

After all, following a life in the West even more privileged than ours, Lady Hester Stanhope had found happiness amongst Arab nomads. Then, while sipping his yoghurt, David glanced at an enormous boulder which must have rolled down the mountain before coming to rest inconveniently close to our host's front door. 'Why don't you move that stone?' David idly asked. Our elderly host slapped his leg and petulantly retorted, 'You have not even been here an hour, and you are already considering changes; after three years here it has never occurred to any of us to alter anything.' The spell was broken; we all laughed, although a little ruefully. Soon after, we parted, rather sadly, deeply touched by the generosity of the only thoroughly contented people we had ever met.

Back in Trebizond we called on our friend the carpet merchant. He received us frigidly. We had clearly offended him, but he would not admit to it at first. Eventually, he conceded that we had hurt his feelings, but he would not tell us how. After many cups of tea, he gently chided us for leaving Trebizond without telling him our plans. Then, when he saw how much we minded having displeased him, he relaxed. 'I will forgive you', he said, 'but you will have to bargain for the carpets from the original figures.' We were only too glad to do so, for we had become genuinely attached to him. And so the nightly haggle was resumed. When our time in Trebizond had run out, the carpets still cost more than when we had first left the town – so we assumed that we would not be able to buy them, and that haggling had only been a game. Therefore, when bidding goodbye, we did not refer to the carpets. Nor did he, until we handed him a parting gift. Then, pointing to a large, carefully corded roll lying on the shop floor, 'There', he said, 'are your carpets. May they remind you of me and my old home.' Their price was derisory.

Many Turks seem to lack imagination, probably because of poverty rather than insensibility. Our grooms were astonished at our concern over a sore on the neck of one of the horses, but when convinced that the wound was tormenting the animal, they unhesitatingly used their neckerchiefs to protect the injury. Turks seldom refuse an appeal for help, whilst a promise once given was in those days invariably, if sometimes belatedly, kept. Two instances of their integrity are typical of the country before its invasion by Western tourists.

Late one evening, at the close of a season's work, we went to Constantinople's covered bazaar to take leave of some of its traders. We decided to buy an icon for ten pounds, only to find that we could not pay for it that night. We promised to collect it and settle up the following evening, our last before an early flight to London. However we were unable to reach the bazaar before it closed. We were very distressed, because we were unable to get in touch with the dealer. We often worried at having let him down. Two years later, when again passing through Istanbul, we hurried to the Bedestan to explain and apologize for breaking our promise. He saw us from afar and started to rummage among his goods. By the time we reached his stall he was holding the icon. 'I kept it for you', he said, 'but had great difficulty for many of your friends wanted it. Your French friend offered me double but I knew you would come back and I could not let you down.' The price remained unchanged.

My second example involves both the cook and the maid whom we employed while excavating the Great Palace's mosaic pavement. Itinerant traders regularly visited our street, selling everything from food to umbrellas; there were also travelling entertainers, some with performing bears. We shopped at a small grocer at its far corner. On passing through Istanbul some years after leaving the district, we decided to look up our grocer. As we entered the shop he showed no surprise, but remarked with obvious relief that he was glad to see us since he would now be able to close an out-of-date account book. Perturbed, I asked whether we were in his debt. On the contrary, he assured us, he was in ours, for he owed us the returns on our empties. Why had he not given that money to our maids, I asked. 'They would not take it,' he assured me, 'it was not rightfully theirs.'

It was not until 1957 that we returned to Trebizond to uncover the murals in the church of Haghia Sophia. The Pension Suisse, Ihsan's father and our friend the carpet merchant were no longer there, but Ihsan was delighted to see us and, as of old, we celebrated Saturday nights by meeting for dinner at the Yasil Yurt restaurant. Now, however, American soldiers were also often dining there, having come down from the radar post established above the town. Ihsan had been obliged to sell the family mansion to a developer, but had built himself a modest villa at the far end of the same street. He still liked to sit among his rose bushes, reading and rereading old copies of *The Times*. He had acquired a jeep and two English pointers, and delighted in camping up in the mountains, to set out at dawn in search of the elusive large white partridge, the Royale. David was sometimes able to join his expeditions and so, on one occasion, was our young son, who was thereby able vicariously to experience some of the thrills in which nineteenth-century English travellers in the Levant revelled.

Trebizond had not greatly changed since our first visit although it had acquired a large and sophisticated hospital as well as several coeducational primary and secondary schools. The pupils were generally friendly but the girls looked much younger than their stated ages, and mature-looking youths claimed to be young teenagers. On persevering, we found that the girls added to their years to find husbands, whilst the men reduced their ages to avoid conscription.

It took five seasons to uncover the frescos in Haghia Sophia. This meant that we could sometimes borrow the expedition's Land Rover, explore more of the hinterland than on our first visit, and check on the condition of the churches we had discovered in the late 1920s. Sadly, many of the best had disappeared without trace, their finely dressed stones having been removed for building purposes. Occasionally we went further afield. Near Divrigi* one spring day we passed a hillside smothered in short, small, vivid red tulips. Later that day we got bogged down in deep, cloying mud. Our struggles to extricate the Land Rover resulted only in exhaustion and the loss of my shoes. No village was in sight, no man or beast visible. We sat on a boulder to catch our breath and wondered where to go for help, when the silhouette of a man, a boy and a donkey appeared on the skyline. I kept my finger pressed on the car's hooter and David ran towards them, shouting. At first they ignored us; then they reluctantly replied. They turned out to be Kurds.

The man agreed to conduct David to the village, an hour's walk away, whilst his young son stayed to mount guard over me. The boy knew no Turkish, I no Kurdish so, apart from giving him some

---

*A large town some 300 kilometres south-west of Trebizond.

sweets, the like of which he had obviously never before seen, let alone eaten, our relationship remained formal. In the end it took eighteen men and two oxen to free the Land Rover. We were so grateful that we increased the sum David had agreed to pay for their help. To our astonishment they angrily refused any money, and explained that my young companion had broken their code of hospitality by accepting my sweets. Although they were obviously very poor, they adamantly refused to change their minds. Sadly, we pushed on.

At dusk, when only a few miles from our destination, we were halted by a swollen river, its bridge swept away in a recent storm. Some miles back we had passed the only village we had seen that day. We decided to return to it to hire helpers, and planned to spend the night in the car. The inhabitants must already have gone to bed when we reached the village, for no lights were visible, yet within seconds we were surrounded by fiercely baying dogs. Soon after, men's shouts added to the noise, and people appeared carrying lanterns. They looked so fierce that I called out to them before David did so, hoping that a woman's voice might propitiate them. Calling off their dogs they surrounded the car and listened to David's request for help.

After much argument conducted in Kurdish, they agreed on a price for their services and the headman asked where we meant to spend the night. We replied that, with their permission, we would do so on the spot, in our car. The headman drew himself up to his full height and remarked with great dignity that even though his house was mean and poor, it could nevertheless provide travellers with shelter. He brushed aside our reluctance to disturb his household, and opened the car door for us. Our hands were seized and we were carefully led down a precipitous path, across stepping stones set in the river bed, and up an even steeper path into the headman's house.

It was obvious that the village was extremely poor. The headman's family had been warned of our arrival and were busily tidying the living-room. The women were unveiled, dignified but sluttish, and talking no Turkish. The room was square, fairly large, a hearth at its centre and divans lining its walls. Hens shared it with its owners. Within minutes the village's entire population had crowded in, and our host's adorable blond and blue-eyed two-year-old son had been woken up to see us. Our host's magnificent purple silk marriage quilt was produced for us to sit on, later to sleep under.

While we answered questions, some about England, we heard much agitated whispering. Eventually we were asked what refreshment we would like. We had eaten nothing since a dawn breakfast and were hungry, but the villagers were so poverty-stricken we hardly knew what to say. Then, remembering that Turkey claimed to be self-sufficient in tea, I said a glass would be pleasant. I should have asked for yoghurt, possibly even for honey, for our hosts had no tea. Hurriedly, men slipped from the house to try to find a spoonful. Eventually we were given a glass each and a hard-boiled egg to share. When we had eaten our host asked his fellow villagers to leave so that we might sleep. Two of his women took my hands. Visions of a harem assailed me as I was led up a steep hillside. I was wondering where I would end up when they gave me a gentle push, let go my hands, and turned their backs. I realized that they had brought me to their lavatory.

Although the room in which we spent the night under the matrimonial purple silk quilt was not clean, I was not troubled by insects. At dawn I was woken by hens, not by bug bites. Soon after, our host appeared and gave us each a spoonful of honey before taking us back to the car, without giving us the opportunity to take leave of our hostesses. There was no question of offering to pay for the warm hospitality, but I had profited from the lesson given to me by the first Kurds the day before, and had secreted what presents I could raise behind the divans on which we had slept. Getting us across the swollen river took far longer than expected, yet the men still refused payment. We parted with expressions of mutual regard and sincere gratitude on our part. Ever since, my sympathies have been with the Kurds for the resentment they feel at being treated as second-class citizens, deprived of education and kept in dire poverty, and for their struggles for political independence.

I I

Mainly of Exhibitions

> It is art that *makes* life, makes interest, makes importance,
> for our consideration and application of these things, and I
> know of no substitute whatever for the force and beauty of
> its process.
>
> Henry James in a letter to H. G. Wells, 10 July 1915

IN 1928 David and I took a three-year lease of an unfurnished
fifth-floor flat in Paris, consisting of a large studio bed-sitting
room, a small bathroom and a kitchen. It was in the Rue Blomet,
opposite the Bal Nègre, the nightly meeting-place of the poorer
Parisian Negroes. The rent of fifty pounds a year included porter-
age, permanent hot water, central heating during the winter, and
lift service. We furnished it with plain deal furniture, choosing
functional pieces with the charm of Shaker furniture. When we had
stippled them a pale green, they acquired an unexpected elegance.
However, we spent twenty-five pounds – at the time a considerable
sum – on having a wide divan bed made to our design by a Russian
carpenter. In order to save room, prompted in part by Goldsmith's
reference in *The Deserted Village* to a piece of furniture which
served as a bed by night and chest of drawers by day,* we had three
immense drawers built into its base; at the time that was an innovation; similar beds are now manufactured commercially.

David and I considered ourselves fortunate in having both
always been able to initiate close friendships with people of
different ages, backgrounds and outlooks. Each possessed a lively
mind, keen if widely differing senses of humour and a highly
developed gift for friendship. We formed many lasting relation-

---

*The chest contrived a double debt to pay,
   A bed by night, a chest of drawers by day.
Describing the village inn: Oliver Goldsmith, *The Deserted Village*, London, 1770, lines
229–30.

ships with our foreign colleagues and these often proved as precious to us as those which dated from our Oxford days, and our times in Gloucestershire and Scotland. These friendships, and the fun they provided, did much to confirm my innately optimistic outlook.

To begin with, our circle consisted of my friends, Tulia and Munia being especially dear. Soon it spread to include friends of David, budding Byzantinists, like him studying for doctorates under Professor Gabriel Millet. Later it embraced such leading figures in the Parisian art world as Georges Salles, director of the Louvre. He gave elegant lunches in his sumptuous flat in the Louvre overlooking the Seine, and here we met notable collectors of Byzantine art.

At this time we met Eustache de Lorey who quickly became a cherished friend. When Syria became a French mandate after the First World War, Eustache was appointed director of that country's antiquities, a post which entitled him when in Damascus to live in the Palais Adjem. Although a distinguished Islamist, his tastes were wide. He was immediately enchanted by the splendour of the Byzantinesque Ommayad mosaics on the Cathedral Mosque of Damascus; their conservation became one of his prime concerns. His appreciation of the best that life on earth has to offer ranged from the finest paintings to food and drink, from the cerebral to the everyday. Like Alexander Benois he was subject to forebodings, but always ready to accept fate's dictates. His letters reflected his warmth, moods and fears, his wit and learning, indeed, his very temperament, as clearly as did his conversation. I wonder whether anyone today writes as freely, elegantly, spontaneously and simply about each passing mood and fancy.

While we were settling into the Rue Blomet, Lennox Berkeley, a friend of David, was living in Montparnasse in an enchanting little house rented from the painter Lurcat, who had decorated it with abstract and cubist murals. Lennox shared the house with John Greenidge, an architect with a fondness for producing plays and films. Lennox was studying musical composition but both had time to enjoy the delights of Paris, especially art exhibitions. We met weekly, sometimes more frequently, and often dined in one of the many inexpensive but excellent local restaurants. In the autumn of 1928, Lennox took us to Ravel's box at the Opéra for the first night of the ballet set to Ravel's *Bolero*.* As the curtain rose, Ravel joined us, immaculately dressed in tails, ebullient in spirit and, to my surprise, with no sign of first-night nerves. The ballet was danced on a table standing in a tavern and, as far as I remember, lasted only fifteen minutes. The curtain fell to tumultuous applause. We then learnt the cause of Ravel's gaiety. Still struggling to control his mirth, he explained that, the train bringing him to Paris running late, he had changed into evening clothes in one of its lavatories. Seldom, he thought, could a composer have dressed for one of his first nights in quite such unexalted surroundings. He carried us off to Le Boeuf sur le Toit, at the time my favourite night-club.† Ravel and Lennox shared an elfin quality but Ravel was the more extrovert, the more sparkling, cerebral and headier of the two, Lennox being dreamier and more contemplative.

Lennox, John, David and I often spent a day in the forest of Fontainebleau. In the early spring we picked wild lilies of the valley there. Their scent mentally transported me to Pavlovsk, but our talks ranged widely over the Barbizon school of painting,‡ current art exhibitions, the music of Les Six,§ Satie's wit or the one-act operettas at the Théâtre Beriza in the Champs-Élysées. I was especially amused by *Angélique* by Jacques Ibert whom I met some thirty years later, when staying in Rome with John and Delia Pilcher. By then Ibert was director of the Villa Medici, the French Academy in Rome. He was every bit as fascinating, witty and elegant as his musical operettas.

In the autumn of 1929 we heard of Evelyn Waugh's marriage break-up. Almost doubting the veracity of the report, we wrote asking whether he would like to come to Paris, staying with us but, as we had no spare room, sleeping out somewhere round the corner.

---

*Fokine produced *Bolero* for Ida Rubinstein's ballet company. The first night was on 22 November 1928.

† The night-club opened by Louis Moyses, called, with the author's permission, after the ballet written and produced by Jean Cocteau, which was immediately successful when premièred in 1921. The night-club was frequented not only by Cocteau, but by social, artistic and literary Paris.

‡An informal association of French landscape painters, named after the village which was their favourite residence. They reproduced landscape in a non-classical manner.

§Les Six – Auric, Durey, Honegger, Milhaud, Poulenc and Tailleferre – composers famous for advanced ideas derived from Satie and Cocteau. From 1917 to the early 1920s they gave concerts together, thereafter going their own way.

His acceptance was instant – short and succinct like so many of his notes, yet leaving no doubt as to the depth of his unhappiness.

By the time he arrived, Bryan Guinness and his first wife, Diana Mitford, were already in Paris. Staying with them was Diana's sister, Nancy. David had long known the Mitford girls and as Evelyn was also a close friend, we saw a good deal of each other. Bryan and Diana wanted to sample some famous Parisian restaurants and so we dined at La Pérouse, one of the prettiest. However, we were to see even more of a young American called Marcella Gump, for she became besotted with Evelyn. She pursued him relentlessly, mercilessly, telephoning several times a day to suggest meetings. To begin with Evelyn refused her invitations, but she gradually wore him down and as she was well-off – her father was a Chicago paint millionaire – he would accept provided we were included. We agreed but only so long as the evening ended at Le Boeuf sur le Toit. As a result, if only for a very short time, we came close to ranking as habitués of that entertaining night-club.

Yet, at heart, Evelyn was miserable. I do not think that he ever fully recovered from the break-up of his first marriage. But he did not permit his unhappiness, or his growing commitment to the Catholic Church, to turn him into a bore. He remained funny and trenchant as ever, but often sought relief by going to the Bal Nègre to watch the dancing. His thank-you note suggests that he found the visit quite agreeable, but it is probably fortunate for us that he does not appear at the time to have kept a diary!

We continued to see quite a lot of Evelyn, both before and after his second marriage in 1937, meeting in London and in Gloucestershire. When Evelyn started to complain of deafness I put this down to depression and was irritated by what I assumed to be a pose. Crossly I suggested that he use an ear-trumpet. He readily agreed to if he could obtain one so, still feeling angry, I offered to get him one. Next morning I discovered two in a junk-shop and bought both, offering him the choice. Evelyn opted for the more elegant, which he went on to use more as a buffer than an amplifier.

In later years Evelyn often stayed with us in Edinburgh. Although we delighted in them, his visits were not trouble-free. Difficulties arose from events as contrasting as social calls or visits to an antiquarian bookseller. Once he went to interview Winifred Peck about his biography of her brother, Ronald Knox. The Pecks were then living in a small top-floor flat in a high house without a lift. Winifred had no domestic help and was unaccustomed to cooking. Under the mistaken impression that Evelyn liked drinking *crème de menthe*, she provided a bottle as an accompaniment to a tepid, undercooked stew. The interview was not a success yet, having failed to discover anything new about Ronald Knox, Evelyn felt obliged to ask for another meeting. Feeling sorry for them both, I telephoned Winifred to suggest cold meat and a bottle of red wine for the following day. That reunion was a success.

On another occasion, Evelyn and I set out on a book hunt. We both collected architectural manuals, Evelyn having first choice of those priced at over five pounds, whilst I had first refusal on anything less. At Grant's we found several books which enchanted Evelyn. While writing out a cheque he asked Grant's to post the books, but lost his temper at being charged postage. He then cancelled the purchase, tore up the cheque, and flounced out of the shop. I thought his behaviour unreasonable and was annoyed. Contrite, he insisted on taking me to lunch at the Café Royal where he demanded oysters in batter, a new venture for that excellent restaurant, one henceforth permanently included on its delectable menu. We gorged.

Our time in Paris was coming to an end. My father-in-law must have sensed that he was mortally ill, for he suddenly insisted on giving us a country house as a belated wedding present. Although he wanted to buy it in our joint names, I thought it more appropriate that David be sole owner. We had great fun hunting for a house of our own. The trouble was, that David wanted some woodland and I longed to live beside running water. I also wanted a family-sized house unencumbered by long kitchen corridors with larders, still-rooms and the like; a house which could be locked up and left when we wanted to go abroad. One perfect summer afternoon, after weeks of leisurely house-hunting, we stumbled on a semi-ruin which enchanted us. Although not the Queen Anne or Georgian house we had in mind, this one rubbed up against a grove at one end, grazed the River Coln at the other and, while essentially Cotswold in style, was curiously evocative of Burgundy. For us Pigeon House in Coln Rogers was to prove a very happy home.

Ghost's death from old age made it easier to move to England.

On giving up our studio we took over my former rooms in my parents' flat in the 16th arrondissement; in May 1931 we finally moved into our own Coln Rogers house. Oxford, within easy reach, continued to play an important part in our lives. However, we were also frequently in London, staying with the Dynevors in Fitzhardinge Street, or with Harry and Blanche Talbot Rice in Montagu Square or, as my mother-in-law's guests, at Brown's Hotel. When De Basil's Ballets Russes came to London, having saved for weeks, we ventured to Covent Garden or the Alhambra to see each of their productions. We often asked members of the company to join us for supper at the Savoy Grill. De Basil and Massine came occasionally, three very young ballerinas of immense talent – Riabouchinska, Baronova and Toumanova – were more frequent guests, but it was Shura Danilova, the company's prima ballerina, who became a real friend.

Shura enjoyed weekends with us in Gloucestershire. She was generally driven down late on Saturday night by Hubert Griffith, an idealistic left-wing journalist. He was a great charmer, a dedicated balletomane with a Celt's verve and fluency. Several years later, when living in Edinburgh, we were to delight in the friendship of Ian Whyte, a Scot, at the time conductor of the BBC's Scottish Symphony Orchestra who resembled Griffith in temperament and equalled him in charm. In contrast to Ian, who disliked politics, Griffith was an ardent upholder of Communism. So, as Danilova was an equally passionate monarchist and profoundly devout, they had agreed not to discuss politics or religion. However, one evening after a good dinner, the talk turned to politics. It flowed smoothly until Griffith enraged Shura by comparing the Communist and Christian doctrines. A bitter argument followed, lasting into the early hours. We went to bed exhausted. Fortunately harmony was restored later in the day and their visits continued for the rest of the season.

Charles des Graz, at the time chairman of Sotheby's, was a frequent guest.* He masked his wide erudition, command of language

---

*Des Graz, Charles Geoffrey Maurice. Educated Eton; Trinity College, Cambridge. Captain of Oppidans, Eton. In the First World War served in the Directorate of Military Intelligence. Assistant Director of Post and Telegraph Censorship in the Second World War. The intervening years were spent at the auction house, Sotheby & Co.; appointed Chairman 1923.

and administrative skills with a keen wit, and was always amusing when talking of travel, books, the arts, wine or food. His main interest centred on Eton, where he had been very happy as a boy, and we used often to look at his collection of watercolours of Eton and Windsor. His bread and butter letters, whether written in Latin, Greek, English or some other European language, were generally in verse. My favourite is perhaps his *Ode to a Pie*, in fact a *kulebiaka,** which I had provided for one of our shooting parties.

In the 1930s, when in London we always saw Vere Pilkington, a close Eton and Oxford friend of David.† Then a junior partner at Sotheby's he was later to succeed Charles as chairman. An accomplished player of the harpsichord and disciple of Violet Gordon Woodhouse, Vere often devoted his lunch hour to transcribing forgotten pieces of music in the British Museum. It was from his flat in Bennet Street, once the property of Byron,‡ that, leaning from one of its balconies, we watched George V's jubilee procession pass down St James's. Like Charles he was an excellent host and a marvellous friend. Once, through my fault, he and I quarrelled; it was a glorious spring day. An invitation to what promised to be a glamorous garden party made me long for a new hat, preferably one which, as in Paris, would be modelled on my head. I was prepared to spend five pounds on it, not a penny more. Where in London could I get one for that price, I asked Vere. He knew exactly; a young friend of his had just set up as a milliner near Sotheby's and Vere would take me there after a picture sale.

Next day, breaking away from luncheon at the Dynevors, I rushed to Sotheby's to collect Vere. His sale was not quite over. The few buyers present were mostly middle-aged men who sat staring at a porter holding a small painting of the Virgin and Child. I was struck by its loveliness. As Vere shouted the figure five I thought, what was a hat compared to such beauty. Why weren't the buyers

---

*An oblong pie made by layering various items between sheets of pastry. The traditional *kulebiaka* consisted of layers of dilled rice, fish, wild mushrooms, thin crêpes and *vesiga*, the dried spinal marrow of the sturgeon. A modern version might contain cabbage, mushrooms, sausage-meat and boiled eggs.
†Pilkington, Charles Vere. Educated Eton; Christ Church, Oxford. Director of the Fine Art auctioneers, Sotheby & Co., 1927; chairman 1953. A keen harpsicord player, he was a member of both the Council of the Royal Musical Association and the Business Committee of *Musica Britannica*. After retirement in 1958 he moved to Portugal.
‡Byron lodged there in 1813. See N. Page, *A Byron Chronology*, London, 1988.

bidding? Impulsively raising my hand I signalled to Vere who seemed not to have seen me do so for he again called, 'Five, any more bids?' I made a more obvious gesture which Vere must have seen, for he shot a glance in my direction, yet, still ignoring me, he again called 'Any more bids?' Furious with him, I raised my bag and waved it above my head, expecting him to raise the figure to seven pounds ten shillings, or even ten guineas. My gesture was inescapable.

It was with horror that I heard him call '1,560 guineas – any more bids?' Realizing that his earlier call must have been for 1,555 guineas, a sum representing our income for three years, I felt sick with apprehension. Tottering from the room I noticed George Spencer-Churchill seated amongst the buyers. Taking myself in hand, I returned to the picture sale to face the consequences of my rash behaviour. To my great relief I heard Vere calling a higher figure and, finally, knocking the painting, the last in the sale, down to a buyer. Minutes later George came up to me, jubilant, saying: 'I have bought the most wonderful painting. I feel sure it is a Dierick Bouts.' And that is what the painting turned out to be.

Vere and I met in anger – he at my recklessness in bidding without knowing what I was letting myself in for, me at his impertinence in disregarding a bid of mine on the assumption, however well founded, that I could not pay it. On reaching the milliner I was still upset. Not surprisingly, the hat was a dismal failure and I never wore it, even though it had cost five pounds. More embittering was the discovery that this, the last hat ever modelled for me, was made on my head by Aage Thaarup, soon to rank as London's finest hat designer, milliner to the Royal Family and also to Mrs Simpson.

In 1929 the Victoria and Albert Museum mounted an exhibition of icons, the first of its kind in England.* It was sent from Russia to display the excellent work of the USSR's State Restoration Workshops. The icons were brought to London by P. J. Yukin, one of the Workshops' most skilled restorers. He stayed in London to guard the panels and see them safely back to Russia. Yukin was a

---

*Ancient Russian Icons from the Twelfth to the Nineteenth Centuries lent by the Government of the USSR to a British Committee. The catalogue dates the exhibition to 18 November–14 December 1929.

very lovable man, simple and deeply religious, a member of the Old Believer sect,* born into a peasant family of hereditary painters. He knew no English and had never before travelled outside Russia. He epitomized much of what I loved best in the Russian character and within minutes of meeting he and I entered into a lifelong friend-ship. It was he who taught me to clean icons, a skill which I put to good use several years later when staying in Cyprus with Rupert Gunnis to list outstanding icons belonging to the island's churches. Our most exciting discovery was in Nicosia, where we found three high and narrow fourteenth-century commemorative icons lying in a church's outhouse, their paintings invisible beneath a thick coat of dirt. When cleaned, the finest, dated to 1356, included the figure of a young girl wearing a dress of sumptuous red brocade.†

By 1930 Leigh Ashton had also become a friend.‡ Within a year he had invited David to help mount the Royal Academy's great winter exhibition of Persian art.§ The creation of Arthur Upham Pope and his wife Phyllis Ackerman this came as a revelation to everyone – even the specialists on Persian miniatures, carpets and ceramics. Touching a work of art somehow extends one's appreci-ation of its quality and David and I were never to forget the thrill we experienced in handling the exhibits, a thrill which we recap-tured in 1958, when mounting the Edinburgh Festival's exhibition of Byzantine art. The Soviet authorities' decision to lend the Royal Academy some of the Hermitage Museum's finest Persian objects excited and enchanted the London art world. That they had agreed to lend these treasures was as much due to Upham Pope's enthusi-asm for Persian art, as to his charm and great persuasive powers. The loans were to be brought by Professor Joseph Orbeli, director of the Hermitage Museum.

---

*Those who left the Orthodox Church as a result of liturgical changes introduced in 1667.
†Illustrated in W. G. Constable and D. Talbot Rice, *The Icons of Cyprus*, London, 1937.
‡Ashton, Sir Arthur Leigh Bollard, Kt. Educated Winchester; Balliol College, Oxford. After serving in the Royal Garrison Artillery in the First World War, Ashton joined the Victoria & Albert Museum, first in the Department of Architecture, subsequently those of Textiles and of Ceramics; in 1937 he became Keeper of Special Collections. After the Second World War, during which he was in the Ministry of Information, he was appointed Museum Director. As such he oversaw a complete redisplay, creating a chronological sequence of galleries in which masterpieces in all media were shown side by side – an innovatory approach at the time.
§*International Exhibition of Persian Art*, 7 January–28 February 1931; Leigh Ashton was the Assistant Director.

I was delighted to be asked to act as Orbeli's interpreter, attending the unpacking of the objects, checking their condition with the descriptions on their invoices, watching while each was locked into its show-case. As the days slipped by without advance news of Orbeli's arrival we started to worry, growing increasingly nervous when our enquiries remained unanswered. Even a telegram sent on Christmas Eve failed to elicit a reply; it was not until New Year's Eve that we learnt that our guest would arrive that night. The news depressed me as, at the time, I still liked to see the New Year in, believing that it could to some extent be propitiated if warmly welcomed. Leigh chided me and promised that, if Orbeli was delayed, he would provide the champagne with which to celebrate the year's entry at Burlington House, amidst the splendour of the exhibition.

We assembled at Burlington House at eight that evening. I brought some caviare sandwiches made for the occasion. The Russian loans aside, the exhibits of Persia's ancient arts, glowing in the carefully contrived lighting, were in place, assembled for the first time and making a stunning impression in all their variety and glory. For a couple of hours we revelled in having the run of the gallery; then anxiety assailed us. Our visitor had still not arrived. What would we do if the Russian loans failed to materialize? Would we rearrange the show-cases or leave gaps on the chance of a late delivery? Fortunately, at about ten-thirty, we were informed that we had only to wait a few more minutes. And indeed almost immediately Professor Orbeli appeared, accompanied by three large tea-chests and Major Longden of the Board of Trade.

Joseph Orbeli was slight, well-groomed, middle-aged and rather Assyrian-looking, with his long and narrow white face framed by longish black hair and a pointed, carefully trimmed black beard. By birth a member of the royal Orbeliani clan, as a young man his radical sympathies had led him to truncate his name and declare himself a socialist. Later he steered clear of politics to become an art historian who, in 1940, was to win world-wide regard for the skill, courage and efficiency with which he masterminded the evacuation of the treasures of the Hermitage.* In London, in 1931,

---

*The Germans reached the outskirts of Leningrad but were unable to capture the city which endured a two-and-a-half-year siege. Some relief was afforded in the winter when supplies were despatched to the besieged across the frozen lakes to the north-east of the city.

his acute intelligence, integrity, keen wit and cultivated outlook won him many friends, especially since he was able to move freely about England, even to accompany David to Oxford, to dine at high table and spend the night in Christ Church. It was with Orbeli's help that I first obtained a visa in time to attend the Congress of Persian Art held in Moscow in September 1935; and my friendship with him probably accounts for the ease with which I have been able to revisit the USSR.

At Burlington House on the last night of 1930 Orbeli's packing-cases were opened by three assistants, Orbeli personally lifting out each object to unwrap it from numerous layers of tissue paper and place it on a baize-covered table for each of us to examine in turn. Only then did Orbeli and I tick off our respective lists and watch it being locked into its allocated show-case. We had almost finished when midnight struck. Leigh poured the champagne as we saw in the New Year, in the customary Soviet manner drinking to universal peace and brotherhood. Then we continued our work, Orbeli lifting the last exhibit from the packing-case, peeling off its wrappings to reveal a late eighteenth-century sword, its gold scabbard covered with diamonds, rubies and emeralds. Its opulence lacked beauty, its flamboyance left us speechless.

It was Major Longden who broke the silence. Suddenly leaning forward he pointed to an empty cavity. The absence of a jewel galvanized us into horrified action. We searched the table, the floor, the packing-cases; we unfolded every scrap of tissue paper; once again we examined the table and the floor beneath. Exhaustion overcame us. 'Ach,' muttered Orbeli, 'who knows when and where the jewel may have fallen out?' I quickly pointed out that the cavity contained some dust. 'Was not that proof', I asked, 'that the loss was not of recent date?' Orbeli agreed; the relevant documents were minuted accordingly, signed and countersigned.

In London, David and I often succumbed to temptation and were running out of money. David overcame his nervousness, gratefully accepting Leigh's invitation to become the exhibition's lecturer. Fortunately, regardless of lack of experience, David's gift for lecturing was evident from the start, and his talks proved so popular that he was soon obliged to increase the number from one to three a day. I was terrified when he lost his voice and, no other speaker being available, I was persuaded to stand in. Shortly before I gave my first talk I saw Robert Byron enter. Having often suffered from his teasing, I appealed to his better nature and implored him not to listen to me. His kinder instincts prevailed on that occasion; letting out a derisive cackle, he had the grace to leave. Fortunately David made a quick recovery, a few days later taking Charlie Chaplin round the exhibition. Chaplin proved extremely appreciative. He passed unnoticed until almost the end of his visit when, on accidentally dropping his walking-stick, he was recognized as he bent to pick it up.*

More important to us were the friendships we formed as a result of the exhibition with eminent collectors, especially dear Mr and Mrs Eumorfopoulos, whose house in Chelsea overlooking the Thames contained contemporary sculptures and marvellous Chinese works of art. We were sad when the exhibition closed.

In 1935 we once again helped mount an exhibition, one sponsored, as part of the Jubilee festivities, by Lady Zia Wernher, daughter of the Grand Duke Michael of Russia and Countess de Torby. Lady Zia's exhibition was devoted to Russia's westernized arts. Her committee included Monsieur A. Polovtsov, once a great landowner and much admired in St Petersburg as a patron of the arts; indeed, the idea for the exhibition may well have originated with him. Also on the executive committee were Lords Conway and Duveen, Professor Tancred Borenius and David. I was entrusted with the section displaying Russia's theatrical arts. The exhibition was held in 1 Belgrave Square, a large and imposing house well suited to the purpose. Although not all the objects were of the finest quality, the general standard was surprisingly high and unexpectedly representative of its period.† King George and Queen Mary came to a special preview and seemed genuinely to like it, although the Queen appeared vexed by the attention with which the King

---

*Sidney C. Hutchison, now Hon. Archivist of the Royal Academy of Arts, previously Secretary, then a very junior staff member, has differing memories of Chaplin's visit. It caused a great stir, Hutchison recalls; people crowded into the courtyard to catch a glimpse of Chaplin. To avoid them, the star had to be smuggled out by the back door.
†See D. T. Rice (ed.), *Russian Art, published in connection with the Exhibition of Russian Art, Belgrave Square, London, 1935*, London & Edinburgh, 1935.

examined Bakst's costume designs, and insisted on hurrying him away.

When we were first married David belonged to only one club, the Cavendish at 119 Piccadilly, a house which had formerly belonged to an uncle. Ladies were not even allowed to wait for a member in its hall, but were obliged to remain outside, pacing the pavement, where I was more than once taken for a tart. When we settled in Gloucestershire David therefore joined the Orleans Club in 29 King Street, noted for its fabulous cuisine as for its furniture and silver, much of it dating from when the house had belonged to Nell Gwyn. Although small it was one of the very few clubs which possessed a ladies' section. I once ventured to ask for the recipe of an especially luscious sauce. The chef brought it to me in person, explaining that it took over twenty-four hours to make. Needless to say I never tried it. During the phoney stage of the Second World War we often invited friends to dine there. They were all enchanted by the staff's friendliness and efficiency which typified the delights of a vanishing age. At the fall of France, after my failure to get through to Paris on the telephone, it was the porter of the Orleans who succeeded in putting me in touch with Tulia and Munia, but by then it was too late for them to be able to join us in England.

In Gloucestershire I was happiest with the friends David had made with members of a previous generation. Violet and John Gordon Woodhouse and George Spencer-Churchill were amongst those who made much of us and to whom we became devoted. The Woodhouses were by then living at Nether Lypiatt Manor, sharing that dream house with Bill Barrington, a superb landscape gardener who was busy laying out their grounds on architectural lines. The elaborate wrought-iron gates date to a previous owner, Judge Coxe. The story goes that he sentenced the local blacksmith to death for murder but the craftsman was reprieved until such time as he had completed the gates he was then making for the judge. Whorl after whorl was added, until it was impossible to fit on any further decoration. Alas, however, the death sentence was not commuted; locals used to say that the blacksmith's spirit still haunts the house.

Violet's nephew John Gwynne was a frequent visitor of theirs and became one of our very special friends.* At the time John was an elegant, slightly arrogant young man about town with a promising legal career ahead and no visible signs of the altruism and passionate enthusiasm for the arts and things spiritual which eventually led him to become a Sufi. It was some searing experience when dropped behind enemy lines in Greece, which turned him into an idiosyncratic but compassionate man who was to devote the remaining years of his life first to running the Outward Bound Trust, and then to furthering the careers of young musicians. It was also at Nether Lypiatt that we got to know many of the local craftsmen such as the carver, W. G. Simmonds, then living at Far Oakridge, as well as the Sitwells, especially Osbert.

We saw almost as much of George Spencer-Churchill as of the Woodhouses, often lunching and spending the rest of the afternoon at Northwick, sometimes weekending there.† Each visit presented us with a surprise, either by revealing some fresh work of art, or some new and unsuspected accomplishment of our host. His versatility ranged from the ability to decipher hieroglyphs to vying at tennis with Fred Perry, or contending with first-class players at bridge and chess. He was reserved but warm-hearted. As his guests came from all walks of life, he placed on their dressing-tables a typewritten note stating that his staff were not to be tipped, for their wages already took account of the extra work entailed by visitors. With the exception of the Buccleuchs, no one else looked after their guests so well. George's concern for people extended beyond his guests. For the men who had fought in his regiment and had

---

*Gwynne, John. Educated Eton; Christ Church, Oxford. Practised as a solicitor until the Second World War. Wounded in France. Trained units for operations behind enemy lines before himself serving with SOE in Greece; invalided home. A lover of early music, inculcated by his aunt, Violet Gordon Woodhouse, who brought him up. A bold rider to hounds and a keen gardener.
†Spencer-Churchill, Captain Edward George, MC. Educated Eton; Royal Military College, Sandhurst. When 13 visited Egypt where he developed an interest in antiquities. Commissioned into the Grenadier Guards in 1894; saw action in the Boer War. During the First World War he was shot through the head and, presumed dead, was laid out for a burial party; rescued when a passing brother officer saw him blink. Once recovered he returned to the trenches. After the war he retired to Northwick Park, Gloucestershire, where he established a brick factory for unemployed soldiers from his regiment. During the depression he sold his coin collection to avoid raising the rents of his tenant farmers. The pick of his collections of paintings, Egyptian figures and Chinese bronzes is now in the Ashmolean Museum, Oxford, and the British Museum.

since become unemployed, he built at Blockley a brickworks that produced bricks of outstanding quality; they were used for Battersea Power Station, now a listed building.

For all that, George's attitude to his women guests was ambivalent. At meals, ladies were offered only one glass of white wine. As no drinks were served before a meal, and only men offered postprandial port, some women guests were apt to think themselves ill done by. One of them felt so deprived that she used her husband's hay fever as an excuse to return to London only a few hours after arriving at Northwick for a long weekend. Regular visitors revelled in George's eccentricity, were touched by his friendship and impressed by his attainments. Everything he sponsored was of the highest quality, his carnations the most fragrant, his peaches and nectarines the most luscious. No visit to Northwick was complete without a tour of his hothouses and no flower smelt sweeter or fruit better than a large, warm, just fully ripened peach, picked off its tree and eaten on the spot.

Between the war years we also saw a lot of the John Masefields.* By then they had left Boars Hill to live at Pinbury, near Sapperton. David had got to know them well during his years at Oxford for he had often taken part in the theatricals the Masefields were so fond of staging. At first I was disconcerted by Mrs Masefield; although she greeted us affably, she seemed abrupt and withdrawn; her voice was either a mutter or else it grated and her eyes appeared to be directed inwards. However, John Masefield's personality did much to offset her melancholic air.

Pinbury was an attractive if slightly gloomy house, standing isolated in the steep and lush Sapperton valley. Initially a nunnery, it became in the 1890s the workshop of the gifted craftsmen Sidney and Ernest Barnsley and Ernest Gimson. Although examples of their work survived in the house, it remained stubbornly cheerless.

---

*Masefield, John, OM, C. Litt., Litt. D., LL D. Educated Warwick School; HMS *Conway*. Trained for a career in the merchant navy, Masefield fell ill on his first sea journey and returned to England, determined to write. He took a job as a bank clerk, and in 1901, with several sea ballads and poems published, abandoned employment for the life of a freelance writer. In 1903 he married Constance de la Charois Crommelin, his senior by eleven and a half years. Too old for soldiering when the First World War broke out, Masefield went to France and Gallipoli as a Red Cross orderly. He then formed a theatrical company at Boars Hill, Oxford. After the almost fatal illness of his wife, they moved in 1932 to Pinbury, in Gloucestershire. He was created Poet Laureate in 1932.

However this was subjugated by Masefield's mischievous smile and lively eyes, above all his innate romanticism, most in evidence in his study where he liked to talk about the sea, hunting, ballet and the paintings of Edward Seago. After lunching, we often played croquet with our hosts on an ancient lawn edged by great yew hedges. On leaving, he usually gave us a neat little parcel for our young daughter. This he had embellished with a seal stencil from one of the fine intaglios in his collections. It contained delicious chocolate truffles made by his cook.

Of our Oxford contemporaries John Dugdale was a dear friend and a close neighbour – until his marriage he spent much of his free time with his parents at Sezincote, a house which they cherished.* It had been built in the early nineteenth century by Samuel Pepys Cockerell for his brother in the Indian style later adapted by Nash for the Royal Pavilion at Brighton. John adored the house probably no less than his parents did, but feeling it would be wrong to own so fine a mansion, always meant to sell it when his parents died. This greatly distressed his father, although John's altruism, a characteristic inherited from his mother, went some way to ease the pain. John lived up to his principles: on becoming an MP he moved into a small suburban house and on inheriting Sezincote, sold it. For the rest of his short life he devoted his energies to campaigning for the underprivileged and for the natives in Africa. His early death was a sad loss both for his friends and the Labour Party, possibly even for Africa.

At Sezincote the only discordant note was struck by the Dugdales' strange and malevolent-looking butler; a ginger-haired, cross-eyed man with a repellent mouth. He had entered their employment in a strange way. Ethel Dugdale had found an intruder in her bedroom one evening examining her jewel-case. She neither fainted nor screamed; instead she persuaded him to sit beside her and tell her about himself. Their conversation ended by her engaging him as butler, a position he retained until the sale of Sezincote. One day we took Charles des Graz to lunch there, and were

---

*Dugdale, Rt. Hon. John, PC. Educated Wellington; Christ Church, Oxford. His first job was as Attaché, British Legation in Peking. Private Secretary to C. R. Atlee 1931–9. After several attempts, returned to Parliament, 1941, as Labour member for West Bromwich, a seat he held until his death in 1963. During the post-war Labour Government, Financial Secretary to the Admiralty, then Member of State for Colonial Affairs.

astonished when he came so close to fainting in the middle of the meal that he had to be driven back to Coln Rogers. He ascribed his indisposition to being suddenly overcome by an acute sense of evil. David and I wondered whether it emanated from the Dugdales' butler.

Although David remained a devoted friend of Robert Byron he saw less of him after our marriage. They tended to meet in London rather than Coln Rogers or at Robert's parents' house deep in the Savernake Forest. This largely stemmed from changes in their work, for although their occupations still obliged them to visit the same countries, their commitments meant travelling at different times of the year.

We often went to London. Even if I could not buy anything I could look longingly at the textiles designed by members of the Omega Workshop. At first we sometimes spent a night in a small hotel in South Molton Street, but after Alastair Graham had introduced us to Rosa Lewis, owner of the Cavendish Hotel in Jermyn Street, we generally stayed with her.* Rosa claimed to have 'known Alastair since before he was born', when she was employed as a cook by one of his uncles. She was devoted to him, as much because of his charm and sheer niceness, as for his uncle's sake, and therefore took to us, and invariably gave us one of the best of the bedrooms normally reserved for her own use, bedrooms still furnished as if for a country house rather than a hotel. We also had an open invitation to use her private sitting-room, a small room with walls covered by photographs of men friends, many of them killed in the Great War. It was then that I first realized the enormity of the losses which Britain had suffered during those terrible years. When Rosa regaled her visitors with glass after glass of excellent vintage champagne, her memory sometimes played tricks on her, and she would see seated among her living guests the image of a boy who had died years ago. Rosa's friendships were as steadfast as her anger was tenacious. Contrary to his expectations she never forgave Evelyn

*Lewis, Rosa (1867–1952). Aged 12 Rosa, née Ovenden, entered domestic service. Four years later she took up a post with the Comte de Paris, working her way up from scullery maid to kitchen maid and eventually cook. In 1887 she became cook to Lady Randolph Churchill. After marriage to Excelsior Lewis in 1893 she set up a catering business, cooking for Edward VII, Mrs Jacob Astor and others of the aristocracy. In 1902 she bought the Cavendish Hotel which she ran until her death.

Waugh for portraying her in *Vile Bodies* as Lottie Crump of Shepheard's Hotel.

In the mornings, at about nine o'clock, Rosa would wake her private guests by entering their bedrooms carrying large bowls of steaming consommé, calling 'soup for my drunks'. Until one became accustomed to it, chicken broth seemed a curious beverage to start the day, but even without a hangover it was surprisingly invigorating. Yet, except for Rosa's delicious game pie, we none of us ate at the Cavendish, in the belief that its restaurant food was disgusting. Its high price probably helped reduce the cost of entertaining her friends. We were among those from whom Rosa resolutely refused to accept any payment so we were very embarrassed when we discovered that an earnest American friend of our Oxford days, fortunately a man of means, who had heard us talking about the Cavendish, had taken his mother to spend a few days there. On leaving, they were presented with a bill for one hundred pounds, an immense sum in the 1930s, but like Rosa's other clients, they did not query the charge. They did, however, think the hotel expensive and indifferently run, its food boring. Much of it was bought daily by Rosa with a keen eye to cost.

The groceries came from the Civil Service Stores, an emporium in the Strand. Rosa had taken a fancy to me and often invited me to come shopping. 'You'll learn a lot, ducks,' she assured me, 'by watching me shop for my hotel.' Soon after ten she would be waiting in the hall, her two terriers at her feet. She carried herself splendidly and although her thick stockings were often wrinkled round her ankles, she was still very impressive. Wearing an Edwardian shirt-blouse, drab ankle-length skirt and a lovely silk jacket, she got into her chauffeur-driven Daimler and seated herself by a window, yelping dogs springing in beside her. I followed. On entering the Civil Service Stores, her yapping dogs still at her feet, Rosa would ask the portly, frock-coated shopwalker who had misguidedly advanced to greet her, 'What's cheap today?' Then, as often as not, noticing a large, open-topped barrel filled with crystallized fruits, she would take a handful and drop it into my gloved hands saying, 'You're fond of these, aren't you, ducks?'

Rosa's bedroom, on the top floor of the Cavendish, was one of several which must originally have served as maids' rooms. It was furnished with two black iron beds decorated with brass knobs, and the painted white deal furniture then found in staff quarters: a tall, narrow cupboard with a full-length mirror fitted into the front of its door; a single upright chair, seldom an arm, a matching chest containing two half-length and two full-length drawers, a dressing-table with a centrally hinged mirror and a marble-topped wash-stand with a narrow full-length top shelf and a lower one to support a slop pail. Rosa must have slept in just such a room when she first went into service. From then until she died, she shared a similar bedroom with Edith Jeffrey, her only close woman friend, a former housemaid. Edith was a financial wizard and could be heard of a morning telephoning instructions to Rosa's stockbroker. Although Rosa had the stronger will, Edith was more clever, with Rosa usually giving in to her wishes.

At the time Boulestin was the most fashionable restaurant in London. One day, on receiving an unexpectedly generous cheque for an article, in gratitude for Rosa's many kindnesses, we invited her to dine there. Surprised and pleased, she accepted. When we called for her, we found her regaling two unattractive subfusc Welshmen with champagne. To David's annoyance she invited them to come with us. As Rosa was wearing her everyday clothes, we attracted a good deal of attention when we entered. Once seated she ordered *truites au bleu* for us all. Never a lively conversationist she was now silent, her two Welshmen taciturn, doubtless sodden.

Waiting for the fish seemed like a prelude to eternity. Eventually a waiter approached carrying a platter with the fish aligned on it. Displaying it before our longing eyes, he pirouetted and was about to deposit the tray on the side-table preparatory to serving it, when the decorous tranquillity of Boulestin was shattered by Rosa's melodious voice with its strong cockney accent shouting, 'Hey, young man, bring 'em here. Call those *truites au bleu*? I cooked them before you was born. They're not right. Take them away; have others done.'

Abashed the waiter fled. The eyes of all the diners turned to stare at us in astonishment; silence reigned, broken only by a few shocked gasps and one or two suppressed giggles. David was hungry and tired, but managed to control his irritation while I dissolved into laughter. Fortunately, Boulestin had witnessed the scene. He hurried to our table; kissed Rosa; ordered champagne. Gradually conversation resumed. Eventually the waiter reappeared with a platter of trout. Were they the same ones? They looked just the same as the first lot, but this time Rosa scarcely glanced at them. We ate in silence. David had just enough money to cover our vast bill. Fortunately, Rosa appeared to have enjoyed her evening.

When in London we saw a good deal of Lucy Norton. She was later to make her name as a writer and translator but at the time, like Nina Hamnett, was considered a promising artist. We relished her for her wit and sheer niceness. Nina Hamnett often joined in, but was less good company.* Stella Locker Lampson, a girl who had teased me immoderately when we were both at Miss Spalding's school, reappeared as a student at the newly founded Courtauld Institute of Art, and became a close friend. About this time we also got to know Joan Eyres Monsell. As her father was First Sea Lord she was able to give amusing parties in the exotic Regency setting of the Admiralty. Diana Gould, who later married Yehudi Menuhin, and her sister Griselda, later the wife of Louis Kentner, were members of the same circle. Sadly the war severed those vastly enjoyable contacts.

During the thirties we often stayed with Stella Locker Lampson's parents, at Barlborough Hall in Derbyshire, a dream house, probably the earliest to have 'more glass than wall'. When Bess of Hardwick saw it, undeterred that the walls of her new house, Hardwick Hall, were already two storeys high, she engaged the builders of Barlborough to make her a second house, the entrancing New Hardwick Hall, alongside the unfinished first house.† Mrs Locker Lampson had inherited Barlborough from her father. It stood above a disused coal-mine, a perfect house of rare beauty. Sometimes Brinsley Ford was a fellow guest.‡ One evening, dressed as Shelley's ghost, he suddenly appeared in one of its galleries and for a moment it seemed we were gazing on a phantom.

---

*Nina Hamnett, artist and writer, exhibited in the Leicester Gallery, Redfern and Tooth's. Her portrait of Lytton Strachey is in the National Portrait Gallery.
†Elizabeth Hardwick, Countess of Shrewsbury (1520–1608). She built or altered several houses, including Chatsworth. A gypsy predicted that she would not die so long as she continued building. A frost set in; building had to stop; within days the countess died, at Hardwick.
‡Sir Richard Brinsley Ford, chairman of the National Art Collections Fund 1975–80 and a former trustee of the National Gallery; currently director of the *Burlington Magazine* and president of the Walpole Society.

Barlborough is situated fairly close to Renishaw. One of our longer visits coincided with a time when Sir George and Lady Sitwell were staying in England. Although Renishaw now belonged to Osbert, Sir George was determined to see his former home and to persuade Osbert to extend its already vast and magnificent garden. However, in order to avoid any queries from the Inspector of Taxes, Sir George decided that he and his wife would sleep at the Renishaw Arms, whilst spending their waking hours at the house. This Osbert had reopened for the occasion, hiring waiters and kitchen staff from Lyons, rather than engaging temporary footmen.

In a stately home setting the difference between the two occupants was surprisingly marked. Lady Ida was frail, withdrawn, and used a stick when walking. We thought her pathetic, but she remained a stately figure. Although Sir George expressed his wishes to Osbert in a dictatorial tone, we found him neither frightening nor distinguished in appearance. His short stature, spats and monocle gave him the appearance of an Edwardian roué rather than a fop.

At the time the drive at Renishaw was overgrown and the brass doorbell tarnished, but the fine gardens were well kept. Osbert used only part of the house; these rooms were enchanting. In the least attractive room, however, he had collected all the ugliest and heaviest pieces of Victorian furniture, investing it with so sinister an atmosphere that he called it 'the haunted room'.

12

Edinburgh Friendships

If a man does not make new acquaintances as he advances
through life, he will soon find himself left alone.

Dr Samuel Johnson, letter to Lord Chesterfield, 7 February 1754

FORTUNATELY for us, when appointed director of the newly
founded Courtauld Institute of Art in 1932, W. G. Constable
included a course on Byzantine art in the Institute's curriculum
and invited David to run it, also arranging for him to teach on two
consecutive days of the week, which meant that he had to spend
only one night a week in London. It was the first time since our
marriage that we were to be parted for even a short time, which
saddened us both.

However the economic crisis continued to erode our finances.
This depressed David, even though his Courtauld lectures attracted
favourable attention. Some student societies and universities were
quick to invite him to lecture. Among the first was the Eton
Archaeological Society. Student societies could only refund
expenses, but a university offered a fee of some five guineas for a
single lecture. Manchester was the first university to invite David to
address its students; Professor and Mrs John Orr were his hosts.

A Tasmanian by birth John was tall, handsome, urbane, charming, witty and extremely learned.* He also had a discerning eye for

---

*Orr, Professor John, D. Litt., LL D, FBA. Educated Launceston High School, Tasmania:
University of Tasmania; Balliol College, Oxford. At Oxford, where he was the first
Rhodes Scholar from Tasmania, Orr became President of the Arnold Society and rowed
in his college eight. He then studied on the Continent, returning to England to serve, from
1915, in the Intelligence Corps. At Manchester University, then at Edinburgh, he was
noted for detailed research, incisive criticism and trenchant writings. His erudition was
recognized by election to a Fellowship of the British Academy and the award of
Commandeur de la Légion d'Honneur. His extensive interests included the arts; he was
Hon. Vice-Principal of the Society of Scottish Artists.

the fine arts. In 1914, having come to Oxford as a Rhodes Scholar, he was on holiday in Switzerland. So too was Tata de Brissac, an enchanting young girl who, although Russian by birth and environment, was French in descent, her forebears having migrated to St Petersburg at the time of the French Revolution. Like other French émigrés of the period, their children and grandchildren had for the most part married westerners and prospered; especially the De Brissacs who, by the end of the nineteenth century, were doing very well, with Tata's mother ranked as St Petersburg's leading court dressmaker. John and Tata fell in love at sight and married shortly after. By then Tata had persuaded John to specialize in the study of Romance languages. Despite the war, Tata encouraged John to stay on in western Europe and pursue his studies.

By 1919 they were living in England, where John was already regarded as an excellent scholar. One day, while at breakfast, each got a letter. Tata's informed her that the Soviets had confiscated all her assets; as a result, she no longer had an income. John's letter notified him of his appointment to Manchester University's Chair of French, the start of a distinguished career. Having lived on Tata's money, they were now to live on his income. Theirs proved a long and happy marriage, but in the early years of it they were saddened by the loss at birth in Italy of two babies, and in their old age by the death of their adored only child, Alan. Aged nineteen, he was killed when serving as a rear gunner during one of the last of the RAF's thousand-bomber raids over Germany.

David's visit to the Orrs was so successful that it changed the course of our lives. It coincided with John's appointment to the Chair of French and Romance Philology at Edinburgh University. At the time Edinburgh was the only university in Britain with a faculty devoted to the fine arts. The Edinburgh chair was founded in 1880 in memory of the distinguished Scottish portrait painter Sir John Watson Gordon, to provide students over two terms with an outline of classical and European art, those qualifying being awarded a diploma. Its first holder, the distinguished medievalist Professor Baldwin Brown, had been appointed for life; as there was then no retiring age for university teachers, he held his chair until shortly before his death in 1932. On its falling vacant John Orr persuaded David to apply. Like the university's Chair of Music, held at the time by Donald Tovey, and that of Archaeology, held by Gordon

Childe, it required only two terms' residence, the third term being free for research. The chair carried a salary of £1,000, two-thirds of the total paid for a full academic year.

John's suggestion appealed to David, but not to me. Edinburgh seemed infinitely far from Paris, even from Coln Rogers which I already loved, nor was I attracted by the idea of living in university circles. I had looked forward to the life of a field archaeologist, working in the Near or Middle East. Although sure he stood no chance of even being short-listed, David was so worried about money that he felt obliged to apply. He was astonished when summoned to Edinburgh for an interview. He spent a few days with the Orrs exploring the city, delighting in its architecture, revelling in its art galleries. He was greatly encouraged when he heard that he had been placed second only to Herbert Read, an established art historian and poet, with a distinguished military record.

We spent most of the next two years in Coln Rogers where we lived quietly and carefully, for we now had a baby daughter and, to placate my mother-in-law, we engaged a nanny for her. We paid Nanny £70 a year and the couple whom we employed £75; this left us £350 a year to live on, no easy matter even when supplemented by fees from magazine articles. Our first couple, the Sparrows, were nice and efficient; we were all sad when family reasons forced them to leave. We replaced them with the Jacksons, an equally nice couple from Oddington, the man working as gardener-houseman, his wife as cook-general. They were delighted to have three days off a fortnight, and two hours each afternoon.

Nanny Teago, from Cirencester, was in her seventies and disliked taking her weekly day off. This meant we could pursue our archaeological interests, conducting small excavations or soundings in Constantinople or at Hira, on the Euphrates near Kufa, or undertaking journeys of exploration in Turkey. As a result we lost touch with the British art world and were astonished to receive a letter in the early summer of 1934 offering David the Watson Gordon Chair of Fine Arts at Edinburgh University. We reacted by telephoning the Orrs to find out whether it was a tiresome joke.

They assured us it was nothing of the sort. Herbert Read had recently abandoned his wife and twelve-year-old son for one of his students and had been forced to resign. David, as runner-up to Read, was now in line for the post. David was so enchanted by the offer he instantly accepted. He never regretted it. My heart sank at the prospect, but I readily conceded that the salary would end our financial difficulties. Luckily I did not foresee the servant problems in store for us. Neither the dear Jacksons, nor any of their Gloucestershire successors, could adapt to Edinburgh life, while Scottish maids suffered acute homesickness in Gloucestershire. Each group begged to be put on board wages for half the year, but even with David's professional salary we could not afford it. As a result we were often oppressed by domestic difficulties.

In August 1934 we went to Edinburgh to house-hunt. We were surprised to find the train crowded until we realized that we were travelling on 11 August, the eve of the grouse-shooting season. When we reached Edinburgh, it was snowing hard and an icy wind blew at gale force. As on the Continent we had never booked hotel rooms, we had not done so in Edinburgh and were appalled to find all the hotels full up.

Eventually we found a room in Princes Street, near the Waverley station. Our bedroom was extremely cold. On asking for the bar, we discovered that we had booked into a temperance hotel. By the following morning I had developed a raging cold. As we drove round the town to get an idea of where we wanted to live, I tried to banish the memory of Dr Johnson's assertion that 'the noblest prospect that a Scotchman ever sees is the highroad that leads to England.'

Soon, however, moved by its architecture, we decided we had to find a flat in the New Town. As nothing was available in Charlotte Square, we opted for a flat in Moray Place, where the architecture was almost as splendid as in the Square. While most of its buildings were large family houses, the corner ones had been designed as flats. However, after the First World War, some of the single houses had been converted into flats extending over two floors. As Moray Place was much sought after, we were lucky to find a basement and ground-floor flat at no. 2. Although it had no view – ironically in a city of magnificent vistas – we decided to rent it in the hope of finding a flat with a view.

This we eventually did, acquiring a top double flat at the north-west corner of Moray Place. There, the front rooms faced the centrally placed garden reserved for residents, whilst the back rooms had a magnificent outlook over Doune Terrace and the Waters of Leith where, up until late Edwardian times, people of fashion continued to gather round St Bernard's Well and 'take the cure'. To the west the gorge was spanned by Telford's magnificent bridge and in the far distance gleamed the sea. Unfortunately in the 1930s none of these houses had lifts or central heating. I suffered permanently from the absence of both, and never ceased to deplore the lack of double glazing in a town situated on the same latitude as Moscow.

We were astonished to learn that the vast cupboards in New Town bedrooms, called 'presses', had probably originally been used as powdering closets and, in late Victorian times, as maids' bedrooms. Indeed, one was still used as such by a very old lady, living almost next door. A year later Jack and Mimi Suffolk became our neighbours and dear friends.*

One way and another, I had seen much bad housing, but the Edinburgh slums came as a great shock. Some Moray Place houses backed on to truly atrocious working-class blocks. In them, a single gas-jet lit the dank and tortuous communal staircases, with a stinking lavatory – and there was only one – on each landing, to serve the floor's numerous occupants. However, the worst slums were in the Old Town near Holyrood Palace. Here a vast seventeenth-century building had been converted into a hostel for male geriatrics, dressed in nightshirts and diminutive dunces' caps, the majority unwashed, huddling on ramshackle beds with horrifically dirty bedding. The overall impression was Hogarthian. All too many slums survived the Second World War, and were so vile that I persuaded Denzil Batchelor to write an article on them for *Picture Post*.† Its appearance angered many in Edinburgh.

---

*Charles Henry George, 20th Earl of Suffolk and Berkshire, GC, BSc, FRSE, FRSSA, FZS. It is surprising that Tamara did not say more about the Suffolks, since Mimi and she became godparents to each other's children. Before the war they saw each other, both in Edinburgh and in the country. During the war David and Tamara often shared hilarious dinners with Jack and his team. As a young man Jack had gone round the world on a sailing ship. It was through his love of the theatre that he met Mimi, whom he married in 1934. When France capitulated Jack was instrumental in getting a vast quantity of diamonds out of that country to prevent their falling into German hands. Then, in charge of the Scientific Research Experimental Unit, he was responsible for finding ways of deactivating new types of bombs. It was whilst working on one of these that he was killed. His George Cross was awarded posthumously.

†Denzil Batchelor, 'The Best and Worst of Some British Cities. 3 – Edinburgh', *Picture Post*, 3 January 1954.

In the thirties many Victorian customs still survived in Edinburgh. The university had nowhere for members of the teaching
staff to meet. It fell to the deans of each faculty to introduce new-
comers to future colleagues, from amongst whom they would draw
most of their friends. In the case of a newly appointed professor, it
was customary for fellow professors each in turn to give a formal
welcoming dinner party. Accordingly, soon after the start of our
first Michaelmas term, we received almost seventy invitations to
dinner parties, carefully spaced out over two terms.

I felt out of place at these functions, which were formal enough
for invitations to stipulate 'white tie'. From this I concluded that I
would have to wear full evening dress rather than a dinner dress. I
had three, including my favourite, a stunning Balenciaga, a present
from my mother-in-law. All three were low cut and sleeveless, to be
worn with long white kid gloves. As they were far too flimsy for
Edinburgh, they turned the dinners into ordeals; rather than ball
gowns, caftans were better suited to the gigantic reception rooms
in Edinburgh's Regency and early Victorian houses.

On arrival, a uniformed parlour maid directed women guests to
an unheated upstairs bedroom to leave their cloaks. The maid then
led each couple to the drawing-room, asking their names. To begin
with I could not understand the maid's request, any more than she
could understand my rendering of our surname, the English pro-
nunciation of the letter 'r' always eluding me. Cowering beside
David, I would leave it to him to give our name as we entered a vast
and icy drawing-room where a small and reluctant fire burned.

The dining-rooms were even colder than the drawing-rooms, for
there the tentative blue flames of a recently lit fire fought a losing
battle with a glacial chimney. As guest of honour I was always
seated to the right of a usually untalkative host. The menu rarely
varied, generally starting with a watery consommé, followed by
tail-in-mouth whiting in parsley sauce; a leg of lamb came next;
then a trifle, with a savoury rounding off the meal. Long before its
end I was shivering with cold and oppressed by gloom.

One particular evening tried me beyond bearing. Our host was
kindly and hospitable, our hostess foolish and opinionated. On
arrival, the parlour maid, who looked just like all the other parlour
maids who had confronted us, said, 'Professor and Mrs Talbot
Rice, isn't it?' How could she have known, I wondered. The

drawing-room was even colder than the others, and in the dining-room the fire had gone out, but a blizzard raged outside. The menu was the same as ever, and as the trying meal neared its end, our hostess enlarged on the merits of Bolshevism. When she turned to me for corroboration my self-control snapped and, forgetting my duties as guest, I hotly contradicted her. It was probably to retrieve the situation that another guest spoke approvingly of the Nazis, whose obnoxious beliefs were already taking hold in Germany. It was more than I could stand. I lost my temper, but back in the drawing-room felt ashamed of my behaviour. We left as soon as we decently could, with me close to tears, convinced that I was unsuited to university life.

As usual, Tata telephoned next day to ask about the dinner party. Again close to tears I said I could not stand another such evening. 'Why?' she asked, with deep concern. 'Well, it's all so awful,' I wailed. 'The intense cold; always the same food; my inability to distinguish one Scottish face from another; and as to the conversation – I cannot stand being repeatedly told about the Franco-Scottish connection. Life here differs greatly to that in France, and the connection seems to boil down to a dish being called an ashet. How can I bear to hear the Communists and Nazis extolled?'

'Let's take first things first,' said Tata. 'Do you realize that it is difficult for people to give large formal dinners nowadays? So, to uphold tradition, they hire the cook and parlour maid from Mackie's for the evening. That's why you often see the same parlour maid and have the same menu. As to the cold – what sort of dress do you wear?' 'Well, since David is in a white tie, I naturally wear an evening dress,' I answered. 'Do you mean a low-cut long one?' she asked. 'Yes, of course, what else with tails?'

'Oh, ma chérie, ma chérie,' cried Tata, 'I should have told you. You should wear a long-sleeved, high-necked silk dress with a thin spencer under it. People no longer regularly use their drawing- and dining-rooms so both are apt to be cold. You ought to appreciate the trouble and expense David's colleagues are taking on your behalf.' Nostalgically, my thoughts flew to cosy evenings in Paris eating bread and ham with fellow émigrés. 'As for last night's conversation,' Tata continued, 'your hostess is known for her extreme left-wing views; you will have to learn to disregard them. Pro-Nazi sentiments are more difficult to deal with, but you will encounter them in all sections of society, in London as much as in Edinburgh. Face up to them, don't retreat.' Feeling thoroughly ashamed of my faintheartedness, I decided to persevere and David cheered me by suggesting that I spend half-term in Paris.

The wives of newly appointed dons met more established wives at the monthly meetings of the Tea and Luncheon clubs. Tata told me that I was expected to become a member of both. Meanwhile she introduced me to some of David's colleagues. One recently retired professor kindly offered David his lecture texts, in the hope that they might be useful. Not wanting to rebuff him David accepted. Glancing through, he was amused to find in one lecture a reminder to announce a holiday in honour of the Queen's birthday, presumably Queen Victoria's. On reading that, David decided to use headings rather than detailed texts which, as he knew, could be hired by undergraduates. This encouraged his students to attend his lectures, so obviating the need for a roll-call or submission of class cards to prove their attendance.*

Tata Orr took me to the first meeting of the Tea Club. It was held in the university's Old College, in the magnificent eighteenth-century room used as a library until, in 1967, the books were rehoused in Basil Spence's less beautiful but more convenient, purpose-built library in George Square.† Obediently I joined the club and was introduced to a succession of ladies. I found the experience intimidating until I met a sympathetic and diverting Belgian, witty and elegant, the wife of a lecturer in the French department.

The Lunch Club met in a private room in Mackie's Princes Street tea-shop. After the meal we were instructed to circulate, and I looked for the attractive Belgian. To my surprise no one knew her, and Tata explained with considerable embarrassment that membership of the Lunch Club was restricted to professors' wives, whilst the Tea Club admitted all teaching staff wives. Horrified by

---

*Class cards had still to be handed in at some lectures in the 1950s.
†Spence, Sir Basil, OM, OBE, RA. Educated George Watson's College, Edinburgh; Edinburgh School of Architecture. Spence began his architectural career in the office of Sir Edwin Lutyens: war intervening, he joined the Royal Artillery and was twice mentioned in despatches. It was not until 1951 that he gained public acclaim as an imaginative designer, both for his 'Sea and Ships' pavilion at the 1951 Festival of Britain, and for his prize-winning designs for rebuilding Coventry Cathedral. Of an evening he would bring these along to Moray Place, eagerly explaining their symbolism to David and Tamara.

such snobbery, I rushed to the club secretary and tendered my resignation. Although such a thing was unprecedented I stood my ground, refusing to join the Lunch Club until it admitted all the wives. This decision made me extremely unpopular.

My brother-in-law Harry had obtained two introductions for us from a fellow officer, married to an Edinburgh girl. One was to her parents who lived in a beautiful Adam house in Charlotte Square. They were quick to invite us to dinner, to which we looked forward with considerable pleasure. David's last lecture of the day took place from five to six every evening, so he had little time in which to get home and change for a formal dinner party. That morning he asked me what to wear for dinner. 'Oh, a dinner-jacket surely,' I assured him, for the invitation had been informally worded, written in long hand with no mention of clothes.

As our flat was within three minutes of Charlotte Square we decided to walk there. As we approached our hosts' door a taxi drew up, a couple descended and entered the house just ahead of us. We followed, and were received by two middle-aged parlour maids wearing elegant beige dresses with écru lace aprons and caps. They directed the ladies to one cloakroom, the men to another. My fellow guest, wearing a long, pale blue satin dress, hardly reacted when I said good evening. On re-entering the hall her husband joined her, and they walked up a lovely curved Adam staircase whilst I waited for David at its foot. There was no sign of him. I was surprised, for he was always quick at leaving his overcoat.

As I waited, further guests arrived. I got more and more worried. After a while I asked the parlour maid if she had by any chance seen my husband go upstairs. 'Yes,' she replied. Horrified at having been abandoned, close to panic, I walked upstairs. On reaching the top landing my advance was blocked by the lady in the pale blue dress and her husband, who were busily assuring yet another maid that they had indeed been asked to dinner that night. 'Your name is not on the list,' the maid insisted. As she spoke a short, plump, elderly lady wearing a black Chantilly lace dress appeared, looked at her guests and squawked, 'You, you were asked for today fortnight, not for today.' As they turned to rush down the stairs, the lady in the Chantilly lace dress and I were left facing each other. Then I too turned and fled, thinking that David must have abandoned me on finding that we had come on the wrong night.

When I collided with him in the hall I was furious. Seizing my arm he forced me to turn and mount the stairs. I quailed as he gave the maid on the landing our name. Fortunately, we were on the guest list. Still speechless, we entered the drawing-room just as dinner was announced. An elderly gentleman offered his arm and silently led me to my place. As I struggled to regain my composure I realized that I, like the other ladies, had only three oysters set before me, while men had four. Surely, I thought, with twenty-two of us at table, by docking the men of their fourth oyster, the lady wearing the pale blue dress and her husband could have been fitted in.

'Are you enjoying yourself?' my neighbour asked. As it was obvious that I was not, I replied, no. 'Why not?' he continued. I told him about the lady in blue. I began to relax, but was still furious with David. 'Why did you leave me?' I queried as we walked home. 'Why, because I had to run home and change,' he explained. 'Didn't you notice that all the men were wearing tails?' I had not. Later it transpired that the parlour maid who received the guests was deaf, and in the habit of replying 'yes' to anything said to her. She had done so, both when David had asked her to explain his absence to me, and when I asked whether he had gone upstairs without waiting for me.

In contrast, Harry's second letter of introduction had much happier results. It was sent to Pat Smythe, a Writer to the Signet,[*] whom Harry had met before the war when both were freshmen at Christ Church. Pat was married to Ysenda Maxtone Graham.[†] They lived with their three young sons in a house in Randolph Cliff with a spectacular view over the Waters of Leith, but were soon to move to an even lovelier house in Heriot Row. They replied to Harry's letter by asking us to a large party. It was fun, and also served as the springboard for several of our most cherished friendships, first and foremost that with our hosts. Their guests, regardless of their different professions, shared Pat and Ysenda's

---

[*]One performing, in the Supreme Court of Scotland, duties similar to those of a solicitor and attorney in England.
[†]Smythe, Patrick Cecil, OBE (Mil.), WS. Educated Charterhouse; Christ Church, Oxford. In the First World War he was mentioned in despatches when serving in France with the 2/6th Battalion Black Watch. He became a Writer to the Signet in 1920, the same year in which he married Ysenda Maxtone Graham.

knowledge of classical music. As in the eighteenth century, Pat, Ysenda and their gifted sons formed a chamber orchestra of real distinction.

Also at that party was Colin Mackenzie who became a special friend.* The five of us were to explore Edinburgh and much of Scotland together. We attended first nights of plays being tried out in Edinburgh or Glasgow, before transferring to London; we never missed an important classical concert; and also regularly went to both of Edinburgh's music-halls, the Empire and the Royal, where the twice-nightly performances were generally filled to capacity. The 'artistes' were for the most part uninhibited comics, whose vulgarity was too earthy to be common. Their most popular songs were lively, often tender and accompanied by that touch of bravado which Nigel had taught me to enjoy.

In addition to being a skilled dry fly fisherman, Pat wrote amusing light verse. For her part, Ysenda, who was an excellent mimic, had the knack of overhearing such startling remarks as those made by a woman at a Buckingham Palace investiture who muttered hopefully to her companion, in a Morningside accent, 'Maybe my feet would not hurt so much if I had my toenails cut.' Or that of a salesgirl at Jenner's who consoled a frustrated customer by assuring her that Jenner's was 'often and often asked for red hair nets but naiver, naiver, kept them'. Perhaps because Ysenda went straight from the schoolroom to nursing in France during the First World War, she was blessed with a deep yet clear-headed sense of compassion which enabled her to help a wide variety of people to face up to life.

Ysenda's mother, Margaret Maxtone Graham of Cultoquhey, was as courageous and amusing as her daughter: erudite, shrewd, broadminded and with an acute sense of humour. She also had that understanding of the world and its ways that Victorian ladies of distinction somehow managed to acquire. She was well travelled,

---

*Mackenzie, Colin Hercules, CMG, Hon. LL B. Educated Eton; King's College, Cambridge. Graduated with a First in Economics and awarded the Chancellor's Medal for English Verse. After losing a leg whilst serving with the Scots Guards in France in the First World War, Mackenzie joined the thread-making firm of J. & A. Coats, becoming director in 1928. During the Second World War he commanded Force 136, the Far Eastern counterpart of Special Operations Executive, receiving decorations from the French and the Dutch, as well as the CMG.

widely read, and herself the author of several delightful family histories and a charming book on the royal children of France. She also revelled in real, not fictitious murders: William Roughead, editor of the accounts of many famous Scottish trials, was one of her favourite dinner guests. Her talent to surprise lasted to the end. When bedridden but mentally alert, she used an early Victorian doll she had had as a child, as a focal point for rounding up several further vintage dolls, and inviting her grandchildren and several of her youngest friends, including our daughter, to a memorable dolls' tea-party.

It was through the Smythes that we got to know, amongst so many more, the Donald Rosses and the Ian Whytes. Although close friends, no two men could have been more different than Donald Ross and Ian Whyte. Donald, a Morayshire laird, was a man of the open air and vast expanses, a sailor, forester, and cattle breeder who was attempting to retrieve the family finances by opening a shop in Queensferry Street. It prospered from the start so that Donald was soon able to transform it into the Aperitif Restaurant, which was to vie in popularity with the Café Royal. At the outbreak of war Donald joined the navy and his wife, Ismay Crichton-Stuart, took over the running of the Aperitif, sitting at its cash desk in the evenings, in a patronne's black dress. On D-Day, Donald was serving on a destroyer involved in the Normandy landings. Amidst the hubbub of the attack he managed to secure a consignment of Camembert and to persuade a friend returning to England to send the cheese to Ismay. Within twenty-four hours of the Allied landing, Camembert featured on the Aperitif's menu. When an astonished customer remarked on it, Ismay nonchalantly assured him that the cheese had been sent by 'our man in Normandy'.

Ian Whyte resembled Donald in his love of good company, food and wine, but music was the essence of his life. In the early 1930s, the BBC Scottish Orchestra was based in Edinburgh and it was a sad day for us when it transferred to Glasgow, as its conductor, Ian, went with it. At the time many of us were captivated by the *Enigma Variations*; following in Elgar's footsteps, Ian delighted in improvising on the piano apt musical interpretations of his friends' personalities. His wife was placid, motherly and immensely hospitable. After the war the atmosphere we associated with Ian was to a large extent recreated for us by Tommy and Eileen Matthews who, although employed by the Scottish National Orchestra – he as leader, she as pianist – preferred to live in Edinburgh and commute.*

Soon after our arrival in Edinburgh we received an invitation from Moray McLaren to a Sunday morning champagne party. At the time Moray lived in Edinburgh and worked for the Scottish BBC. We had not experienced the pre-war Scottish sabbath, so Moray's invitation did not strike us as in any way unusual. We arrived at midday to find the party in full swing, excellent champagne flowing like water, but no food. The party was immensely enjoyable and lasted into the early evening. As we walked home at dusk along cobbled, dimly lit streets powdered with snow, we savoured the beauty of the town's late Georgian architecture and concluded that such parties would greatly enhance university life. All too soon we found that the party was unique. The champagne was just a windfall – a present from a Polish friend of Moray.

Thanks to Moray we quickly got to know many of Edinburgh's leading intellectuals; amongst the first was David Scott-Moncrieff who wanted to spend a small legacy on mounting an exhibition of modern art. On finding that we were both fascinated by the portraits of Modigliani, an artist then almost unknown in Edinburgh, he decided to give that artist a one-man show and generously suggested that I join him in the enterprise. We were anxious to present the paintings in the right sort of setting, and were delighted when Whytock & Reid, a leading local firm of decorators and furniture-makers, offered us their Charlotte Square premises. This meant we could show the paintings in furnished surroundings as at the Hermitage at Leningrad and, to some extent, at the Fitzwilliam at Cambridge. The resulting exhibition attracted much favourable comment.†

---

*Before appointment to the Scottish National Orchestra (now RSNO) as Assistant Conductor and Leader, Thomas Matthews had led the LSO, the LPO and Covent Garden Orchestra. He appeared as a soloist. In 1961 he took up an appointment as Resident Conductor of the Tasmanian Symphony Orchestra. His pianist wife was Australian.

†Arranged on behalf of the Leith Unemployed Men's Club – one of the many clubs set up in Edinburgh in the thirties to cater for the high numbers of unemployed – the November 1937 Modigliani exhibition included drawings and one or two pieces of sculpture as well as oils. Of the latter, the *Scotsman* singled out for mention portraits of Lounia Czechowsjka (Mme Monnier) and *Young Girl with Red Hair*. David Scott-Moncrieff was then a partner in the law firm Tody, Murray & Jamieson. A member of the Royal Company of Archers. Purse Bearer to the Queen's Commissioner, the Earl of Wemyss and March, at the General Assemblies of 1959 and 1960; Baillie, Palace of Holyrood House 1957–79.

It was at Moray's also that we first met the Maitlands, whom we often visited in the years that followed in their Heriot Row house, either for a stimulating concert or to see their ever-growing collection of fine Post-Impressionist paintings – later bequeathed to the National Gallery of Scotland.*

Of all the arts practised in Edinburgh, painting came first. We spent much of our free time with artists such as James Cowie, Johnny Maxwell, Willie MacTaggart, William Gillies and, later, Anne Redpath, Robin Philipson, Victorine Foot and her husband the sculptor Eric Schilsky, Elizabeth Blackadder and her painter-husband John Houston, and the stained-glass artist Willie Wilson. But we spent even more time with Joan and Basil Spence and Jas Tarnowski.†

Once settled in Edinburgh we soon discovered the auction rooms of Dowell's and of Lyon & Turnbull, both of which regularly held picture sales. David had wanted to acquire works by contemporary Scottish artists but even their modest prices were more than we could afford. However, older pictures cost so little that we seldom missed a sale; soon David's colleagues, especially John Orr and A. H. Coxon, were following our example. Eventually we were nicknamed the five-pound brigade, that being our limit. I still regret not buying an adorable Guardi for £31, an exquisite Boudin for £38 and a huge John Martin with a hole at its centre for only £28.

One of the first pictures I bought at Dowell's was a small early Victorian oil of a large house poised on a cliff overlooking the sea. It was the work of a skilled artist with an eye for the picturesque and a mind attuned to the romanticism of Walter Scott. We were enchanted with it, but a few days later we received a letter, signed Victoria Wemyss, asking whether we would consider ceding the painting to her, as it was a view of her house. Since it seemed only

---

*In 1960 Alexander Maitland QC (later Kt.) presented twenty-one superb nineteenth- and twentieth-century French paintings to the National Gallery of Scotland in memory of his wife, Rosalind Gertrude née Craig-Sellar. Throughout their married life, the couple had collected the paintings with the Gallery in view as their final home, choosing them not only because they both loved each work, but because each painting would fill a gap in the Gallery's collections. See D. Baxendall and C. Thompson, *The Maitland Gift and Related Pictures*, National Gallery of Scotland, 1963.

†Count Jan (Jas) Tarnowski. Tarnowski served in the Polish Army during the war and settled thereafter in Scotland. Having before the war made his Warsaw home into a museum, and studied a wide range of arts and crafts, he was an ideal choice for the appointment of artistic adviser to the Scottish Craft Centre.

right that the owner of the house should also own the picture, we readily agreed, if with a tinge of regret.

The incident led to our forming a lifelong friendship with Michael and Victoria Wemyss, an equally close and precious one with David and Mary Crawford, and other treasured friends living in Fife and Perthshire. Until the launch of the new Forth road bridge, our visits to them were relatively rare, for they depended on the sailings of the Queensferry ferries, the demands for which were sometimes so heavy that we had to choose between queuing for an hour or so, or taking the long alternative route through romantic Culross. After the war, when especially depressed by currency restrictions which virtually ruled out foreign travel, I used to give myself the illusion of embarking on a long journey by taking the children across the Forth by the Burnt Island ferry; the length of the crossing entitled that ferry to open its bar as though on the high seas.

13

A Gathering of Dark Clouds

Now I fear disturbance of the quiet seasons:
Winter shall come bringing death from the sea,
Ruinous spring shall beat at our doors,
Root and shoot shall eat our eyes and our ears . . .
Some malady is coming upon us. We wait, we wait.

T. S. Eliot, *Murder in the Cathedral*

WHEN Geoffrey Knox was in England, either on leave or on a home posting, we often met, dining at such delicious restaurants as Prunier's, Scott's or Boulestin. He also greatly enjoyed staying at Pigeon House, photographing the garden we were making; meeting our friends; above all sightseeing with a luscious picnic. Those picnics were always immensely enjoyable, whether held in the Konya plain, verdant England, the Saar or Hungary.

1935 was plebiscite year in the Saar.* Geoffrey went there the year before to administer the region during that critical period, to ensure that there was no intimidation during the election. In December 1934 we stayed with him in Saarbrucken, in a house requisitioned as his residence. It must have belonged to a prosperous burgher with dissolute tastes because the bathroom had a glass wall and the bedrooms extremely suggestive frescos. This erotic atmosphere was reflected in the behaviour of Klaxon, Geoffrey's Siamese tom-cat, who walked along the parapet screeching, his antics helping to ease the tense atmosphere.

Geoffrey was quick to assess the dangerous situation and soon realized that his entire staff consisted of Nazis who might well make an attempt on his life. Seemingly carefree, Geoffrey was at pains never to let his chauffeur know his movements in advance.

---

*Although the smallest of the German states, the Saar was of great importance because of its coal and steel production. After the First World War it was administered by the League of Nations. In a plebiscite held in 1935, over 90 per cent of the population voted for a return to Germany.

When planning a picnic, he invariably ordered enough food for his driver and filled up with petrol. Only when the car had been loaded, and David and I were seated in it, would Geoffrey dismiss his chauffeur. Shortly before Christmas we visited Trier without the driver. It was a clear, sunny winter day with snow deep on the ground. Christmas trees were on sale in the markets, the church doors were open to reveal their candlelit interiors but, although the scene evoked a bygone memory, the atmosphere was tense.

Geoffrey's next posting was to Hungary. We often stayed with him in Budapest, in the fine eighteenth-century house on the hill overlooking the Danube and the more modern part of the city. Benjie and Tamara (née Karsavina, Diaghilev's ballerina) Bruce were in another equally beautiful eighteenth-century mansion, in a ground-floor flat filled with their lovely English and Russian furniture. Benjie was acting as financial adviser to the Hungarian Government.* He and Tamara were very happy there, and so much loved that, on the outbreak of war, the Hungarians packed and stored their belongings, returning them when the war was over. However they were mostly in fragments, having suffered a direct hit from a bomb.

Hungary was then undergoing an economic crisis, and many once wealthy citizens were living in greatly reduced circumstances. However, they refused to alter their way of life, partly out of obstinacy, partly because money passed from one pocket to the other with such speed that few realized when they were short of it. If a butler's white cotton gloves were not as spotless as in the past, the dishes he handed round at luncheon or dinner had lost little of their excellence. Class distinctions were still of almost medieval severity.

In Bucharest, only a couple of years later, a friend of David, a delightful regular soldier, became engaged to a young Romanian aristocrat. They were very much in love and she hurried to invite her girl-friends to a tea-party to tell them of her happiness. 'Was he a commoner?' one of them asked. 'Yes, indeed,' she was assured.

---

*Henry James Bruce (Benjie), CMG, MVO, joined the Foreign Office in 1904. In 1913 he was posted to St Petersburg, an appropriate move since he already spoke Russian. He was promoted First Secretary in May 1918 but within three months had been transferred to Tangier. In 1915 he had married the beautiful prima ballerina Tamara Karsavina, leading dancer of Diaghilev's Ballets Russes from 1909 to 1922. She continued to make guest appearances with Diaghilev's company until 1929. Now retired from the Foreign Office, Bruce became, in 1931, adviser to the National Bank of Hungary.

'How awful,' exclaimed another, 'toute une vie de bout de table', as she considered the question of precedence.

For all our gaiety, our giggles over such remarks and our genuine liking and respect for the many educated Hungarians and Romanians, our minds were often filled with more sinister considerations. When alone with Geoffrey in his study, with ever-increasing revulsion we surveyed neighbouring Germany, a setting for inescapably sinister developments which all pointed to the imminence of war. Despite supporting evidence, Geoffrey's reports expressing this conviction seemed to have no impact on the Foreign Office. Even the German reoccupation of the Rhine seemed to leave the Foreign Office unmoved. We felt that time was running out, that another war would involve the whole of Europe. Believing that the civilization we loved was under threat, we lived in the present, setting great store on friendship and the arts. Since artistry expresses all that is best in human nature, we sought it in the contemporary arts, in *haute cuisine*, in the remains of ancient civilizations and the beauties of nature.

At the outbreak of the Second World War, Geoffrey begged to be given some form of war work in England. Instead he was appointed ambassador to Rio de Janeiro, Brazil – a city swarming with German spies. As he could not control their activities he resigned from the Diplomatic Service, went to live in Jamaica, and died soon after.

From about 1936 travelling in parts of Europe became unpleasant. On one occasion we were driving through southern Bavaria. I was waiting for David in the hotel lobby when, perhaps because there were a lot of Nazi officers about, the hotel manager greeted me with the Hitler salute. I said 'Good morning'. Again he clicked his heels, raised his arm and shouted 'Heil Hitler'. So I said 'Guten Tag'. Once more he gave the Nazi salute. Concealing that I was losing my temper, I used the Bavarian greeting, 'Grüss Gott'. Fortunately, David arrived just as some German officers moved menacingly around me.

In 1938 Charles des Graz came to stay at Pigeon House for our first partridge shoot of the season. His arrival coincided with that of Chamberlain's return from his meeting with Hitler in Munich.*

---

*29 September 1938. Munich was the venue of a conference on the future of Czechoslovakia attended by Hitler, the British Prime Minister Neville Chamberlain, and the French and Italian leaders. Czechoslovakia was not represented but was forced, by Chamberlain's policy of appeasement, to surrender one-fifth of her territory and great economic resources.

Charles had travelled to Kemble by the 4.45, the train we always tried to catch because of the delectable 3s. 6d. tea served in its dining-car. Driving back from the station we stopped at our local, the Hare and Hounds, to hear Chamberlain's announcement on the wireless. Most of the local agricultural workers were already there and we arrived just in time to hear the Prime Minister report that he had returned from Germany bringing peace with honour. At the Hare and Hounds at Foss Cross the news was received in grim silence, with consternation and shame, whatever the reaction to the speech may have been in the rest of Britain. We all sensed the agreement was contemptible. Everyone felt dishonoured, unable to look his companions in the eye. Charles broke the tension by calling for a round of drinks.

Nine months later, after I had applied for employment in the event of war, I was sent to London to a course on postal censorship. To my astonishment Charles addressed the opening session. Only then did I learn he had been a postal censor during the First World War, as he was to be in the Second.

Although David belonged to a reserved occupation, in the autumn of 1938 he had volunteered for military service, asking to join the Welsh Guards. To his regret he was posted to military intelligence, attending a training course in the spring of 1939.

By the outbreak of the war we were both already in London, David having been called up in mid-August and I on 1 September.* There, things were made easy for us by the kindness of friends, first John and Prim Codrington, then Francis Watson. The Codringtons offered us a room in their longish, single-storeyed Regency villa, set in an acre of garden. Recently bought, it was flanked to the west by Onslow Square houses, and on the east by those of Pelham Street, where the Codringtons also owned a studio, let to Augustus John. Their beautiful garden was balm to our spirits during the glorious autumn evenings of that ominous month.

Later we shared Francis Watson's attractive house in Ebury Street. Later still I was to move into a small top-floor service flat in Park Place, opposite the Overseas League. By that time night

---

*At the time of Munich Tamara had volunteered for service in the event of war and prepared herself for the outbreak by passing the St Andrew's Ambulance Association examination in Ambulance Work and First Aid to the Injured in December 1938 and that on Air Raid Precautions in March 1939.

bombing had become a feature of London life, yet however late I returned to my flatlet, the elderly butler who served my dinner was always waiting up for me. It took me some time to discover that he lived somewhere in north London, yet his courage and professional pride were such that he never hurried over my dinners. His refusal to leave earlier so worried me that I often said I would eat out when I had no intention of doing so.

I was in Park Place when the West End suffered its worst air raids and I had my busiest night of fire-fighting.* Round us the whole of London seemed ablaze. With bombs raining down, some firemen were ordered to clear the Overseas League. A group of them emerged carrying a soldier, inert but with no signs of blood on him.

Conquering my terror, trying to remember my first aid training, I told the men to lay him on the pavement for me to examine. Very gingerly, as I had been taught, I felt his body, starting with his toes. During training I had practised this on healthy volunteers and his body felt no different from theirs but he remained inert. My terror returned as I reached his chest. I had no idea what was the matter. His heart seemed to be normal. Not until my head was level with his and I smelt his breath did I realize that my casualty, mercifully my only one throughout the war, was merely dead drunk. Rising from the pavement I laughed and asked some firemen to dip him in a nearby emergency tank.

Quickly sizing up the situation, laughing as heartily as I, they did so, to the horror of some onlookers in my block of flats. It was hard to convince them that we were not suffering from hysterics, until my poor drunk regained consciousness and slunk off in shame.

As I was walking to work along King Street next morning I suddenly saw a hole where the Orleans had stood. The house had received a direct hit, and nothing was left but a void. Fortunately its entire staff had sought safety in a shelter and no one was hurt. As I stood looking at the gaping hole, I was ashamed to find myself crying; crying for all the innocent pleasures, the many convivial hours David and I had enjoyed there; crying not so much for the loss of the Orleans itself, as for the loss of a setting emblematic of a way of life sustained by standards of good fellowship, service and excellence that were unlikely to survive.

---

*London suffered its most damaging raid of 1941 on 10 May, when 1,400 civilians were killed, 5,000 houses destroyed and 12,000 people made homeless.

The Second World War

Both David and Tamara volunteered at the time of Munich, and were called up before war was declared on 3 September 1939. Tamara's mother had been persuaded to extend her annual visit to Gloucestershire from France, so was still in this country. Maykins, Tamara's governess from Russian days, came to Pigeon House to look after their daughter Elizabeth.

Apart from a brief intermission when her second daughter, Nina, was born in 1941, Tamara was in London from mid-1939 until the birth of her son, Nicholas, in mid-1944. First, she worked in censorship but on 17 May 1940 she heard from the Establishment Officer of the Ministry of Information of her appointment as a temporary Junior Assistant Specialist in the Foreign Division at an annual salary of £260, with a leave entitlement of twenty-four days. Whether the move was at her request is not known, but she used often to say how uncongenial she had found censorship.

The Ministry of Information, housed in the Bloomsbury building of the University of London, came into being a few days after the outbreak of hostilities, to provide an overseas news service. It did not handle propaganda, which was the responsibility of the Political War Executive. Tamara was posted to the division dealing with neutral countries, in particular to the Middle Eastern section then covering Turkey, Syria and Palestine but later expanded to include all Arabic and Persian countries. Her old friend, Leigh Ashton, was already at the Ministry, first in charge of Finance; then, from 1941, Deputy Director of Neutral Countries and finally Director of the British Information Office, Istanbul.

In the years immediately preceding the outbreak of war, France and Britain on the one hand, Germany on the other, paid court to Turkey who flirted with both. Eventually, in October 1939, Britain and Turkey signed a Treaty of Mutual Assistance which committed the Allies to assist should Turkey be engaged in a war with a European power, but did not impose a similar commitment on Turkey.

Turkey was determined on non-involvement, a course which appeared particularly sagacious in 1941, when the Germans swept through Yugoslavia, Greece and Crete. Yet a Turkish-German Treaty of Friendship and Non-Aggression was signed in June 1941, Turkey thus resourcefully completing treaties with both Allies and Axis.

As the Allies slowly gained the upper hand in late 1942 and 1943, Turkish partiality veered back to her first friends, but not until 23 February 1945 did she declare war on Germany and Japan.

The aims of the Ministry so far as Turkey was concerned are set out in a Planning Committee summary now in the Public Record Office. The principal objectives were to convince the Turks that the Allies had confidence in Turkish integrity and admired her progressive outlook; that the Turks' future depended on an Allied victory; and that the Allies had the resources and morale necessary to gain the final victory.

The increased difficulty in putting this across after the signing of the Turko-German Pact, is evident from a detailed report by Tamara of 25 August 1941 (PRO/FO371/30096/7942). The Turks now eagerly exploited any utterance in the British press which could be interpreted as favourable to the Axis, or unfavourable to the Allies.

Turkish rules regarding the dissemination of news were strict. No free distribution of leaflets was allowed; none could be in Turkish; only factual material could be included; Germany was not to be attacked verbally; no direct distribution of press features to newspapers was permitted. The only practicable course was to get insertions into magazines which were already accepted, such as *War in Pictures*, BBC broadsheets, and *Réalité*, a magazine produced in French by the British Embassy.

Entertainment films were allowed. However, whereas Germany subsidized a cinema in Istanbul, few British films were screened because of difficulties over payment. Tamara suggested that such comedy films as *Sailors Three* and George Formby's *Let George Do It* be made available. Gossip was influential but, she pointed out, the MoI had no staff in Istanbul to counter it. Her forceful pleas for an increase in local staffing were eventually acted upon.

In April 1941 Tamara wrote to the Establishment Division requesting upgrading to Senior Assistant Specialist (PRO/Inf 1/83). She made a persuasive case:

Not only do I look after Turkey, but I also do a good deal of the work connected with Iran and likewise endeavour to be fully informed on general matters concerning the rest of the Middle East, in order to be able to answer questions put during the Head of the Section's absence ... To the best of my belief, I am the only regional officer who provides as many as three different newsreels each week, plus a considerable number of shorts. Furthermore, no other officer in the Foreign Division is – like myself – responsible for the British news supplied to a foreign press agency (the Anatolian Agency, Turkey) and is assisted in this by a journalist lacking all knowledge of the country for which she is writing.

Her superiors admitted that an unfair burden had been placed on Tamara; as well as the prolonged absence on sick leave of the department head, another senior specialist was in Oxford and the third spent most afternoons in Whitehall. So Tamara had to 'hold the work of the section and often take quite important decisions'. Her request was also endorsed: 'her work is extremely important to the official working of the section and she performs it with the utmost skill and competence.' However, another member of the section had recently been promoted, and Management was unhappy at again asking Treasury for an upgrading. Moreover, Tamara did not number 'among her many good qualities those of discretion and calmness in a crisis'.

Nevertheless, in June 1941, she was granted a special gratuity of £40 in respect of duties 'superior to those normally allocated to her grade', undertaken during the past seven or eight months, and she was promoted to Senior Assistant Specialist at a salary of £320 per annum on 22 June when the departure of another member of staff created a vacancy. By 1944 the Middle East Division had been subdivided into four sections – Arab States, Persia, Turkey, and Production: Tamara was then Specialist in charge of the Turkish section (PRO/Inf 1/47).

Tamara kept memorabilia relating to two events that she organized, which were ideally suited to her capabilities and experience. In May 1941 she helped plan the British Pavilion at the 10th Izmir International Trade Fair and she succeeded in persuading the authorities to take part again in the 1943 Fair.

In neither year was participation easy. In 1941 the problem was transport; time was short, and communications were fraught with difficulty since Yugoslavia, Greece and Crete had all fallen to the Axis. Two years later the main problems were different. British industry was entirely geared to the war so there was a profound shortage of non-war industrial goods. Since the aim of the fair was the development of Turkey's foreign trade, exhibits of a propaganda, political or war nature were rigorously excluded. So although the quantity and variety of British goods had declined, the aim of the British Pavilion was to show that the quality remained as high as in peace-time.

Tamara told the London-Turkish Society that most of the exhibits at the fair were photographs. Movement was introduced in the display by two cranes illuminated by flashing lights, one raising loads depicting Turkey's exports to Britain, the other lowering loads of British imports. A small collection of clothes displayed utility wear – designed under strict regulations to cut out any excess material.

British fashion must have held a particular interest for Turkish women; Tamara preserved photographs of an early 1943 Austerity Dress Show arranged for them in Norman Hartnell's London establishment. Since the sumptuousness of the dresses was strictly limited by utility clothing rules, glamour was added to the show by the display of models for stage productions.

In 1944 Tamara resigned from the Ministry of Information, returning to Gloucestershire to care for her new-born son, who became seriously ill on release from hospital, where he had been poisoned. In the summer of 1945 her elder daughter's school, which had been evacuated to Dorset, returned to London, so alternative arrangements had to be made at very short notice.

Tamara tried to interest herself in the farm, and to supplement rations by keeping hens. At a later stage attempts to rear turkeys were a continuing problem. Was it now, or after the war, that two beautiful Jersey cows, Juno and Juniper, were added to the menagerie? Certainly Tamara did not milk them herself, but she did make butter – hard work in those days since the cream was churned by hand – and the loft was commandeered for ripening cheeses, sometimes successfully, at others less so. I believe the attempt to cure sides of pork which involved daily turning and rubbing with salt, was tried only once. Bottling produce gave way at some stage to home-canning.

These domestic chores did not come naturally to Tamara, any more than did farm management, so it was a great relief when David was demobilized. Most important, they were able to resume their close-knit lives, but Tamara was also free again to pursue, with pleasure, her academic and archaeological interests.

14
Mostly about David

He's gone, and all our plans
Are useless indeed.
We'll walk no more on Cotswold
Where the sheep feed
Quietly and take no heed.

Ivor Gurney, *To His Love*

REGARDLESS of our financial preoccupations, until the seventies the post-war years were very happy. They seemed to come as a bonus from grudging fate, their felicity contrasting with the unhappiness of the war years, and later the misery of David's illness, which coincided with the death of the elm trees he so greatly loved for their intrinsic beauty, as well as for their role in English painting.

During the war, when David was in England and our leaves coincided, we snatched at the pleasures that came our way. On one of these, in the autumn of 1943, Robert Henriques, also on leave, decided to have a partridge shoot.* Vi, recently back from the States, provided the lunch. The weather was perfect, the autumn colours resplendent, the blackberries at their best, the birds plentiful. We were in excellent spirits when we assembled for lunch, but David's happiness was shattered on receiving a telephoned summons to report back to the War Office immediately. 'But how had they known where he was?' we miserably asked. Vi hesitated, before replying that Miss Bridges, our much loved postmistress,

---

*Henriques, Col. Robert David Quixano, MBE. Educated Rugby; New College, Oxford. The Henriques were the closest of neighbours and friends. Robert served in the Royal Artillery 1926–33; he then became a writer, winning the International Prize for Literature with his first novel, *No Arms, No Armour*, and then the James Tait Black Memorial Prize for *Through the Valley*; and a broadcaster, appearing regularly on *Any Questions*. During the war he served in the RA, in a Commando and at Combined Operations HQ. He was awarded the US Silver and Bronze Stars. In 1928 he married Vivien Doris Levy.

had enlightened the authorities. Our chagrin at David's recall was slightly tempered by amusement and a sense of guilt, for had we not always encouraged Miss Bridges to keep us abreast of the local news? She was admirably placed for so doing, for she not only ran our local post office, sorting letters, scanning postcards and delivering them twice daily on her bicycle, but she also worked our telephone exchange.

David's early enlistment entitled him to very early demobilization. Partly because I longed to go abroad, but chiefly because David was too tired to relax at home where so much needed his attention, I persuaded him to apply for permission to take the car to France for a short holiday. Whilst waiting for the answer, as the weather was glorious, we had another partridge shoot. We asked Charles des Graz to stay, and also invited Michael Maclagan, a recent but already close friend, to come over from Oxford.* For all the shabby setting – one sitting-room still stacked with furniture which Leigh Ashton had stored with us at the outbreak of war – we had an idyllic day. Both Charles and Michael wrote their bread and butter letters to us in verses which expressed the happiness we all felt at being at peace, at home, together among friends.

Pre-war, David had loved France. However he found it hard to condone much that had happened, and was reluctant to revisit the country. All the same, we left for France in early October 1945, heading for Rouen, a city we both loved. We planned to spend the night at a favourite hotel, only to find it full. My heart sank. It was dusk, much of the town lay in ruins, street lighting was poor, few people were about and food was scarce. The hotel staff reassured us, persuading us to go to the restaurant, while they solved our sleeping problem. We were soon enjoying an omelette and a bottle of wine. Meanwhile the hall porter had found us a bedroom nearby, in a small house belonging to an artisan and his wife. They welcomed us with delight, and plied us with questions about England. Next day, when serving us large cups of delicious coffee, they explained that some Americans had given them the beans. They

---

*Maclagan, Michael, CVO, FSA, FRHist.S. Educated Winchester; Christ Church, Oxford. Fellow, Trinity College, Oxford 1939–81. Slains Pursuivant 1948–70, Portcullis Pursuivant 1970–80, Richmond Herald of Arms 1980–9. Lord Mayor of Oxford 1970–1. For part of the war, Michael was among David's staff in a section of Military Intelligence dealing with Italy and the Balkans.

had been saving them for a special occasion, but 'what could be more special than this one?' David was deeply touched. We spent the next night in an ugly, pretentious house belonging to a retired grocer and his wife. There, having heard that writing paper was in short supply in England, our hosts pressed large quantities of it on us. The last shred of David's resentment collapsed. The France we had loved had survived after all.

Back in Coln Rogers we had meant to resume our pre-war ways but soon found we had too much to do. Anticipating a post-war food shortage David, whilst still in the army, had decided that the best way to combat it was to expand his small herd of pedigree Hereford cattle. The herd's size largely depended on how many beasts he could comfortably rear in his three Cotswold barns, the total being slightly larger if the animals were hornless. My intense dislike of de-horning young calves could well have fostered David's interest in the flourishing herds of pedigree Polled Hereford cattle already firmly established in the USA, Australia and New Zealand. So he decided to try to breed hornless cattle of his own. He was fully aware of the difficulties involved, and reminded me of the limerick that summarizes the Mendelian theory of genetics. This asserts that, of every four offspring by similar parents of mixed race, two would be horned; one with mixed genes; and only one polled.

David was preparing to embark on the long process of breeding out a Hereford's horns when a short cut seemed to present itself. Sadly, however, these advantages were, in the long run, to hobble him. Failure to avoid this set-back was partly due to an oversight of the close friend running our farm for us during the war, but chiefly to the failure of the owner of a pedigree Hereford cow which had recently given birth to a polled heifer, a 'sport', to register the birth or to inform David of the omission when David, whilst home on short leave, bought the calf.

On acquiring the heifer David wrote to Dr J. Hammond, the leading animal geneticist, for advice on breeding from it. His letter reached Dr Hammond just as Hammond was all set to test his carefully researched conclusions on artificial insemination. To this end, in late 1948 Hammond obtained permission to import a small amount of semen from the magnificent pedigree poll Hereford bull, C. M. R. Advance Domino 81st., bred by W. P. Moore at Senatobia,

Mississippi, USA. In due course enough semen to inseminate four cows arrived in England but due to flight delay it lost much of its potency and only one beast, David's heifer, proved fertile. On 4 April 1949, with the fates still smiling, she produced a hornless bull calf which David named Coln Arthur.

It was only when trying to register his birth in the society's records that we found that the birth of his dam had never been entered. The full consequences of that oversight struck home five years later with the birth of Coln Arthur's first calves. Persuaded by David, the Hereford Herd Book Society eventually recognized the polled variant, but still stubbornly insisted on entering Coln Arthur's progeny in a demeaning subsidiary herd book. Yet the *Daily Telegraph* Peterborough column declared that David had 'left his mark on British agriculture', and to our further delight the Bull Hotel at Fairford asked permission to portray Coln Arthur on its inn sign.

Soon after the birth of Coln Arthur's first calves, two neighbours joined our venture. So also did Douglas McDougall, manager of Messrs Cooper, McDougall & Robertson's farming enterprises and, shortly after, Robert Henriques and Oscar Colburn, both close friends and neighbours. They all agreed that it was now essential to introduce new blood into the strain to avoid inbreeding, and that the only way to do so quickly was to import several pedigree beasts from the USA, Australia or New Zealand.

When Douglas McDougall approached the Ministry of Agriculture for permission to do this, they learnt that licences could be granted only to an established breed society, hence the formation of the Poll Hereford Breeders of Great Britain Ltd, in May 1955, with David as their chairman. The society applied to import the prize-winning bull Toko Excelsior from New Zealand as well as four in-calf heifers. The beasts reached London on 23 September, and in July 1956 the society was at last granted full recognition of the Polled Herefords together with permission to exhibit the cattle at agricultural shows. With over eighty farmers breeding poll Herefords, the agricultural shows at Thame and Moreton-in-Marsh decided to exhibit them in special classes. Other shows followed suit including, the final accolade, the Royal Agricultural Show, in 1961.

In January 1946 we returned to Edinburgh, to a flat which we had not lived in since March 1939. It was let during the war to a wing commander's family and was now a slum with mattresses so filthy that the authorities instantly issued us with coupons to enable us to get replacements. When we had last lived in the flat there had been ourselves, our young daughter, her nanny, and two domestic staff. Now we had no staff and three children, the youngest still delicate, the middle one almost too fit, and the eldest temperamentally upset at having to change schools. However, the warmth with which we were welcomed back to Edinburgh, not only by our friends, colleagues and acquaintances, but also by our former tradesmen, including our Musselburgh fishwife, raised our spirits.

I managed to engage a formidable live-in cook who would not do any housework. Her idiosyncrasies were diverting especially when she emerged from her room in the early afternoon looking very dolled up. Several hours later she unsteadily returned from the bar of the North British Hotel. We assumed that she would walk out on us one day; and so she did, within a month. Rather than live in, her replacement preferred to come daily; she stayed for just about a fortnight. She always arrived wearing a chef's hat and carrying several very long, sharp carving knives. One morning, picking up the largest and brandishing it, she attempted to chase me round the kitchen table. Too surprised and angry to be frightened, I stood my ground and gave her instant notice. Abashed, she left without fuss.

Her successor, supplied by the Labour Exchange, proved scarcely less hostile. Choosing an evening when she knew that, but for the children, I would be alone, she persuaded her lover to telephone to demand money, threatening, if refused, to attack me when I took the dogs for their evening run. I encouraged him to do just that, but was sufficiently unnerved to inform the police. As the duty officer refused to attach any importance to the threat, when I took the dogs out that evening I armed myself with a poker. Outside, there was no policeman to protect me, nor any sign of my potential assailant. Nor, next day, was there any sign of the cook. Instead Noel Fergusson, a dear friend and splendid cook, came every morning to prepare our main meal. Eventually I was able to employ two pleasant and efficient German girls who stayed for two years.

David's farming activities did not affect his academic pursuits. Rather the reverse, perhaps because, while still in the army, he had assumed – wrongly as it transpired – that the technological advances triggered off by the war, combined with the determination to avoid unemployment, would result in a shorter working day. In that event David feared that many workers might find it hard to fill their leisure hours, yet he felt certain that, if given the chance, many would derive great pleasure from the arts.

He set out to convince the university authorities of the need to extend his curriculum from two to three teaching terms a year, and establish a three-year honours degree course in history of art. He also suggested that students following honours degree courses in such disciplines as history, languages and the like, be encouraged to obtain credits by studying their related arts. At the time nothing comparable was available at any other British university. David also collaborated with the Edinburgh College of Art to enable students with both creative and intellectual aspirations to follow a five-year course; this combined the university's and the college's curricula, to qualify for an honours degree in fine arts, thus fitting them for senior administrative posts offered by the Arts Council, colleges of art, and similar institutions.

Undergraduates were quick to take advantage of these various opportunities and David gradually increased his staff from one in 1946, to ten by 1972. By that time postgraduates were coming to Edinburgh from countries as far apart as Iraq and the USA to study for their doctorates under his supervision. Nevertheless, whilst concentrating on those students specializing in Byzantine, Anglo-Saxon or Islamic art, David continued to devote a good deal of time to teaching his first-year students. During the immediate post-war years he also lectured regularly to members of the Workers Educational Association studying at Newbattle Abbey, a college of further education near Dalkeith.

David's intellectual activities were not confined to the visual arts. As a music lover he persuaded Raymond Russell to present his important collection of keyboard instruments to Edinburgh University.* David then prevailed on the university to restore St

---

*In 1958 Russell decided to present his collection of keyboard instruments to a British university. Negotiations with Edinburgh proved inconclusive despite the acquisition of St Cecilia's Hall by the university in 1959. After Russell's death in 1964 his mother presented the greater part of the collection to the university 'in memory of her son and to fulfil a wish long entertained by him'. See *The Russell Collection and other Early Keyboard Instruments in Saint Cecilia's Hall, Edinburgh*, Edinburgh, 1968.

Cecilia's Hall, Edinburgh's eighteenth-century concert hall, as a show-place for the instruments which, when repaired, could be played there. Ian Lindsay, at the time architect to the Iona Community, was commissioned to restore the hall. As so often, the cost far exceeded the estimate. However, this difficulty overcome, students and music-lovers were soon admiring the instruments and listening to concerts. It was also due to David that a workshop was eventually established in Edinburgh for the conservation and restoration of Scotland's medieval mural and easel paintings.

The increase in the number of undergraduates in the early sixties resulting from the post-war bulge created considerable problems for Scottish students. In the past they had lived in lodgings where they were fed and housed, but after the war the lack of domestic help put an end to all that. As a result many students shared furnished flats and did all the chores. David regretted the time they had to spend in clearing up after themselves and pressed the university, which thanks to the generosity of Sir Donald Pollock had land available, to build several halls of residence where students could enjoy a collegiate way of life. He was extremely disappointed to find that, rather than live communally, the majority preferred to share with friends. But once he had persuaded the university authorities to convert the splendid medieval flats on the Mound, the romance of their setting resulted in their being constantly over-subscribed.

I greatly regretted the post-war loss of our free annual third term. Although we had never spent more than three months on field work in Turkey, it now seemed to me that we would have no time at all for any. In the event, from the early 1950s David took charge of the second phase of excavating the magnificent mosaic pavement of the Great Palace of the Byzantine Emperors at Constantinople. Somewhat later we uncovered the thirteenth-century Byzantine frescos in the church of St Sophia at Trebizond.

During these post-war years we were also able, on occasion, to accept pressing invitations from the Yugoslav Government to study the country's antiquities. Similar invitations followed from the Romanian, Bulgarian and Polish governments, as well as a couple of extended British Council lecture tours in Afghanistan and the Near and Middle East. And on a sabbatical, we went to both Greece and the USA.

The visits proved immensely rewarding and enjoyable and did not interfere with David's activities as an assiduous member on the boards of the British Schools of Archaeology at Athens, Ankara, and Tehran, as well as on those of the Scottish Arts Council, the Scottish Craft Centre, and the National Trust for Scotland. His appointment as a trustee of the National Galleries of Scotland gave him particular pleasure, as did his election to the Royal Scottish Academy as an honorary member. However the children and I were especially pleased by his appointment in 1958 to the board of the Independent Television Authority as this obliged him to acquire a television, a luxury for which we had been longing. David, however, derived greater satisfaction being on the committee responsible for controlling the export of works of art.

By the 1960s the combined activities of the university's Department of Fine Arts and of Edinburgh's annual festival of the arts were making an impact on many of the town's circles. Public lectures on the arts grew in number, so did their audiences; commercial art galleries attracted more and more visitors and the university's members increasingly devoted free time to painting and sculpting. As the university already owned a number of important works of art, notably those of the Torrie Bequest,* David increasingly longed for a centre where the works could be displayed and people, regardless of status or occupation, could enjoy the arts. Ideally he saw a centre as consisting of three sections: one for permanent exhibition, another for temporary shows and the third, a common room provided with British and foreign periodicals.

There seemed little prospect of this dream becoming reality until the university's main library was transferred from the splendid hall in Old College to larger premises specially designed by Basil Spence. A passionate scramble for the empty space broke out among heads of departments. David emerged triumphant – with three stock-rooms and above them two enchanting domed rooms, the large downstairs space for exhibitions, the smaller upstairs spaces studios for use by people other than art students. A generous grant from the Gulbenkian Foundation and the first of two

---

*In 1834 Sir James Erskine of Torrie bequeathed forty-six paintings by old masters, twenty-one bronzes and sixteen marbles to Edinburgh University 'for the purpose of laying a foundation for a Gallery for the encouragement of the Fine Arts'.

important contributions from Bill Younger of Scottish and Newcastle Breweries, got off to a good start the structural changes. As David lay dying, he was profoundly touched to learn that the university had decided to call the centre after him. At his death many friends spontaneously presented it with important works of art in his memory, and Giles Robertson, David's former colleague and successor to his chair, also set up an annual art lecture in David's name. Supported by its Friends, the Talbot Rice Gallery continues to make a valuable contribution to Edinburgh's intellectual life.

EPILOGUE

WITH its concentration on David's career, the last chapter of my mother's memoirs is very different in tone from those preceding it; I believe it was written soon after plans for a biography of David fell through. Among other things she had long been anxious to correct the impression given in *Poll Hereford Cattle in Great Britain* – the first publication on the subject, written and privately printed by two of the society's earliest members – that David bought, rather than bred, Coln Arthur. This was her opportunity.

When asked for their recollections of her, her surviving Edinburgh friends found it impossible to separate memories of Tamara from those of David. Together they had planned the 1958 Edinburgh exhibition *Masterpieces of Byzantine Art*: this was the first exhibition on Byzantine art on British soil: only two others, my father wrote in the introduction to the catalogue, had been staged in Europe, a small one at Grottaferrata in Italy in 1905 and one on a more extensive scale, at Paris in 1931.

Together they gave Sunday lunch-time parties, invitations to which were apparently eagerly hoped for. At evening receptions, mulled wine was served to fine art students to help them thaw out, both physically and figuratively. After David became Vice-Principal of the university, there were countless official receptions: the advantage of being the wife of the Vice-Principal was, Tamara said, that one could often chose whom to sit next to.

In Gloucestershire her large garden was a source of both enjoyment and labour; she was also fully involved in village affairs. The flow of guests did not abate so, as domestic help became scarce, cooking must have taken up much time; this was mostly done after the visitors had retired to bed. Thinking back, one remembers my parents' joy in meeting their friends – so many of whom have not been mentioned by name – and Tamara's interest in their troubles and in the progress of their children and grandchildren.

After my father's death in 1972, my mother made the best of things, although she continued to miss him deeply until her own death twenty-one years later. The Edinburgh flat was soon disposed of and she remained at Pigeon House for the next few years. Then, in 1976, she moved into a charming little house in Donne Place in Chelsea, partly so that her son, who now had young children, could take over the family home, and partly persuaded by her children and an old friend, Enriqueta Frankfort, who all felt the change would facilitate her writing and enable her Scottish friends to visit her more easily.

The move she found 'traumatic'; the accumulation of forty-five years of collecting had to be reduced to fit into what she called her 'doll's house'. Sadly Chelsea had its drawbacks, the most serious of which was the parking problem. Tamara found that, if she went out during the day, only a parking space some distance away was free on her return. Since she was no great walker by then, this dismayed her. The lack of a garden had a twofold disadvantage. She derived much pleasure from gardening, but even more from her dog. There had been a continual succession of these since Ghost's death. The current one, a Tibetan terrier named Gengi, whom she adored, was very obstinate – if anyone but Tamara tried to walk him, he would plant his forefeet solidly on the pavement, and all attempts to get him to move in any direction but the few yards home were doomed to failure.

In July 1979 she decided that, although the prospect of another move appalled her, she 'did not like London enough to continue living in it'. Fortunately she owned a cottage in a village less than a mile from Pigeon House, and she enjoyed modernizing it, and recounting to all and sundry her battles with the local authorities and the Department of the Environment over building on a second bathroom, which she won, and a garage, which she lost. She also turned a wilderness into the most charming little garden.

She had already returned to Russia several times, first, against the advice of the Foreign Office, in 1935, for the 3rd International Congress of Persian Art and Archaeology. After David's death Sir Mortimer Wheeler encouraged her to become a tour lecturer with Swan Hellenic and Serenissima. Two Chicagoans, James and Mary Gormley, who went on a number of tours under her aegis, remember 'her gregarious and sympathetic spirit – with every fellow traveller meaning a new friendship which she spontaneously cultivated and nurtured'. Whenever baggage failed to arrive or Intourist changed the itinerary at the last moment, Tamara's patrician tones demolished the passive obstructionism so widespread in Russia: on hearing her pre-revolutionary accent, minor officials were swift to trace mislaid effects and local guides rapidly rejigged schedules, sometimes improving on the original tour. Tamara also added unforgettable flourishes of her own, such as a visit to Tolstoy's home in Moscow, now a museum, and the Tolstoy family church nearby where, Gormley recalls, she 'slipped coins inconspicuously to some poor elderly women in the old Russian spirit of personal charity'.

At other times, Tamara's reputation as an art historian preceded her. At Tbilisi, in Georgia, she was very touched when the curator of the State Museum presented her with an article 'from one author to another'. At the ancient walled city of Maracanda, the original Samarkand, the chief archaeologist on the site, knowing her work, showed her party round the dig and gave a commentary which Tamara interpreted. And, to fill in a half-day gap caused by a flight delay at Samarkand airport, she met Gormley's request for a second look at the Shakhi-Zinda, a cluster of thirteenth- to fifteenth-century mosques. Her reputation also gained them entry to a number of then virtually inaccessible places, such as the museum at Zagorsk, the great centre of the Russian Orthodox Church, with its magnificent collection of religious fabrics.

As ever, Tamara proved a magnetic and resourceful hostess. The Gormleys remember her as the focal point of a 'rollicking banquet' at Slavansky's; and, in the interval of *Eugene Onegin* at the Bolshoi, they delighted in the dexterity with which she appropriated a large table in the opera buffet 'so that we could knock off a couple of bottles of *shampanskoye*'. An unflagging shopper and a haggler *par excellence*, Tamara frequently secured for members of her group bargains such as pottery from a factory in Samarkand – 'Although the shop was a state establishment, the workers were willing to sell us on most considerate terms items they tactfully called "seconds"' – and bolts of robust but attractively patterned cotton from a backyard outlet in Tashkent.

On returning home to Chicago, James Gormley wrote a letter of thanks to which Tamara sent a warm and – true to her wartime conditioning in the Civil Service – prompt reply, encouraging them both to keep in touch. They did, and, as so often with Tamara, the relationship ripened into a close friendship between the Gormley family and Tamara's. Gormley notes that, throughout the late 1970s, calling on her extraordinary 'reservoir of stamina and energy' and generously bestowing on her groups 'her lifetime of scholarship, insight and humanity and, beyond that, her companionship', she was always embarking on her final lecture tour – there were at least eighteen – but in fact these continued to 1983 when, leading a party of friends, she returned to Leningrad and Moscow 'chiefly to see old friends for the last time'. She also took particular delight in showing her younger daughter, who was on the trip, her native land.

But if these tours were all to places she knew well, in 1978 she was to break new ground, with a visit to Pakistan, as chief guest of the Chughtai Academy of Arts at celebrations commemorating the third anniversary of the death of the artist; she was asked to lecture on the Art of Chughtai. Abdur Rahman Chughtai (1897–1975), although a traditionalist, integrated with the ancient Mogul and Persian schools, influences of Western artists whose work he had studied on two visits to Europe. To quote the *Pakistan Times* of 19 January 1978, Tamara 'in her brief and learned speech dwelt on the Islamic content of Chughtai's art, finding beneath the imagery the profound mysticism which imbues the religion of Islam'. Even in her address she laments the absence of David who, she says, should be occupying her place on the dais.

Invitations were received to visit other countries including, in 1980, one to Holland with the suggestion that she might like, when there, to lecture on Cypriot icons. But the invitation she certainly appreciated most was one to return and take up residence in Russia. Strangely she did not preserve the offer. I now deeply regret the look of horror which, I fear, suffused my face when she told me of the proposal.

During the fifties and sixties Tamara's reputation had brought her numerous commissions for books and articles on her chosen fields of interest. Her contributions ranged from academic volumes in Thames & Hudson's 'Ancient Peoples and Places' series, to works designed for a younger audience on life in Byzantium and on the lives of Russian sovereigns. Several dealt with Russian art and icons. After reading her authoritative *A Concise History of Russian Art*, James Gormley sent her a page from Martin Cruz Smith's *Gorky Park* which mentioned her book. In thanks she wrote: 'I am amused and enchanted at figuring in a whodunnit.' She also contributed specialist chapters to art histories and encyclopaedias.

Nor was her pen sheathed during the following decades. Besides reviews and contributions to several encyclopaedias, she now embarked on a lengthy biography of Tsar Paul, the 'Gentle Czarevitch, Mad Czar' as she described him in *Czars and Czarinas of Russia*, who reigned from 1796 to 1801, and for whom his mother Catherine had built a palace at

Pavlovsk, employing for this the Scottish architect Charles Cameron. Though the book, alas, failed to find a publisher, she then courageously started work on these memoirs.

In January 1988 she wrote to James Gormley, 'I found last year very depressing. I don't know whether that is due to our sunless weather or to the constant bickering in the media and parliament or to old age, but I found it an unpleasant year even though no misfortunes befell us – on reflection my dissatisfaction may be due to boredom.' And that November she wrote, 'I don't enjoy old age and do not wish it on any of my friends. However, if enforced, it has to be endured with as good a grace as possible so I think of Dr Coué and try to count my blessings.' (Coué, the pioneer of auto-suggestion, had counselled the formula 'Every day, in every way, I am becoming better and better.') Now that they were all beyond the baby stage which she disliked, the company of her four grandchildren gave her much enjoyment: 'the grandchildren are now old enough to be really companionable so that is a great pleasure.'

Part of her despondency was undoubtedly due to pain. In the autumn of 1988 she underwent a serious operation necessitating the insertion of a metal rod into her spine where several vertebrae had collapsed because of osteoporosis. Although the operation was a success, from then on movement became increasingly difficult. Gardening was now an impossibility and, for the first time since a teenager, she had no dog to keep her company.

She maintained a vivid interest in *perestroika* and all that was happening in Russia, although that too filled her with foreboding. She always thought regional nationalism would put an end to the Communist regime. But the end came too fast, without giving the Russians time to learn how to manage possessions, how to have bank accounts. She feared that, if the people were hungry, or cold, rage would follow: she dreaded extreme nationalism and foresaw inter-republic jealousy leading to bitter violence: she mistrusted Yeltsin. But, with only a slight hesitation, she concurred that it was better that it should happen than that it should not. Thinking back, she remembered the excitement with which the Revolution had been greeted, the enthusiasm for a Utopia which, all too soon, turned to disappointment: after all they had suffered, she hoped the Russians would not be disappointed once more.

In March 1993 her spine started to crumble again. In what was to be almost her last letter to Gormley she wrote that Tolstoy 'was not wholly mistaken in his belief of man's power to control events being limited'. She dreaded becoming dependent on others, and was adamant that her children had their own lives to lead, and were not to move to Gloucestershire to look after her. Fortunately the end came peacefully. One evening she asked to be taken into the local cottage hospital. The next day she died, quickly, willingly and thankfully.

Bibliography

PUBLICATIONS OF TAMARA TALBOT RICE

Although every attempt has been made to trace articles and reviews, so wide were Tamara's interests that some may inadvertently have been omitted. Foreign language editions of her publications are not included.

'Angora as Seen by the Afghan King', *Illustrated London News*, 1928
'Georgian Art in the Middle Ages', *Asiatic Review*, 1929
'Role of Georgia in the Art of the Middle Ages', *Asiatic Review*, 1930
'Persian Bird and Beast in Art's Pleasure', *Asia*, 1931
Caravan Cities, by M. I. Rostovtsev, translated by D. and T. Talbot Rice, Oxford, 1932
Review, 'Splendours of the Persian Book', *Asia*, 1933
'Russian Ballet', *Listener*, 1934
'Art Movements in the Ballet', *Listener*, 1934
'Evolution of the Russian Ballet', *Apollo*, 1934
'Industrialism in the Stroud Valley', *Archaeological Review*, 1934
'Decorative Art – Theatre and Ballet' in *Russian Art*, ed. D. Talbot Rice, London, 1935
'The Russian Table – Exhibition of Russian Art', *Apollo*, 1935
'The Petersburg of Alexander I', *Architectural Review*, 1935
'The Evolution of the Ballet', *Dancing Times*, 1936
'Russian Icon Painting', *Apollo*, 1936
'The Costume of Cyprus in the Middle Ages' and 'Some Aspects of Social Life in Medieval Cyprus' in *The Icons of Cyprus*, ed. W. G. Constable and D. Talbot Rice, Courtauld Institute Publication on Near Eastern Art II, London, 1937
'Evolution of Russian Ballet', *Apollo*, 1937
'Russian Metalwork', *Apollo*, 1937
Russian Art, London, 1949
The Scythians, London, 1957
'The Holy City of Byzantium', *Times Literary Supplement*, 1957
'Royal Doors for the Priesthood', *Connoisseur* (American edn), 1958
'The Russian Setting', *Connoisseur* (American edn), 1958

Icons, introduction and descriptive notes to illustrations, London, 1959

'Some Reflections on Nineteenth-Century Russian Painting', *Burlington Magazine*, 1959

The Seljuks in Asia Minor, London, 1961

'Homage to Andrew Rublev', *Connoisseur*, 1961

Review, *Histoire Illustrée de la Russie* by J. Carmichael, *Connoisseur*, 1961

'Yugoslav Icons at Ohrid', *Connoisseur*, 1962

Finding out about Early Russians, London, 1963

Russian Icons, London, 1963

A Concise History of Russian Art, London, 1963

'Northern Iran', *Vogue*, 1964

'The Ancient Cultures 2500BC–AD200' and 'The Civilization of the South West 800BC–AD1600', in *Art Treasures in Russia: Monuments, Masterpieces, Commissions and Collections*, intr. Prince Dimitri Obolenski, London, 1964

Ancient Arts of Central Asia, London, 1965

'The Crucible of Peoples: Eastern Europe and the Rise of the Slavs', in *The Dark Ages*, ed. D. Talbot Rice, London, 1965

Everyday Life in Byzantium, London, 1967

'The USSR Shows its Treasures: An Exhilarating Exhibition now at Zurich', *Connoisseur*, 1967

'Charles Cameron, Catherine the Great's British Architect', *Connoisseur*, 1967

'Charles Cameron, Architect to the Imperial Russian Court', in catalogue of an exhibition of Cameron's architectural drawings, Arts Council, London, 1967

'The Scytho-Sarmatian Tribes of South-Eastern Europe', in F. Millar, *The Roman Empire and its Neighbours*, London, 1967

Czars and Czarinas of Russia, New York, 1968

Icons: The Natasha Allen Collection Catalogue, with D. Talbot Rice, Dublin, 1968

'Analysis of the Decorations in the Seljukid Style', in *The Church of Hagia Sophia at Trebizond*, ed. D. Talbot Rice, Edinburgh, 1968

Byzantium, London, 1969

Elizabeth, Empress of Russia, London, 1970

'Some Reflections on the Subject of Arm Bands', *Forschungen zur Kunst Asiens*, Istanbul, 1970

'Byzantium', *Times Literary Supplement*, 1970

'Palermo's Ancient Summer Plaisances', *Connoisseur*, 1970

'Classical Turkey', *Scotsman*, 1973

Icons and their Dating, with D. Talbot Rice, London, 1974

'Animal Combat Scenes in Byzantine Art', in *Studies in Memory of David Talbot Rice*, Edinburgh, 1975

Review, *Early Russian Architecture* by H. Faenson and V. Ivanov, *Times Literary Supplement*, 1975

Review, *Byzantine Style and Civilization* by Sir Steven Runciman, *Times Literary Supplement*, 1976

Review, *Russian Porcelain in the Hermitage Collection* by L. Nikiforova, *Connoisseur*, 1976

Review, *Iconoclasm: Papers given at the 9th Spring Symposium of Byzantine Studies* by A. Bryar and J. Herrin, *Times Literary Supplement*, 1977

Review, *Moscow: An Architectural History* by K. Berton, *Times Literary Supplement*, 1978

Review, *Russia on Canvas* by I. Repin, F. and S. J. Parker, *Burlington Magazine*, 1982

CONTRIBUTIONS TO ENCYCLOPAEDIAS

Encyclopaedia Britannica
Chambers Encyclopaedia
Concise Encyclopaedia of Antiques
The Cambridge Encyclopaedia of Russia and the Soviet Union
Encyclopaedia of Decorative Arts
Oxford Companion to Gardens
Oxford Companion to the Decorative Arts
Oxford Junior Encyclopaedia

BROADCASTS

Backdrop for Petrushka, Radio 3, 23 December 1968
Rasputin's Coffin, Radio 3, 30 December 1968
Contributor to *Rus* by M. Mason, Radio 3, 9 May 1968

OTHER SOURCES

The books listed below are amongst those consulted by the editor, and are recommended as background to those interested in particular periods of Tamara's life. The list is in no way comprehensive.

The place of publication is London unless otherwise stated.

H. M. M. Acton, *Memoirs of an Aesthete*, 1948

C. Bede, *The Adventures of Mr Verdant Green*, 1853

C. E. Black (ed.), *The Transformation of Russian Society: Aspects of Social Change since 1861*, Harvard, 1960

M. Buchanan, *Petrograd, the City of Trouble 1914–18*, 1918

H. Carpenter, *The Brideshead Generation: Evelyn Waugh and His Friends*, 1989

Sir Fife Clark, *The Central Office of Information*, The New Whitehall Series No. 15, 1970

H. E. Counsell, *37 The Broad: The Memoirs of an Oxford Doctor*, 1943

C. Day Lewis, *The Buried Day*, 1960

A. de Jonge, *The Life and Times of Grigorii Rasputin*, 1982

J. Delage, *La Russie en exil*, Paris, 1930

S. Deringil, *Turkish Foreign Policy during the Second World War: An Active Neutrality*, Cambridge, 1989

L. H. Dudley Buxton and S. Gibson, *Oxford University Ceremonies*, Oxford, 1935

M. Ferro, *The Russian Revolution of February 1917*, 1972

G. Finlay, *The History of Greece and of the Empire of Trebizond 1204–1461*, Edinburgh, 1851

J. R. Fothergill, *An Innkeeper's Diary*, 1931

J. Frumkin, G. Aronson and A. Goldenweiser, tr. M. Ginsburg, *Russian Jewry (1860–1917)*, New York, 1966

R. Gessain and M. Doré, *Facteurs comparées d'assimilation chez les Russes et les Arméniens*, Paris, 1946

H. Green, *Pack my Bag: A Self-Portrait*, 1940

Carlton J. H. Hayes, *France: A Nation of Patriots*, Columbia University Press, 1930

H. Hobson, *Indirect Journey: An Autobiography*, 1978

C. Hollis, *Oxford in the Twenties: Recollections of Five Friends*, 1976

Sir John Hope Simpson, *The Refugee Problem: Report of a Survey*, Oxford, 1939

S. Huddleston, *Bohemian Literary and Social Life in Paris*, 1928

L. Iremonger, *The Ghosts of Versailles: Miss Moberley and Miss Jourdain and their Adventure*, 1957

J. B. Kinross, *Atatürk: The Rebirth of a Nation*, 1964

Major-General Sir A. Knox, *With the Russian Army 1914–1917, being chiefly extracts from the diary of a Military Attaché*, 2 vols., 1921

L. Kochan and R. Abraham, *The Making of Modern Russia*, 2nd edn. 1983

G. Leggett, *The Cheka: Lenin's Political Police*, Oxford, 1981

W. Le Gros Clark, *Chant of Pleasant Exploration*, Edinburgh, 1968

B. Lewis, *The Emergence of Modern Turkey*, Oxford, 1961

V. Littauer, *Royal Hussar*, 1965. The quotations are from pp. 156–7, 229 and 248

D. McDougall and O. Colburn, *Poll Hereford Cattle in Great Britain*, privately published, 1977

A. Masters, *Rosa Lewis, an Exceptional Edwardian*, 1977

S. Mstislavskii, *Five Days which Transformed Russia*, 1988

M. Occleshaw, *The Romanov Conspiracies*, 1993

T. C. Owen, *Capitalism and Politics in Russia: A Social History of the Moscow Merchants 1855–1905*, Cambridge, 1981

Oxford Home Students (Miscellaneous Papers 1912–) Bodleian Library G A Oxon. 4 532)

A. Powell, *To Keep the Ball Rolling*, Vol. I: *Infants of the Spring*, 1976

M. P. Price, *A History of Turkey from Empire to Republic*, 1956

M. Raeff, *Russia Abroad: A Cultural History of the Russian Emigration 1919–1939*, Oxford, 1990

W. Rutherford, *The Tsar's War 1914–1917: The Story of the Imperial Russian Army in the First World War*, rev. edn. Cambridge, 1992

N. Stone and M. Glenny, *The Other Russia*, 1990

E. Waugh, *A Little Learning*, 1964

Frank G. Weber, *The Evasive Neutral: Germany, Britain and the Quest for a Turkish Alliance in the Second World War*, Missouri, Columbia, 1979

R. F. Wilson, *Paris on Parade*, Indianapolis, 1924

Reports of various Committees to the Assembly of the League of Nations, 1925, 1926, 1927, Geneva, 1926, 1927, 1929

The newspapers and journals consulted include *The Times*, *Isis*, *Cherwell*, *Morning Post*

Biographical details from, *inter alia*, *Who's Who* and national editions, *Burke's Peerage*, *Burke's Landed Gentry*, obituaries in *The Times*, *The Scotsman*

Index

Entries relating to Tamara refer to her likes and dislikes, her health and financial state. Friendships and activities are indexed under alternative entries. Since she and her husband were so closely involved, references to David have been included only up to his marriage.

Artists, authors and performers mentioned *en passant* are indexed under collective headings. Russian sovereigns appear under 'Romanov'.